AWS Certified Machine Learning Specialty: MLS-C01 Certification Guide

The definitive guide to passing the MLS-C01 exam on the very first attempt

Somanath Nanda

Weslley Moura

BIRMINGHAM—MUMBAI

AWS Certified Machine Learning Specialty: MLS-C01 Certification Guide

Group Product Manager: Kunal Parikh

Publishing Product Manager: Aditi Gour

Senior Editor: David Sugarman

Content Development Editor: Joseph Sunil

Technical Editor: Arjun Varma

Copy Editor: Safis Editing

Project Coordinator: Aparna Nair

Proofreader: Safis Editing

Indexer: Rekha Nair

Production Designer: Vijay Kamble

First published: March 2021
Production reference: 1180321

Published by Packt Publishing Ltd.
Livery Place
35 Livery Street
Birmingham
B3 2PB, UK.

ISBN 978-1-80056-900-3

www.packt.com

Contributors

About the authors

Somanath Nanda has 10 years of working experience in the IT industry, which includes prod development, DevOps, and designing and architecting products from end to end. He has also worked at AWS as a big data engineer for about 2 years.

Weslley Moura has 17 years of working experience in information technology (the last 9 years working on data teams and the last 5 years working as a lead data scientist).

He has worked in a variety of industries, such as financial, telecommunications, healthcare, and logistics. In 2019, he was a nominee for data scientist of the year at the European DatSci & AI Awards.

About the reviewer

Arunabh Sahai is a results-oriented leader who has been delivering technology solutions for more than 16 years across multiple industries around the globe. He is also a forward-thinking technology enthusiast and a technology coach, helping learners to polish their technology skills. Arunabh holds a master's degree in computer science and has in-depth knowledge of cloud (AWS/Azure/GCP) technologies. He holds multiple certifications attesting to his cloud technology knowledge and experience. He is also passionate about intelligent automation using predictive analytics. You can connect with him on his LinkedIn, and he will be happy to help you with your technology questions.

Table of Contents

Section 2: Data Engineering and Exploratory Data Analysis

3

Data Preparation and Transformation

4
Understanding and Visualizing Data

5
AWS Services for Data Storing

6
AWS Services for Data Processing

Section 3: Data Modeling

7
Applying Machine Learning Algorithms

8
Evaluating and Optimizing Models

9
Amazon SageMaker Modeling

Other Books You May Enjoy

Index

Preface

The AWS Machine Learning Specialty certification exam tests your competency to perform **machine learning (ML)** on AWS infrastructure. This book covers the entire exam syllabus in depth using practical examples to help you with your real-world machine learning projects on AWS.

Starting with an introduction to machine learning on AWS, you'll learn the fundamentals of machine learning and explore important AWS services for **artificial intelligence (AI)**. You'll then see how to prepare data for machine learning and discover different techniques for data manipulation and transformation for different types of variables. The book also covers the handling of missing data and outliers and takes you through various machine learning tasks such as classification, regression, clustering, forecasting, anomaly detection, text mining, and image processing, along with their specific ML algorithms, that you should know to pass the exam. Finally, you'll explore model evaluation, optimization, and deployment and get to grips with deploying models in a production environment and monitoring them.

By the end of the book, you'll have gained knowledge of all the key fields of machine learning and the solutions that AWS has released for each of them, along with the tools, methods, and techniques commonly used in each domain of AWS machine learning.

Who this book is for

This book is for professionals and students who want to take and pass the AWS Machine Learning Specialty exam or gain a deeper knowledge of machine learning with a special focus on AWS. Familiarity with the basics of machine learning and AWS services is necessary.

What this book covers

Chapter 1, Machine Learning Fundamentals, covers some machine learning definitions, different types of modeling approaches, and all the steps necessary to build a machine learning product, known as the modeling pipeline.

Chapter 2, AWS Application Services for AI/ML, covers details of the various AI/ML applications offered by AWS, which you should know to pass the exam.

Chapter 3, Data Preparation and Transformation, deals with categorical and numerical features, applying different techniques to transform your data, such as one-hot encoding, binary encoding, ordinal encoding, binning, and text transformations. You will also learn how to handle missing values and outliers on your data, two important topics to build good machine learning models.

Chapter 4, Understanding and Visualizing Data, teaches you how to select the most appropriate data visualization technique according to different variable types and business needs. You will also learn about available AWS services for visualizing data.

Chapter 5, AWS Services for Data Storing, teaches you about AWS services used to store data for machine learning. You will learn about the many different S3 storage classes and when to use each of them. You will also learn how to handle data encryption and how to secure your data at rest and in transit. Finally, we will present other types of data store services, still worth knowing for the exam.

Chapter 6, AWS Services for Processing, teaches you about AWS services used to process data for machine learning. You will learn how to deal with batch and real-time processing, how to directly query data on Amazon S3, and how to create big data applications on EMR.

Chapter 7, Applying Machine Learning Algorithms, covers different types of machine learning tasks, such as classification, regression, clustering, forecasting, anomaly detection, text mining, and image processing. Each of these tasks has specific algorithms that you should know about to pass the exam. You will also learn how ensemble models work and how to deal with the curse of dimensionality.

Chapter 8, Evaluating and Optimizing Models, teaches you how to select model metrics to evaluate model results. You will also learn how to optimize your model by tuning its hyperparameters.

Chapter 9, Amazon SageMaker Modeling, teaches you how to spin up notebooks to work with exploratory data analysis and how to train your models on Amazon SageMaker. You will learn where and how your training data should be stored in order to be accessible through SageMaker and the different data formats that you can use.

To get the most out of this book

You will need a system with a good internet connection and an AWS account.

If you are using the digital version of this book, we advise you to type the code yourself or access the code via the GitHub repository (link available in the next section). Doing so will help you avoid any potential errors related to the copying and pasting of code.

Download the example code files

You can download the example code files for this book from GitHub at `https://github.com/PacktPublishing/AWS-Certified-Machine-Learning-Specialty-MLS-C01-Certification-Guide`. In case there's an update to the code, it will be updated on the existing GitHub repository.

We also have other code bundles from our rich catalog of books and videos available at `https://github.com/PacktPublishing/`. Check them out!

Download the color images

We also provide a PDF file that has color images of the screenshots/diagrams used in this book. You can download it here: `https://static.packt-cdn.com/downloads/9781800569003_ColorImages.pdf`.

Conventions used

There are a number of text conventions used throughout this book.

`Code in text`: Indicates code words in text, database table names, folder names, filenames, file extensions, pathnames, dummy URLs, user input, and Twitter handles. Here is an example: To check each of the versions and the latest one of them we use aws s3api list-object-versions --bucket version-demo-mlpractice to which S3 provides the list-object-versions API, as shown here."

A block of code is set as follows:

```
"Versions": [
{
"ETag":
"\"b6690f56ca22c410a2782512d24cdc97\"",
"Size": 10,
"StorageClass": "STANDARD",
```

```
"Key": "version-doc.txt",
"VersionId":
"70wbLG6BMBEQhCXmwsriDgQoXafFmgGi",
"IsLatest": true,
"LastModified": "2020-11-07T15:57:05+00:00",
"Owner": {
"DisplayName": "baba",
"ID": "XXXXXXXXXXXX"
}
} ]
```

When we wish to draw your attention to a particular part of a code block, the relevant lines or items are set in bold:

```
[default]
exten => s,1,Dial(Zap/1|30)
exten => s,2,Voicemail(u100)
exten => s,102,Voicemail(b100)
exten => i,1,Voicemail(s0)
```

Any command-line input or output is written as follows:

```
$ aws s3 ls s3://version-demo-mlpractice/
$ echo "Version-2">version-doc.txt
```

Bold: Indicates a new term, an important word, or words that you see onscreen. For example, words in menus or dialog boxes appear in the text like this. Here is an example: "Select **System info** from the **Administration** panel."

> **Tips or important notes**
> Appear like this.

Get in touch

Feedback from our readers is always welcome.

General feedback: If you have questions about any aspect of this book, mention the book title in the subject of your message and email us at customercare@packtpub.com.

Errata: Although we have taken every care to ensure the accuracy of our content, mistakes do happen. If you have found a mistake in this book, we would be grateful if you would report this to us. Please visit www.packtpub.com/support/errata, selecting your book, clicking on the Errata Submission Form link, and entering the details.

Piracy: If you come across any illegal copies of our works in any form on the Internet, we would be grateful if you would provide us with the location address or website name. Please contact us at copyright@packt.com with a link to the material.

If you are interested in becoming an author: If there is a topic that you have expertise in and you are interested in either writing or contributing to a book, please visit authors.packtpub.com.

Reviews

Please leave a review. Once you have read and used this book, why not leave a review on the site that you purchased it from? Potential readers can then see and use your unbiased opinion to make purchase decisions, we at Packt can understand what you think about our products, and our authors can see your feedback on their book. Thank you!

For more information about Packt, please visit packt.com.

Section 1: Introduction to Machine Learning

This section provides details about the AWS Machine Learning Specialty Exam. It also introduces machine learning fundamentals and covers the most important AWS application services for artificial intelligence.

This section contains the following chapters:

- *Chapter 1, Machine Learning Fundamentals*
- *Chapter 2, AWS Application Services for AI/ML*

1
Machine Learning Fundamentals

For many decades, researchers have been trying to simulate human brain activity through the field known as **artificial intelligence**, **AI** for short. In 1956, a group of people met at the Dartmouth Summer Research Project on Artificial Intelligence, an event that is widely accepted as the first group discussion about AI as we know it today. Researchers were trying to prove that many aspects of the learning process could be precisely described and, therefore, automated and replicated by a machine. Today, we know they were right!

Many other terms appeared in this field, such as **machine learning** (ML) and **deep learning** (DL). These sub-areas of AI have also been evolving for many decades (granted, nothing here is new to the science). However, with the natural advance of the information society and, more recently, the advent of **big data** platforms, AI applications have been reborn with much more power and applicability. Power, because now we have more computational resources to simulate and implement them; applicability, because now information is everywhere.

Even more recently, cloud services providers have put AI in the cloud. This is helping all sizes of companies to either reduce their operational costs or even letting them sample AI applications (considering that it could be too costly for a small company to maintain its own data center).

That brings us to the goal of this chapter: being able to describe what the terms AI, ML, and DL mean, as well as understanding all the nuances of an ML pipeline. Avoiding confusion on these terms and knowing what exactly an ML pipeline is will allow you to properly select your services, develop your applications, and master the AWS Machine Learning Specialty exam.

The main topics of this chapter are as follows:

- Comparing AI, ML, and DL
- Classifying supervised, unsupervised, and reinforcement learning
- The CRISP-DM modeling life cycle
- Data splitting
- Modeling expectations
- Introducing ML frameworks
- ML in the cloud

Comparing AI, ML, and DL

AI is a broad field that studies different ways to create systems and machines that will solve problems by simulating human intelligence. There are different levels of sophistication to create these programs and machines, which go from simple, rule-based engines to complex, self-learning systems. AI covers, but is not limited to, the following sub-areas:

- Robotics
- Natural language processing
- Rule-based systems
- ML

The area we are particularly interested in now is ML.

Examining ML

ML is a sub-area of AI that aims to create systems and machines that are able to learn from experience, without being explicitly programmed. As the name suggests, the system is able to observe its running environment, learn, and adapt itself without human intervention. Algorithms behind ML systems usually extract and improve knowledge from the data that is available to them, as well as conditions (such as **hyperparameters**), and feed back after trying different approaches to solve a particular problem:

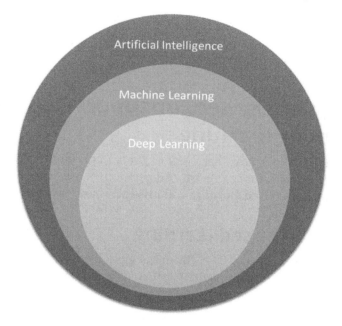

Figure 1.1 – Heirarchy of AI, ML, DL

There are different types of ML algorithms; for instance, we can list decision tree-based, probabilistic-based, and neural networks. Each of these classes might have dozens of specific algorithms. Most of them will be covered in later sections of this book.

As you might have noticed in *Figure 1.1*, we can be even more specific and break the ML field down into another very important topic for the Machine Learning Specialty exam: DL.

Examining DL

DL is a subset of ML that aims to propose algorithms that connect multiple layers to solve a particular problem. The knowledge is then passed through layer by layer until the optimal solution is found. The most common type of DL algorithm is deep neural networks.

At the time of writing this book, DL is a very hot topic in the field of ML. Most of the current state-of-the-art algorithms for machine translation, image captioning, and computer vision were proposed in the past few years and are a part of DL.

Now that we have an overview of types of AI, let's look at some of the ways we can classify ML.

Classifying supervised, unsupervised, and reinforcement learning

ML is a very extensive field of study; that's why it is very important to have a clear definition of its sub-divisions. From a very broad perspective, we can split ML algorithms into two main classes: **supervised learning** and **unsupervised learning**.

Introducing supervised learning

Supervised algorithms use a class or label (from the input data) as support to find and validate the optimal solution. In *Figure 1.2*, there is a dataset that aims to classify fraudulent transactions from a bank:

Day of the week	EST Hour	Transaction amount	Merchant Type	Is Fraud?
Mon	09:00	$1000	Retail	No
Tue	23:00	$5500	e-commerce	Yes
Fri	14:00	$500	Travel	No
Mon	10:00	$100	Retail	No
Tue	22:00	$100	e-commerce	No
Tue	22:00	$6000	e-commerce	Yes

Figure 1.2 – Sample dataset for supervised learning

The first four columns are known as **features**, or **independent variables**, and they can be used by a supervised algorithm to find fraudulent patterns. For example, by combining those four features (day of the week, EST hour, transaction amount, and merchant type) and six observations (each row is technically one observation), you can infer that e-commerce transactions with a value greater than $5,000 and processed at night are potentially fraudulent cases.

> **Important note**
>
> In a real scenario, we should have more observations in order to have statistical support to make this type of inference.

The key point is that we were able to infer a potential fraudulent pattern just because we knew, *a priori*, what is fraud and what is not fraud. This information is present in the last column of *Figure 1.2* and is commonly referred to as a target variable, label, response variable, or dependent variable. If the input dataset has a target variable, you should be able to apply supervised learning.

In supervised learning, the target variable might store different types of data. For instance, it could be a binary column (yes or no), a multi-class column (class A, B, or C), or even a numerical column (any real number, such as a transaction amount). According to the data type of the target variable, you will find which type of supervised learning your problem refers to. *Figure 1.3* shows how to classify supervised learning into two main groups: **classification** and **regression** algorithms:

Data type of the target variable	Sub data type of the target variable	Type of supervised learning applicable
Categorical	Binary	Binary classification
Categorical	Multi class	Multi classification
Numerical	N/A	Regression

Figure 1.3 – Choosing the right type of supervised learning given the target variable

While classification algorithms predict a class (either binary or multiple classes), regression algorithms predict a real number (either continuous or discrete).

Understanding data types is important to make the right decisions on ML projects. We can split data types into two main categories: numerical and categorical data. Numerical data can then be split into continuous or discrete subclasses, while categorical data might refer to ordinal or nominal data:

- *Numerical/discrete data* refers to individual and countable items (for example, the number of students in a classroom or the number of items in an online shopping cart).

- *Numerical/continuous data* refers to an infinite number of possible measurements and they often carry decimal points (for example, temperature).

- *Categorical/nominal data* refers to labeled variables with no quantitative value (for example, name or gender).

- *Categorical/ordinal data* adds the sense of order to a labeled variable (for example, education level or employee title level).

In other words, when choosing an algorithm for your project, you should ask yourself: do I have a target variable? Does it store categorical or numerical data? Answering these questions will put you in a better position to choose a potential algorithm that will solve your problem.

However, what if you don't have a target variable? In that case, we are facing unsupervised learning. Unsupervised problems do not provide labeled data; instead, they provide all the independent variables (or features) that will allow unsupervised algorithms to find patterns in the data. The most common type of unsupervised learning is **clustering**, which aims to group the observations of the dataset into different clusters, purely based on their features. Observations from the same cluster are expected to be similar to each other, but very different from observations from other clusters. Clustering will be covered in more detail in future chapters of this book.

Semi-supervised learning is also present in the ML literature. This type of algorithm is able to learn from partially labeled data (some observations contain a label and others do not).

Finally, another learning approach that has been taken by another class of ML algorithms is **reinforcement learning**. This approach rewards the system based on the good decisions that it has made autonomously; in other words, the system learns by experience.

We have been discussing learning approaches and classes of algorithms at a very broad level. However, it is time to get specific and introduce the term **model**.

The CRISP-DM modeling life cycle

Modeling is a very common term used in ML when we want to specify the steps taken to solve a particular problem. For example, we could create a binary classification model to predict whether those transactions from *Figure 1.2* are fraudulent or not.

A model, in this context, represents all the steps to create a solution as a whole, which includes (but is not limited to) the algorithm. The **Cross-Industry Standard Process for Data Mining**, more commonly referred to as **CRISP-DM**, is one of the methodologies that provides guidance on the common steps we should follow to create models. This methodology is widely used by the market and is covered in the AWS Machine Learning Specialty exam:

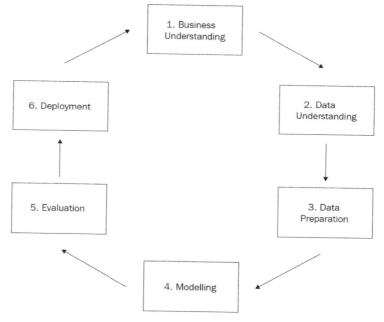

Figure 1.4 – CRISP-DM methodology

Everything starts with business understanding, which will produce the business objectives (including success criteria), situation assessment, data mining goals, and project plan (with an initial assessment of tools and techniques). During the situation assessment, we should also look into an inventory of resources, requirements, assumptions and constraints, risks, terminology, costs, and benefits. Every single assumption and success criterion matters when we are modeling.

Then we pass on to data understanding, where we will collect raw data, describe it, explore it, and check its quality. This is an initial assessment of the data that will be used to create the model. Again, data scientists must be skeptical. You must be sure you understand all the nuances of the data and its source.

The data preparation phase is actually the one that usually consumes most of the time during modeling. In this phase, we need to select and filter the data, clean it according to the task that needs to be performed, come up with new attributes, integrate the data with other data sources, and format it as expected by the algorithm that will be applied. These tasks are often called **feature engineering**.

Once the data is prepared, we can finally start the modeling phase. Here is where the algorithms come in. We should start by ensuring the selection of the right technique. Remember: according to the presence or absence of a target variable (and its data type), we will have different algorithms to choose from. Each modeling technique might carry some implicit assumptions of which we have to be aware. For example, if you choose a multiple linear regression algorithm to predict house prices, you should be aware that this type of model expects a linear relationship between the variables of your data.

There are hundreds of algorithms out there and each of them might have its own assumptions. After choosing the ones that you want to test in your project, you should spend some time checking their specifics. In later chapters of this book, we will cover some of them.

> **Important note**
> Some algorithms incorporate in their logic what we call **feature selection**. This is a step where the most important features will be selected to build your best model. Decision trees are examples of algorithms that perform feature selection automatically. We will cover feature selection in more detail later on, since there are different ways to select the best variables for your model.

During the modeling phase, you should also design a testing approach for the model, defining which evaluation metrics will be used and how the data will be split. With that in place, you can finally build the model by setting the hyperparameters of the algorithm and feeding the model with data. This process of feeding the algorithm with data to find a good estimator is known as the **training process**. The data used to feed the model is known as **training data**. There are different ways to organize the training and **testing data**, which we will cover in this chapter.

> **Important note**
>
> ML algorithms are built by parameters and hyperparameters. These are learned from the data. For example, a decision-tree-based algorithm might learn from the training data that a particular feature should compose its root level based on information gain assessments. Hyperparameters, on the other hand, are used to control the learning process. Taking the same example about decision trees, we could specify the maximum allowed depth of the tree by specifying a pre-defined hyperparameter of any decision tree algorithm (regardless of the underlining training data). Hyperparameter tuning is a very important topic in the exam and will be covered in fine-grained detail later on.

Once the model is trained, we can evaluate and review results in order to propose the next steps. If results are not acceptable (based on our business success criteria), we should come back to earlier steps to check what else can be done to improve the model results. It can either be a small tuning in the hyperparameters of the algorithm, a new data preparation step, or even a redefinition of business drivers. On the other hand, if the model quality is acceptable, we can move to the deployment phase.

In this last phase of the CRISP-DM methodology, we have to think about the deployment plan, monitoring, and maintenance of the model. We usually look at this step from two perspectives: training and inference. The **training pipeline** consists of those steps needed to train the model, which includes data preparation, hyperparameter definition, data splitting, and model training itself. Somehow, we must store all the model artifacts somewhere, since they will be used by the next pipeline that needs to be developed: the **inference pipeline**.

The inference pipeline just uses model artifacts to execute the model against brand-new observations (data that has never been seen by the model during the training phase). For example, if the model was trained to identify fraudulent transactions, this is the time where new transactions will pass through the model to be classified.

In general, models are trained once (through the training pipeline) and executed many times (through the inference pipeline). However, after some time, it is expected that there will be some model degradation, also known as **model drift**. This phenomenon happens because the model is usually trained in a static training set that aims to represent the business scenario at a given point in time; however, businesses evolve, and it might be necessary to retrain the model on more recent data to capture new business aspects. That's why it is important to keep tracking model performance even after model deployment.

The CRISP-DM methodology is so important to the context of the AWS Machine Learning Specialty exam that, if you look at the four domains covered by AWS, you will realize that they were generalized from the CRISP-DM stages: data engineering, exploratory data analysis, modeling, and ML implementation and operations.

We now understand all the key stages of a modeling pipeline and we know that the algorithm itself is just part of a broad process! Next, let's see how we can split our data to create and validate ML models.

Data splitting

Training and evaluating ML models are key tasks of the modeling pipeline. ML algorithms need data to find relationships among features in order to make inferences, but those inferences need to be validated before they are moved to production environments.

The dataset used to train ML models is commonly called the training set. This training data must be able to represent the real environment where the model will be used; it will be useless if that requirement is not met.

Coming back to our fraud example presented in *Figure 1.2*, based on the training data, we found that e-commerce transactions with a value greater than $5,000 and processed at night are potentially fraudulent cases. With that in mind, after applying the model in a production environment, the model is supposed to flag similar cases, as learned during the training process.

Therefore, if those cases only exist in the training set, the model will flag **false positive** cases in production environments. The opposite scenario is also valid: if there is a particular fraud case in production data, not reflected in the training data, the model will flag a lot of **false negative** cases. False positives and false negatives ratios are just two of many quality metrics that we can use for model validation. These metrics will be covered in much more detail later on.

By this point, you should have a clear understanding of the importance of having a good training set. Now, supposing we do have a valid training set, how could we have some level of confidence that this model will perform well in production environments? The answer is: using testing and validation sets:

Figure 1.5 – Data splitting

Figure 1.5 shows the different types of data splitting that we can have during training and inference pipelines. The training data is the one used to create the model and the testing data is the one used to extract final model quality metrics. The testing data *cannot* be used during the training process for any reason other than to extract model metrics.

The reason to avoid using the testing data during training is simple: we *cannot* let the model learn on top of the data that will be used to validate it. This technique of holding one piece of the data for testing is often called **hold-out validation**.

The box on the right side of *Figure 1.5* represents the production data. Production data usually comes in continuously and we have to execute the inference pipeline in order to extract model results from it. No training, nor any other type of recalculation, is performed on top of production data; we just have to pass it through the inference pipeline as it is.

From a technical perspective, most of the ML libraries implement training steps with the .fit method, while inference steps are implemented by the .transform *or* .predict method. Again, this is just a common pattern used by most ML libraries, but be aware that you might find different name conventions across ML libraries.

Still looking at *Figure 1.5*, there is another box, close to the training data, named **validation data**. This is a subset of the training set often used to support the creation of the best model, before moving to the testing phase. We will talk about that box in much more detail, but first, let's explain why we need them.

Overfitting and underfitting

ML models might suffer from two types of fitting issues: **overfitting** and **underfitting**. Overfitting means that your model performs very well in the training data, but cannot be generalized to other datasets, such as testing and, even worse, production data. In other words, if you have an overfitted model, it only works on your training data.

When we are building ML models, we want to create solutions that are able to generalize what they have learned and infer decisions on other datasets that follow the same data distribution. A model that only works on the data that it was trained on is useless. Overfitting usually happens due to the large number of features or the lack of configuration of the hyperparameters of the algorithm.

On the other hand, underfitted models cannot fit the data during the training phase. As a result, they are so generic that they can't perform well with the training, testing, or production data. Underfitting usually happens due to the lack of good features/ observations or due to the lack of time to train the model (some algorithms need more iterations to properly fit the model).

Both overfitting and underfitting need to be avoided. There are many modeling techniques to work around that. For instance, let's focus on the commonly used **cross-validation** technique and its relationship with the validation box showed in *Figure 1.5*.

Applying cross-validation and measuring overfitting

Cross-validation is a technique where we split the training set into training and validation sets. The model is then trained on the training set and tested on the validation set. The most common cross-validation strategy is known as **k-fold cross validation**, where k is the number of splits of the training set.

Using k-fold cross-validation and assuming the value of k equals 10, we are splitting the train set into 10 folds. The model will be trained and tested 10 times. On each iteration, it uses nine splits for training and leaves one split for testing. After 10 executions, the evaluation metrics extracted from each iteration are averaged and will represent the final model performance during the training phase, as shown in *Figure 1.6*:

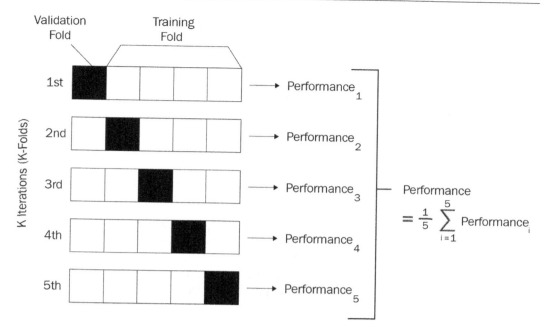

Figure 1.6 – Cross-validation in action

Another common cross-validation technique is known as **leave one out cross-validation** (**LOOCV**). In this approach, the model is executed many times and, with each iteration, one observation is separated for testing and all the others are used for training.

There are many advantages of using cross-validation during training:

- We mitigate overfitting in the training data, since the model is always trained on a particular chunk of data and tested on another chunk that hasn't been used for training.

- We avoid overfitting in the test data, since there is no need to keep using the testing data to optimize the model.

- We expose the presence of overfitting or underfitting. If the model performance in the training/validation data is very different from the performance observed in the testing data, something is wrong.

Let's elaborate a little more on the third item on that list, since this is covered in the AWS Machine Learning Specialty exam. Let's assume we are creating a binary classification model, using cross-validation during training and using a testing set to extract final metrics (hold-out validation). If we get 80% accuracy in the cross-validation results and 50% accuracy in the testing set, it means that the model was overfitted to the train set, and cannot be generalized to the test set.

On the other hand, if we get 50% accuracy in the training set and 80% accuracy in the test set, there is a systemic issue in the data. It is very likely that the training and testing sets do not follow the same distribution.

> **Important note**
> Accuracy is a model evaluation metric commonly used on classification models. It measures how often the model made a correct decision during its inference process. We have selected this metric just for the sake of example, but be aware that there are many other evaluation metrics applicable for each type of model (which will be covered at the appropriate time).

Bootstrapping methods

Cross-validation is a good strategy to validate ML models, and you should try it in your daily activities as a data scientist. However, you should also know about other resampling techniques available out there. **Bootstrapping** is one of them.

While cross-validation works **with no replacement**, a bootstrapping approach works **with replacement**. With replacement means that, while you are drawing multiple random samples from a population dataset, the same observation might be duplicated across samples.

Usually, bootstrapping is not used to validate models as we do in the traditional cross-validation approach. The reason is simple: since it works with replacement, the same observation used for training could potentially be used for testing, too. This would result in inflated model performance metrics, since the estimator is likely to be correct when predicting an observation that was already seen in the training set.

Bootstrapping is often used by ML algorithms in an embedded way that requires resampling capabilities to process the data. In this context, bootstrapping is not being used to *validate* the model, but to *create* the model. **Random forest**, which will be covered in the algorithms chapter, is one of those algorithms that uses bootstrapping internally for model building.

Designing a good data splitting/sampling strategy is crucial to the success of the model or the algorithm. You should come up with different approaches to split your data, check how the model is performing on each split, and make sure those splits represent the real scenario where the model will be used.

The variance versus bias trade-off

Any ML model is supposed to contain errors. There are three types of errors that we can find on models: **bias** error, **variance** error, and **unexplained** error. The last one, as expected, cannot be explained. It is often related to the context of the problem and the relationships between the variables, and we can't control it.

The other two errors can be controlled during modeling. We usually say that there is a trade-off between bias and variance errors because one will influence the other. In this case, increasing bias will decrease variance and vice versa.

Bias error relates to assumptions taken by the model to learn the target function, the one that we want to solve. Some types of algorithms, such as linear algorithms, usually carry over that type of error because they make a lot of assumptions during model training. For example, linear models assume that the relationship present in the data is linear. Linear regression and logistic regression are types of algorithms that, in general, contain high bias. Decision trees, on the other hand, are types of algorithms that make fewer assumptions about the data and contain less bias.

Variance relates to the difference of estimations that the model performs on different training data. Models with high variance usually overfit to the training set. Decision trees are examples of algorithms with high variance (they usually rely a lot on specifics of the training set, failing to generalize), and linear/logistic regression are examples of algorithms with low variance. It does not mean that decision trees are bad estimators; it just means that we need to prune (optimize) them during training.

That said, the goal of any model is to minimize both bias and variance. However, as already mentioned, each one will impact the other in the opposite direction. For the sake of demonstration, let's use a decision tree to understand how this trade-off works.

Decision trees are nonlinear algorithms and often contain low bias and high variance. In order to decrease variance, we can prune the tree and set the `max_depth` hyperparameter (the maximum allowed depth of the tree) to 10. That will force a more generic model, reducing variance. However, that change will also force the model to make more assumptions (since it is now more generic) and increase bias.

Shuffling your training set

Now that you know what variance and data splitting are, let's dive a little deeper into the training dataset requirements. You are very likely to find questions around data shuffling in the exam. This process consists of randomizing your training dataset before you start using it to fit an algorithm.

Data shuffling will help the algorithm to reduce variance by creating a more generalizable model. For example, let's say your training represents a binary classification problem and it is sorted by the target variable (all cases belonging to class "0" appear first, then all the cases belonging to class "1").

When you fit an algorithm on this sorted data (especially some algorithms that rely on **batch processing**), it will take strong assumptions on the pattern of one of the classes, since it is very likely that it won't be able to create random batches of data with a good representation of both classes. Once the algorithm builds strong assumptions about the training data, it might be difficult for it to change them.

> **Important note**
> Some algorithms are able to execute the training process by fitting the data in chunks, also known as batches. This approach lets the model learn more frequently, since it will make partial assumptions after processing each batch of data (instead of making decisions only after processing the entire dataset).

On the other hand, there is no need to shuffle the test set, since it will be used only by the inference process to check model performance.

Modeling expectations

So far, we have talked about model building, validation, and management. Let's complete the foundations of ML by talking about a couple of other expectations while modeling.

The first one is **parsimony**. Parsimony describes models that offer the simplest explanation and fits the best results when compared with other models. Here's an example: while creating a linear regression model, you realize that adding 10 more features will improve your model performance by 0.001%. In this scenario, you should consider whether this performance improvement is worth the cost of parsimony (since your model will become more complex). Sometimes it is worth it, but most of the time it is not. You need to be skeptical and think according to your business case.

Parsimony directly supports **interpretability**. The simpler your model is, the easier it is to explain it. However, there is a battle between interpretability and **predictivity**: if you focus on predictive power, you are likely to lose some interpretability. Again, be a proper data scientist and select what is better for your use case.

Introducing ML frameworks

Being aware of some ML frameworks will put you in a much better position to pass the AWS Machine Learning Specialty exam. There is no need to master these frameworks, since this is not a framework-specific certification; however, knowing some common terms and solutions will help you to understand the context of the problems/questions.

scikit-learn is probably the most important ML framework that you should be aware of. This is an open source Python package that provides implementations of ML algorithms such as decision trees, support vector machines, linear regression, and many others. It also implements classes for data preprocessing, for example, one-hot encoding, a label encoder, principal component analysis, and so on. All these preprocessing methods (and many others) will be covered in later sections of this book.

The downside of scikit-learn is the fact that it needs customization to scale up through multiple machines. There is another ML library that is very popular because of the fact that it can handle multiprocessing straight away: **Spark's ML library**.

As the name suggests, this is an ML library that runs on top of **Apache Spark**, which is a unified analytical multi-processing framework used to process data on multiple machines. AWS offers a specific service that allows developers to create Spark clusters with a few clicks, known as **EMR**.

The Spark ML library is in constant development. As of the time of writing, it offers support to many ML classes of algorithms, such as classification and regression, clustering, and collaborative filtering. It also offers support for basic statistics computation, such as correlations and some hypothesis tests, as well as many data transformations, such as one-hot encoding, principal component analysis, min-max scaling, and others.

Another very popular ML framework is known as **TensorFlow**. This ML framework was created by the Google team and it is used for numerical computation and large-scale ML model development. TensorFlow implements not only traditional ML algorithms, but also DL models.

TensorFlow is considered a low-level API for model development, which means that it can be very complex to develop more sophisticated models, such as **transformers**, for text mining. As an attempt to facilitate model development, other ML frameworks were built on top of TensorFlow to make it easier. One of these high-level frameworks is **Keras**. With Keras, developers can create complex DL models with just a few lines of code. More recently, Keras was incorporated into TensorFlow and it can be now called inside the TensorFlow library.

MXNet is another open source DL library. Using MXNet, we can scale up neural network-based models using multiple GPUs running on multiples machines. It also supports different programming languages, such as Python, R, Scala, and Java.

Graphical processing unit (**GPU**) support is particularly important in DL libraries such as TensorFlow and MXNet. These libraries allow developers to create and deploy neural network-based models with multiple layers. The training process of neural networks relies a lot on matrix operations, which perform much better on GPUs than on CPUs. That's why these DL libraries offer GPU support. AWS also offers EC2 instances with GPU enabled.

These ML frameworks need a special channel to communicate with GPU units. NVIDIA, the most common supplier of GPUs nowadays, has created an API called the **Compute Unified Device Architecture** (**CUDA**). CUDA is used to configure GPU units on NVIDIA devices, for example, setting up caching memory and the number of threads needed to train a neural network model. There is no need to master CUDA or GPU architecture for the AWS Machine Learning Specialty exam, but you definitely need to know what they are and how DL models take advantage of them.

Last, but not least, you should also be aware of some development frameworks widely used by the data science community, but not necessarily to do ML. These frameworks interoperate with ML libraries to facilitate data manipulation and calculations. For example, **pandas** is a Python library that provides data processing capabilities, and **NumPy** is an open source Python library that provides numerical computing.

These terms and libraries are so incorporated into data scientists' daily routines that they might come up during the exam to explain some problem domain for you. Being aware of what they are will help you to quickly understand the context of the question.

ML in the cloud

ML has gone to the cloud and developers can now use it as a service. AWS has implemented ML services in different levels of abstraction. ML application services, for example, aim to offer out-of-the-box solutions for specific problem domains. **AWS Lex** is a very clear example of an ML application as a service, where people can implement chatbots with minimum development.

AWS Rekognition is another example, which aims to identify objects, people, text, scenes, and activities in images and videos. AWS provides many other ML application services that will be covered in the next chapter of this book.

Apart from application services, AWS also provides ML development platforms, which is the case with **SageMaker**. Unlike out-of-the-box services such as AWS Lex and Rekognition, SageMaker is a development platform that will let you build, train, and deploy your own models with much more flexibility.

SageMaker speeds up the development and deployment process by automatically handling the necessary infrastructure for the training and inference pipelines of your models. Behind the scenes, SageMaker orchestrates other AWS services (such as EC2 instances, load balancers, auto-scaling, and so on) to create a scalable environment for ML projects. SageMaker is probably the most important service that you should master for the AWS Machine Learning Specialty exam, and it will be covered in detail in a separate section. For now, you should focus on understanding the different approaches that AWS uses to offers ML-related services.

The third option that AWS offers for deploying ML models is the most generic and flexible one: you can deploy ML models by combining different AWS services and managing them individually. This is essentially doing what SageMaker does for you, building your applications from scratch. For example, you could use EC2 instances, load balancers, auto-scaling, and an API gateway to create an inference pipeline to a particular model. If you prefer, you can also use AWS serverless architecture to deploy your solution, for example, using **AWS Lambda functions**.

Summary

We are now heading to the end of this chapter, where we have covered several important topics about the foundations of ML. We started the chapter with a theoretical discussion about AI, ML, and DL and how this entire field has grown over the past few years due to the advent of big data platforms and cloud providers.

We then moved on to the differences between supervised, unsupervised, and reinforcement learning, highlighting some use cases related to each of them. This is likely to be a topic in the AWS Machine Learning Specialty exam.

We discussed that an ML model is built in many different stages and the algorithm itself is just one part of the modeling process. We also covered the expected behaviors of a good model.

We did a deep dive into data splitting, where we talked about different approaches to train and validate models, and we covered the mythic battle between variance and bias. We completed the chapter by talking about ML frameworks and services.

Coming up next, you will learn about AWS application services for ML, such as Amazon Polly, Amazon Rekognition, Amazon Transcribe, and many other AI-related AWS services. But first, let's look into some sample questions to give you an idea of what you could expect in the exam.

Questions

1. You have been hired to automate an audible response unit from a call center company. Every time a new customer's call comes in, the system must be able to understand the current load of the service as well as the goal of the call and recommend the right path in the audible response unit. The company does not have labeled data to supervise the model; it must take an approach to learn by experience (trial and error) and every time the algorithm makes a good recommendation of path, it will be rewarded. Which type of machine learning approach would best fit this project?

    a) Unsupervised learning

    b) Reinforcement learning

    c) Supervised learning

    d) DL

> **Answer**
>
> b, Since there is no labeled data and the agent needs to learn by experience, reinforcement learning is more appropriate for this use case. Another important fact in the question is that the agent is rewarded for good decisions.

2. You are working in a marketing department of a big company and you need to segment your customers based on their buying behavior. Which type of ML approach would best fit this project?

   a) Unsupervised learning

   b) Reinforcement learning

   c) Supervised learning

   d) DL

   > **Answer**
   >
   > a, Clustering (which is an unsupervised learning approach) is the most common type of algorithm to work with data segmentation/clusters.

3. You are working in a retail company that needs to forecast sales for the next few months. Which type of ML approach would best fit this project?

   a) Unsupervised learning

   b) Reinforcement learning

   c) Supervised learning

   d) DL

   > **Answer**
   >
   > c, Forecasting is a type of supervised learning that aims to predict a numerical value; hence, it might be framed as a regression problem and supervised learning.

4. A manufacturing company needs to understand how much money they are spending on each stage of their production chain. Which type of ML approach would best fit this project?

    a) Unsupervised learning.

    b) Reinforcement learning.

    c) Supervised learning.

    d) ML is not required.

    Answer

    d, ML is everywhere, but not everything needs ML. In this case, there is no need to use ML since the company should be able to collect their costs from each stage of the production chain and sum it up.

5. Which one of the following learning approaches gives us state-of-the-art algorithms to implement chatbots?

    a) Unsupervised learning

    b) Reinforcement learning

    c) Supervised learning

    d) DL

    Answer

    d, DL has provided state-of-the-art algorithms in the field of natural language processing.

6. You receive a training set from another team to create a binary classification model. They have told you that the dataset was already shuffled and ready for modeling. You have decided to take a quick look at how a particular algorithm, based on a neural network, would perform on it. You then split the data into train and test sets and run your algorithm. However, the results look very odd. It seems that the algorithm could not converge to an optimal solution. What would be your first line of investigation on this issue?

a) Make sure the algorithm used is able to handle binary classification models.

b) Take a look at the proportion of data of each class and make sure they are balanced.

c) Shuffle the dataset before starting working on it.

d) Make sure you are using the right hyperparameters of the chosen algorithm.

> **Answer**
>
> c, Data scientists must be skeptical about their work. Do not make assumptions about the data without prior validation. At this point in the book, you might not be aware of the specifics of neural networks, but you know that ML models are very sensitive to the data they are training on. You should double-check the assumptions that were passed to you before taking other decisions. By the way, shuffling your training data is the first thing you should do. This is likely to be present in the exam.

7. You have created a classification model to predict whether a banking transaction is fraud or not. During the modeling phase, your model was performing very well on both the training and testing sets. When you executed the model in a production environment, people started to complain about the low accuracy of the model. Assuming that there was no overfitting/underfitting problem during the training phase, what would be your first line of investigation?

a) The training and testing sets do not follow the same distribution.

b) The training set used to create this model does not represent the real environment where the model was deployed.

c) The algorithm used in the final solution could not generalize enough to identify fraud cases in production.

d) Since all ML models contain errors, we can't infer their performance in production systems.

> **Answer**
>
> b, Data sampling is very challenging, and you should always make sure your training data can represent the production data as precisely as possible. In this case, there was no evidence that the training and testing sets were invalid, since the model was able to perform well and consistently on both sets of data. Since the problem happens to appear only in production systems, there might have been a systematic issue in the training that is causing the issue.

8. You are training a classification model with 500 features that achieves 90% accuracy in the training set. However, when you run it in the test set, you get only 70% accuracy. Which of the following options are valid approaches to solve this problem (select all that apply)?

    a) Reduce the number of features.

    b) Add extra features.

    c) Implement cross-validation during the training process.

    d) Select another algorithm.

> **Answer**
>
> a, c, This is clearly an overfitting issue. In order to solve this type of problem, you could reduce the excessive number of features (which will reduce the complexity of the model and make it less dependent on the training set). Additionally, you could also implement cross-validation during the training process.

9. You are training a neural network model and want to execute the training process as quickly as possible. Which of the following hardware architectures would be most helpful to you to speed up the training process of neural networks?

    a) Use a machine with a CPU that implements multi-thread processing.

    b) Use a machine with GPU processing.

    c) Increase the amount of RAM of the machine.

    d) Use a machine with SSD storage.

> **Answer**
>
> b, Although you might take some benefits from multi-thread processing and large amounts of RAM, using a GPU to train a neural network will give you the best performance. You will learn much more about neural networks in later chapters of this book, but you already know that they perform a lot of matrix calculations during training, which is better supported by the GPU rather than the CPU.

10. Which of the following statements is *not* true about data resampling?

    a) Cross-validation is a data resampling technique that helps to avoid overfitting during model training.

    b) Bootstrapping is a data resampling technique often embedded in ML models that needs resampling capabilities to estimate the target function.

    c) The parameter k in k-fold cross-validation specifies how many samples will be created.

    d) Bootstrapping works without replacement.

> **Answer**
>
> d, All the statements about cross-validation and bootstrapping are correct except option d, since bootstrapping works with replacement (the same observations might appear on different splits).

2
AWS Application Services for AI/ML

In this chapter, we will learn about the AWS AI services for building chatbots, advanced text analysis, document analysis, transcription, and so on. This chapter has been designed in such a way that you can solve different use cases by integrating AWS AI services and get an idea of how they work. AWS is growing every day and they are adding new AI services regularly.

In this chapter, you will approach different use cases programmatically or from the console. This will help you understand different APIs and their usages. We will use S3 for storage and AWS Lambda to execute any code. The examples in this chapter are in Python, but you can use other supported languages such as Java, Node.js, .NET, PowerShell, Ruby, and so on.

We are going to cover the following topics:

- Analyzing images and videos with Amazon Rekognition
- Text to speech with Amazon Polly
- Speech to text with Amazon Transcribe
- Implementing natural language processing with Amazon Comprehend
- Translating documents with Amazon Translate

- Extracting text from documents with Amazon Textract
- Creating chatbots on Amazon Lex

Let's get started!

Technical requirements

All you will need for this chapter is an AWS account.

You can download the code examples for this chapter from GitHub at `https://github.com/PacktPublishing/AWS-Certified-Machine-Learning-Specialty-MLS-C01-Certification-Guide/tree/master/Chapter-2`.

Analyzing images and videos with Amazon Rekognition

If you need to add powerful visual analysis to your applications, then **Amazon Rekognition** is the service to opt for. **Rekognition Image** lets you easily build powerful applications to search, verify, and organize millions of images. **Rekognition Video** lets you extract motion-based context from stored or live stream videos, and helps you analyze them. Rekognition Video also allows you to index metadata such as objects, activities, scene, celebrities, and faces, making video searches easy. Rekognition Image uses deep neural network models to detect and label thousands of objects and scenes in your images. It helps you capture text in an image, a bit like **Optical Character Recognition (OCR)**. A perfect example is a T-shirt with quotes on it. If you were to take a picture of one and ask Amazon Rekognition to extract the text from it, it would be able to tell you what the text says. You can also perform celebrity recognition using Amazon Rekognition. I am not a celebrity, so I won't be using the celebrity recognition API for my face; instead, I will use the face comparison API.

The official documentation, available at `https://aws.amazon.com/rekognition/faqs/`, states the following:

> *"With Rekognition Image, you only pay for the images you analyze and the face metadata you store. You will not be charged for the compute resources if, at any point of time, your training fails."*

Some common uses of Amazon Rekognition include the following:

- Image and video analysis
- Searchable image library

- Face-based user verification

- Sentiment analysis

- Text in image

- Facial recognition

- Image moderation

- Search index for video archives

- Easy filtering for videos, for explicit and suggestive content

- Examples of explicit nudity – sexual activity, graphical nudity, adult toys, and so on

- Examples of suggestive content – partial nudity, swimwear or underwear, and so on

Exploring the benefits of Amazon Rekognition

Let's look at some of the benefits of using Amazon Rekognition:

- AWS manages the infrastructure it runs on. In short, just use the API for your image analysis. We just need to focus on building and managing our deep learning pipelines.

  With or without knowledge of image processing, you can perform image and video analysis just by using the APIs provided in Amazon Rekognition, which can be used for any application or service on several platforms.

- The Labels API's response will identify real-world entities within an image through the DetectLabels API. These labels include city, town, table, home, garden, animal, pets, food, drink, electronics, flowers, and more. The entities are classified based on their **Confidence** score, which indicates the probability that a given prediction is correct: the higher the better. Similarly, we can use the DetectText API to extract the text in an image. Amazon Rekognition may detect multiple lines based on the gap between words. Periods don't represent the end of a line.

- Amazon Rekognition can be integrated with AWS Kinesis Video Stream, AWS S3, and AWS Lambda for seamless and affordable image and video analysis. With the AWS IAM service, Amazon Rekognition API calls can easily be secured and controlled.

- Low cost. You only pay for the images and videos that are analyzed.

- Through AWS CloudTrail, all the API calls for Amazon Rekognition can be captured as events. It captures all calls made from the console, or the CLI, or code calls for APIs, which further enables the user to create Amazon SNS notifications based on CloudTrail events.

- You can create a VPC Endpoint policy for specific API calls to establish a private connection between your VPC and Amazon Rekognition. This helps you leverage enhanced security. As per the AWS shared responsibility model, AWS takes care of the security of the infrastructure and software, and we have to take care of the security of our content in the cloud.

Getting hands-on with Amazon Rekognition

In this section, we will learn how to integrate AWS Lambda with Amazon Rekognition to detect the labels in our image (uploaded at `https://github.com/PacktPublishing/AWS-Certified-Machine-Learning-Specialty-MLS-C01-Certification-Guide/tree/master/Chapter-2/Amazon%20Rekognition%20Demo/images`) and print the detected objects in the CloudWatch console. We will use the `detect_labels` API from Amazon Rekognition in the code.

We will begin by creating an IAM role for Lambda:

1. Navigate to the IAM console page.

2. Select **Roles** from the left-hand menu.

3. Select **Create role**.

4. Select **Lambda** from the **Choose a use case** section.

5. Add the following managed policies:

- `AmazonS3ReadOnlyAccess`

- `AmazonRekognitionFullAccess`

- `CloudWatchLogsFullAccess`

6. Name the role `rekognition-lambda-role`:

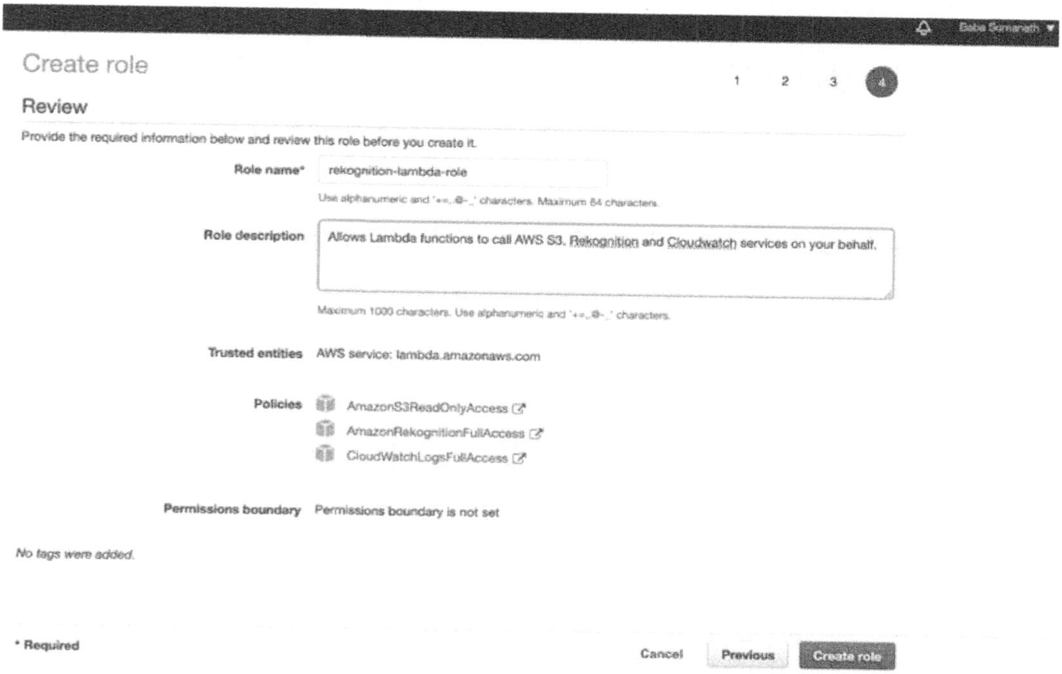

Figure 2.1 – The Create role dialog

Next, we will create a Lambda function.

7. Navigate to the AWS Lambda console page.

8. Select **Create function**.

9. Create a function:

- Select **Author from scratch**.

- Give the function a name, such as `lambda-rekognition`.

- Choose `Python 3.6` from the **Runtime** dropdown.

- Select **Use an existing role**. Add the name of the role you created previously; that is, `rekognition-lambda-role`:

Figure 2.2 – Creating the Lambda function

10. Enter the following code in `lambda_function.py`:

```
from __future__ import print_function
import boto3
def lambda_handler(event, context):
    print("========lambda_handler started=======")
    # read the bucket name (key) from the event
    name_of_the_bucket=event['Records'][0]['s3']['bucket']['name']
    # read the object from the event
    name_of_the_photo=event['Records'][0]['s3']['object']['key']
    detect_labels(name_of_the_photo,name_of_the_bucket)
    print("Labels detected Successfully")
def detect_labels(photo, bucket):
    client=boto3.client('rekognition')
    response=client.detect_labels(Image={'S3Object':{'Bucket':bucket,'Name':photo}})
    print('Detected labels for ' + photo)
```

```
        print('==============================')
        for label in response['Labels']:
            print ("Label: " + label['Name'])
            print ("Confidence: " +
str(label['Confidence']))
            print ("Instances:")
            for instance in label['Instances']:
                print ("   Bounding box")
                print ("Top:
"+str(instance['BoundingBox']['Top']))
                print ("Left: \
"+str(instance['BoundingBox']['Left']))
                print ("Width: \
"+str(instance['BoundingBox']['Width']))
                print ("Height: \
"+str(instance['BoundingBox']['Height']))
                print ("Confidence:
"+str(instance['Confidence']))
                print()
            print ("Parents:")
            for parent in label['Parents']:
                print ("   " + parent['Name'])
            print ("----------")
            print('==============================')
    return response
```

Now, we will create a trigger for the Lambda Function.

11. Navigate to the AWS S3 console page. Create a bucket, for example, `rekognition-test-baba`, as shown in the following screenshot:

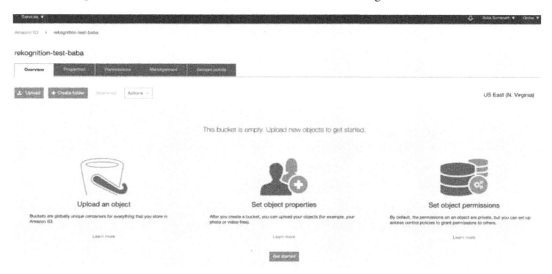

Figure 2.3 – AWS S3 console page

12. Click on **Create folder** and name it `images`. Click **Save**.

13. Click the **Properties** tab of our bucket.

14. Scroll to **Events** for that bucket.

15. Inside the **Events** window, select **Add notification** and set the following properties:

- **Name**: `rekognition_event`
- **Events**: `All object create events`
- **Prefix**: `images/`
- **Send to**: `Lambda Function`
- **Lambda**: `lambda-rekognition:`

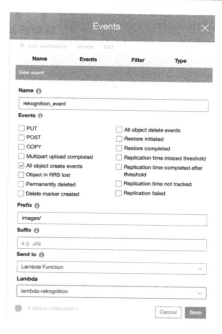

Figure 2.4 – S3 bucket Events window

Next, we will upload the image from the shared GitHub repository to the S3 bucket `images` folder.

16. As soon as you upload, you can check the **Monitoring** tab in the Lambda console to monitor the events, as shown in the following screenshot:

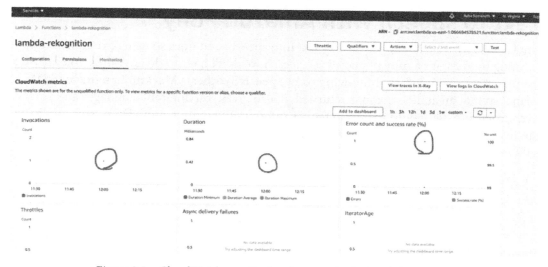

Figure 2.5 – CloudWatch monitoring the event in the Lambda console

17. Navigate to **CloudWatch > CloudWatch Logs > Log groups > /aws/lambda/ lambda-rekognition**. Select the latest stream from all the streams and scroll down in the logs to see your output, as shown in the following screenshot:

Figure 2.6 – CloudWatch logs

In this section, we learned how to implement the Amazon Rekognition AI service to detect objects in an image and get a confidence score for each. We will see more use cases for Amazon Rekognition in the upcoming sections, when we detect text in images. In the next section, we will learn about Amazon's text-to-speech service and implement it.

Text to speech with Amazon Polly

Amazon Polly is all about converting text into speech, and does so using pretrained deep learning models. It's a fully managed service, so we don't have to do anything. You provide the plain text as input for synthesizing or in **Speech Synthesis Markup Language** (**SSML**) format so that an audio stream is returned. It also gives you different languages and voices to choose from, with both male and female options. The output audio from Amazon Polly can be saved in MP3 format for further usage in the application (web or mobile) or can be a JSON output for written speech.

For example, if we were to input the text "Baba went to the library" into Amazon Polly, the output speech mark object would look as follows:

```
{"time":370,"type":"word","start":5,"end":9,"value":"went"}
```

The word `"went"` begins 370 milliseconds after the audio stream begins, and starts at byte 5 and ends at byte 9 of the given input text.

It also returns output in `ogg_vorbis` and `pcm` format. When `pcm` is used, the content that's returned is audio/pcm in a signed 16-bit, 1 channel (mono), little-endian format.

Some common uses of Amazon Polly include the following:

- Can be used as an accessibility tool for reading web content.

- Can be integrated with Amazon Rekognition to help visually impaired people read signs. You can click a picture of the sign with text and feed it to Amazon Rekognition to extract text. The output text can be used as input for Polly, and it will return a voice as output.

- Can be used in a public address system, where the admin team can just pass on the text to be announced and Amazon Polly does the magic.

- By combining Amazon Polly with **Amazon Connect** (telephony backend service), you can build an **audio/video receiver** (**AVR**) system.

- Smart devices such as smart tvs, smart watches, and **Internet of Things** (**IoT**) devices can use this for audio output.

- Narration generation.

- When combined with Amazon Lex, full-blown voice user interfaces for applications can be developed.

Now, let's explore the benefits of Amazon Polly.

Exploring the benefits of Amazon Polly

Some of the benefits of using Amazon Polly include the following:

- This service is fully managed and doesn't require any admin cost to maintain or manage resources.

- It provides an instant speech corrections and enhancements facility.

- You can develop your own access layer using the HTTP API from Amazon Polly. Development is easy due to the huge amount of language support that's available, such as Python, Ruby, Go, C++, Java, and Node.js.

- For certain neural voices, speech can be synthesized by using the Newscaster style, to make them sound like a TV or radio broadcaster.

- Amazon Polly also allows you to modify the pronunciation of particular words or the use of new words.

Next, we'll get hands-on with Amazon Polly.

Getting hands-on with Amazon Polly

In this section, we will build a pipeline where we can integrate AWS Lambda with Amazon Polly to read a text file, and then generate an **MP3** file of the same to another folder in the same bucket. We will monitor the task's progress in CloudWatch logs.

We will begin by creating an IAM Role for Lambda. Let's get started:

1. Navigate to the IAM console page.
2. Select **Roles** from the left-hand menu.
3. Select **Create role**.
4. Select **Lambda** as the trusted entity.
5. Add the following managed policies:

    - `AmazonS3FullAccess`
    - `AmazonPollyFullAccess`
    - `CloudWatchFullAccess`

6. Save the role as `polly-lambda-role`.

Next, we will create a Lambda function:

1. Navigate to **Lambda > Functions > Create Function**.

    - Name the function `polly-lambda`
    - Set the runtime to `python 3.6.`
    - Use an existing role; that is, `polly-lambda-role`

2. Paste the code at `https://github.com/PacktPublishing/` `AWS-Certified-Machine-Learning-Specialty-MLS-C01-` `Certification-Guide/tree/master/Chapter-2/Amazon%20` `Rekognition%20Demo/lambda_code` into your lambda function and check its progress in the CloudWatch console. We will be using the `start_speech_` `synthesis_task` API from Amazon Polly for this code; it is an asynchronous synthesis task.

3. Scroll down and in **Basic Settings** section, change **Timeout** to 5 9 **sec**, as shown in the following screenshot, and click **Save**:

> **Important note**
> The default is 3 sec. Since this is an asynchronous operation, any retried attempts will create more files.

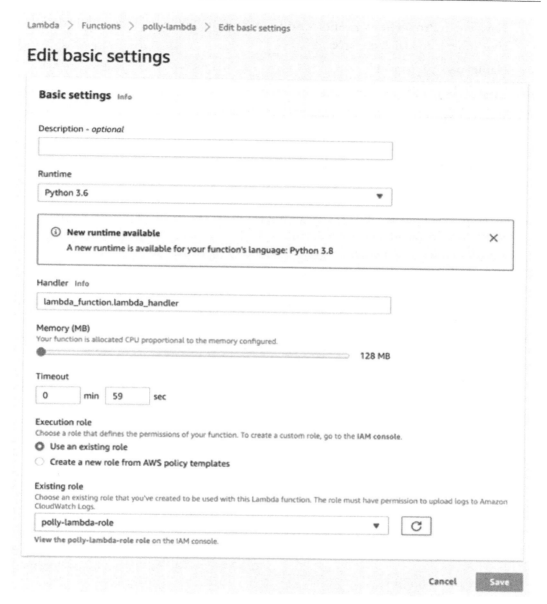

Figure 2.7 – Edit basic settings window

Now, we will create a bucket to trigger an event.

4. Navigate to the AWS S3 console and create a bucket called `polly-test-baba`.

5. Create a folder called `input-text` (in this example, we will only upload `.txt` files).

6. Navigate to **Properties > Events > Add notification**. Fill in the required fields, as shown here, and click on **Save**:

-   **Name**: polly_event
-   **Events**: All object create events
-   **Prefix**: input-text/
-   **Suffix**: .txt
-   **Send to**: Lambda Function
-   **Lambda**: polly-lambda

7. Next, we will upload a file in order to trigger an event and check its progress in CloudWatchUpload, in this case, a file test_file.txt in input-text, as shown in the following screenshot. You can download the sample file from this book's GitHub repository at https://github.com/PacktPublishing/ AWS-Certified-Machine-Learning-Specialty-MLS-C01- Certification-Guide/tree/master/Chapter-2/Amazon%20Polly%20 Demo/text_file:

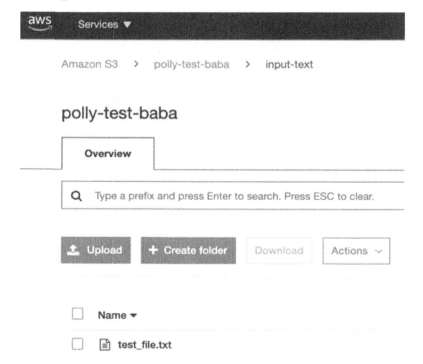

Figure 2.8 – The S3 bucket after uploading a text file for further processing

8. This will trigger the lambda function. You can monitor your logs by going to **CloudWatch> CloudWatch Logs> Log groups> /aws/lambda/polly-lambda**:

Figure 2.9 – Log groups in the CloudWatch console

9. Click on the latest stream; the log will look as follows:

```
File Content:  Hello Everyone, Welcome to Dublin. How
are you doing today?
{'ResponseMetadata': {'RequestId': '74ca4afd-5844-
47d8-9664-3660a26965e4', 'HTTPStatusCode': 200,
'HTTPHeaders': {'x-amzn-requestid': '74ca4afd-5844-
47d8-9664-3660a26965e4', 'content-type':
'application/json', 'content-length': '471', 'date':

'Thu, 24 Sep 2020 18:50:57 GMT'}, 'RetryAttempts': 0},
'SynthesisTask': {'Engine': 'standard', 'TaskId':
'57548c6b-d21a-4885-962f-450952569dc7', 'TaskStatus':
'scheduled', 'OutputUri': 'https://s3.us-east-
1.amazonaws.com/polly-test-baba/output-
audio/.57548c6b-d21a-4885-962f-450952569dc7.mp3',
'CreationTime': datetime.datetime(2020, 9, 24, 18, 50,
57, 769000, tzinfo=tzlocal()), 'RequestCharacters':
59, 'OutputFormat': 'mp3', 'TextType': 'text',
'VoiceId': 'Aditi', 'LanguageCode': 'en-GB'}}
```

The logs sample is shown in the following screenshot:

```
▸  2020-09-24T19:07:04.054+01:0...   Task Status is : scheduled
▸  2020-09-24T19:07:04.094+01:0...   Task Status is : scheduled
▸  2020-09-24T19:07:04.105+01:0...   Task Status is : scheduled
▸  2020-09-24T19:07:04.184+01:0...   Task Status is : scheduled
▸  2020-09-24T19:07:04.254+01:0...   Task Status is : inProgress
▸  2020-09-24T19:07:04.497+01:0...   Task Status is : completed
▸  2020-09-24T19:07:04.534+01:0...   Audio File Saved Successfully
▸  2020-09-24T19:07:04.553+01:0...   END RequestId: 1d57151b-8462-434c-89b4-9b318c2437d8
▸  2020-09-24T19:07:04.553+01:0...   REPORT RequestId: 1d57151b-8462-434c-89b4-9b318c2437d8 Duration: 15832.73 ms Billed Duration:
                                     No newer events at this moment. Auto retry paused. Resume
```

Figure 2.10 – The logs in the CloudWatch console

10. It will create output in MP3 format, as shown in the following screenshot. Download and listen to it:

Figure 2.11 – The output file that was created in the S3 bucket

> **Important note**
>
> The most scalable and cost-effective way for your mobile apps or web apps is to generate an AWS pre-signed URL for S3 buckets and provide it to your users. These S3 Put events asynchronously invoke downstream AI workflows to generate results and send a response to the end users. Many users can be served at the same time through this approach, and it may increase performance and throughput.

In this section, we learned how to implement text to speech. In the next section, we will learn about Amazon Transcribe, a speech-to-text AI service.

Speech to text with Amazon Transcribe

In the previous section, we learned about text to speech. In this section, we will learn about speech to text and the service that provides this: **Amazon Transcribe**. It is an automatic speech recognition service that uses pre-trained deep learning models, which means that we don't have to train on petabytes of data to produce a model; Amazon does this for us. We just have to use the APIs that are available to transcribe audio files or video files; it supports a number of different languages and custom vocabulary too. Accuracy is the key and through custom vocabulary, you can enhance it based on the desired domain or industry:

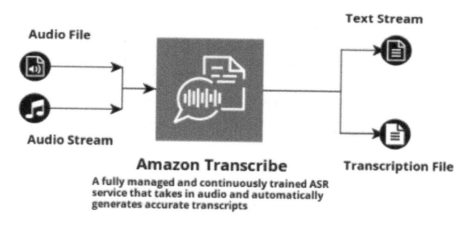

Figure 2.12 – Block diagram of Amazon Transcribe's input and output

Some common uses of Amazon Transcribe include the following:

- Real-time audio streaming and transcription.
- Transcripting pre-recorded audio files.
- Enable text searching from a media file by combining AWS Elasticsearch and Amazon Transcribe.
- Performing sentiment analysis on recorded audio files for voice helpdesk (contact center analytics).
- Channel identification separation.

Next, we'll explore the benefits of Amazon Transcribe.

Exploring the benefits of Amazon Transcribe

Let's look at some of the benefits of using Amazon Transcribe:

- *Content Redaction*: Customer privacy can be ensured by instructing Amazon Transcribe to identify and redact **personally identifiable information (PII)** from the language transcripts. You can filter unwanted words from your transcript by supplying a list of unwanted words with `VocabularyFilterName` and `VocabularyFilterMethod`, which are provided by the `StratTranscriptionJob` operation. For example, in financial organizations, this can be used to redact a caller's details.

- *Language Identification*: It can automatically identify the most used language in an audio file and generate transcriptions. If you have several audio files, then this service would help you classify them by language.

- *Streaming Transcription*: You can send recorded audio files or live audio streams to Amazon Transcribe and output a stream of text in real time.

- *Custom Vocabulary or Customized Transcription*: You can use your custom vocabulary list as per your custom needs to generate accurate transcriptions.

- *TimeStamp Generation*: If you want to build or add subtitles for your videos, then Amazon Transcribe can return the timestamp for each word or phrase from the audio.

- *Cost Effectiveness*: Being a managed service, there is no infrastructure cost.

Now, let's get hands-on with Amazon Transcribe.

Getting hands-on with Amazon Transcribe

In this section, we will build a pipeline where we can integrate AWS Lambda with Amazon Transcribe to read an audio file stored in a folder in an S3 bucket, and then store the output JSON file in another S3 bucket. We will monitor the task's progress in CloudWatch logs too. We will use the `start_transcription_job` asynchronous function to start our job and we will constantly monitor the job through `get_transcription_job` until its status becomes COMPLETED. Let's get started:

1. First, create an IAM role called `transcribe-demo-role` for the Lambda function to execute. Ensure that it can read and write from/to S3, use Amazon Transcribe, and print the output in CloudWatch logs. Add the following policies to the IAM role:

   - `AmazonS3FullAccess`
   - `CloudWatchFullAccess`
   - `AmazonTranscribeFullAccess`

2. Now, we will create a Lambda function called `transcribe-lambda` with our existing IAM role, `transcribe-demo-role`, and save it.

   Please make sure you change the default timeout to a higher value in the **Basic settings** section of your lambda function. I have set it to 10 min and 20 sec to avoid timeout errors. We will be using an asynchronous API call called `start_transcription_job` to start the task and monitor the same by using the `get_transcription_job` API.

3. Paste the code available at `https://github.com/PacktPublishing/AWS-Certified-Machine-Learning-Specialty-MLS-C01-Certification-Guide/blob/master/Chapter-2/Amazon%20Transcribe%20Demo/lambda_function/lambda_function.py` and click on **Deploy**.

   This should give us the following output:

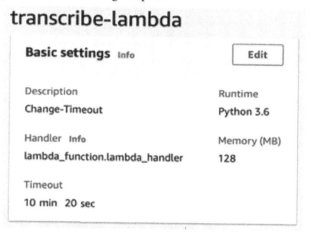

Figure 2.13 – The Basic settings section of our created lambda function

4. Next, we will be creating the an S3 bucket called `transcribe-demo-101` and a folder called `input`. Create an event by going to the **Properties** tab of the **Create event notification** section. Enter the following details:

- **Name**: `audio-event`
- **Events**: `All object create events`
- **Prefix**: `input/`
- **Destination**: `Lambda Function`
- **Lambda**: `transcribe-lambda`

5. Upload the audio file in .mp4 format to the input folder. This will trigger the Lambda function. As per the code, the output will be stored in the S3 bucket in JSON format, which you can then use to read the contents of the file.

6. Navigate to **CloudWatch > CloudWatch Logs > Log groups > aws/lambda/ transcribe-lambda**. Choose the latest stream from the list. It will look as follows:

Figure 2.14 – The logs in a Log Stream for the specified log groups in the CloudWatch console

7. The output is saved to the S3 bucket in JSON format, as per the jobname mentioned in your code (you can use the the S3 getObject API to download and read it):

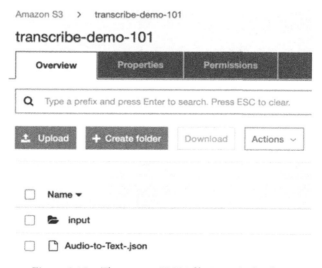

Figure 2.15 – The output JSON file in an S3 bucket

> **Important note**
>
> It is a best practice not to overprovision your function's timeout settings. Always understand your code performance and set a function timeout accordingly. Overprovisioning a function timeout results in Lambda functions running longer and it causes unexpected costs. If you're using asynchronous API calls in your Lambda function, then it's good to write them into SNS topics on success and trigger another Lambda function from that. If it needs human intervention, then it is suggested that you use AWS Step Functions.

In this section, we learned and applied Amazon Transcribe to convert speech into text. In the next section, we will learn about one of the most powerful AWS AI services we can use to get the maximum amount of insight from our text data.

Implementing natural language processing with Amazon Comprehend

This service helps you extract insights from unstructured text. Unstructured text information is growing exponentially. A few data source examples are as follows:

- *Customer engagement*: Call center, issue triage, customer surveys, and product reviews

- *Business processes*: Customer/vendor emails, product support messages, and operation support feedback

- *Records and research*: Whitepapers and medical records

- *News and social media*: Social media analytics, brand trends, and correlated events

Now, the question is, what can we do with this data? How can we analyze it and extract any value out of it? The answer is Amazon Comprehend, which is used to get insights from your unstructured data.

Some common uses of Amazon Comprehend include the following:

- Information management system

- More accurate search system on organized topics

- Sentiment analysis of users

- Support ticket classification

- Language detection from a document and then translating it into English using Amazon Translate

- Creating a system to label unstructured clinical data to assist in research and analysis purposes

- Extracting topics from the saved audio files of company meetings or TV news

Next, we'll explore the benefits of Amazon Comprehend.

Exploring the benefits of Amazon Comprehend

Some of the advantages of using Comprehend can be seen in the following image:

Figure 2.16 – A block diagram showing Amazon Comprehend's capabilities

Let's look at these in more detail:

- It detects the language of the text and extract key phrases. Amazon Comprehend can be used for sentiment analysis and topic modeling too.

- Amazon Comprehend Medical can be used to extract medical information.

- You pay for what you use since this is a fully managed service; you do not have to pay for the infrastructure. You don't need to train, develop, and deploy your own model.

- The topic modeling service works by extracting up to 100 topics. A topic is a keyword bucket so that you can see what's in the actual corpus of documents.

- It's accurate, continuously trained, and easy to use.

Next, we'll get hands-on with Amazon Comprehend.

Getting hands-on with Amazon Comprehend

In this section, we will build a pipeline where we can integrate AWS Lambda with Amazon Rekognition and Amazon Comprehend. We will then read an image file stored in an S3 bucket and detect the language of the text that's been extracted from the image. We will also use CloudWatch to print out the output. The following is a diagram of our use case:

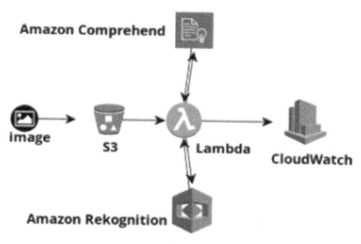

Figure 2.17 – Architecture diagram of the required use case

Let's begin by creating an IAM Role:

1. Navigate to the IAM console page.
2. Select **Roles** from the left-hand menu.
3. Select **Create role**.
4. Select **Lambda** as the trusted entity.
5. Add the following managed `policies`:

    *   `AmazonS3ReadOnlyAccess`
    *   `AmazonRekognitionFullAccess`
    *   `ComprehendFullAccess`
    *   `CloudWatchFullAccess`

6. Save the role as `language-detection-from-image-role`.
7. Now, let's create the Lambda function. Navigate to **Lambda** > **Functions** > **Create Function**.

8. Name the function `language-detection-from-image`.

9. Set the runtime to `Python 3.6`.

10. Use our existing role; that is, `language-detection-from-image-role`.

11. Download the code from `https://github.com/PacktPublishing/AWS-Certified-Machine-Learning-Specialty-MLS-C01-Certification-Guide/tree/master/Chapter-2/Amazon%20Transcribe%20Demo/lambda_function`, paste it into the function, and click **Deploy**.

    This code will read the text from the image that you uploaded and detect the language of the text. We have used the `detect_text` API from Amazon Rekognition to detect text from an image and the `batch_detect_dominant_language` API from Amazon Comprehend to detect the language of the text.

12. Now, go to your AWS S3 console and create a bucket called *language-detection-image*.

13. Create a folder called `input-image` (in this example, we will only upload `.jpg` files).

14. Navigate to **Properties > Events> Add notification**.

15. Fill in the required fields in the **Events** section with the following information; then, click on **Save**:

- **Name**: `image-upload-event`
- **Events**: `All object create events`
- **Prefix**: `input-image/`
- **Suffix**: `.jpg`
- **Send to**: `Lambda Function`
- **Lambda**: `language-detection-from-image`

16. Navigate to **Amazon S3>language-detection-image>input-image**. Upload the `sign-image.jpg` image in the folder. (This file is available in this book's GitHub repository at `https://github.com/PacktPublishing/AWS-Certified-Machine-Learning-Specialty-MLS-C01-Certification-Guide/tree/master/Chapter-2/Amazon%20Comprehend%20Demo/input_image`).

17. This file upload will trigger the lambda function. You can monitor the logs from **CloudWatch> CloudWatch Logs> Log groups> /aws/lambda/language-detection-from-image**.

18. Click on the streams and select the latest one. The detected language is printed in the logs, as shown in the following screenshot:

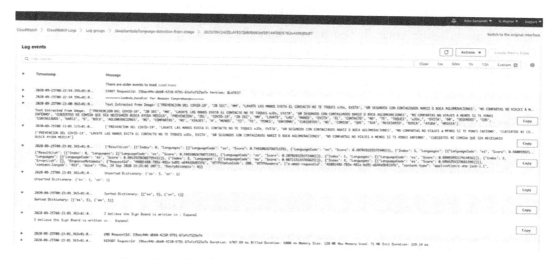

Figure 2.18 – The logs in CloudWatch for verifying the output

> **Important note**
>
> It is suggested that you use batch operations such as `BatchDetectSentiment` or `BatchDetectDominantLanguage` in your production environment. This is because single API operations can cause API-level throttling. More details are available here: `https://docs.aws.amazon.com/comprehend/latest/dg/functionality.html`.

In this section, we learned how to use Amazon Comprehend to detect the language of texts. The text is extracted into our Lambda function using Amazon Rekognition. In the next section, we will learn about translating the same text into English via Amazon Translate.

Translating documents with Amazon Translate

Most of the time, people prefer to communicate in their own language, even on digital platforms. Amazon Translate is a text translation service. We can provide documents or strings of text in various languages and get it back in a different language. It uses pre-trained deep learning techniques, so we shouldn't be worried about the models, nor how they are managed. We can make API requests and get the results back.

Some common uses of Amazon Translate include the following:

- If there's an organization-wide requirement to prepare documents in different languages, then Translate is the solution for converting one language into many.

- Online chat applications can be translated in real time to provide a better customer experience.

- To localize website content faster and more affordably into more languages.

- Sentiment analysis can be applied to different languages once they have been translated.

- To provide non-English language support for a news publishing website.

Next, we'll explore the benefits of Amazon Translate.

Exploring the benefits of Amazon Translate

Some of the benefits of using Amazon Translate include the following:

- It uses neural machine translation, which mimics the way the human brain works.

- No need to maintain your resources.

- Produces high-quality results and maintains their consistency.

- You can customize your brand names and model names, and any other unique terms get translated using the Custom Terminology Feature.

- Can be easily integrated with applications through APIs.

- Amazon Translate scales itself when you need it to do more.

Next, we will get hands-on with Amazon Translate.

Getting hands-on with Amazon Translate

In this section, we will build a product by integrating AWS Lambda with Amazon Rekognition, Amazon Comprehend, and Amazon Translate to read an image file stored in an S3 bucket. Then, we will detect the language of the text that's been extracted from the image so that we can translate it into English. We will also use CloudWatch to print the translated output. The following is a diagram of our use case:

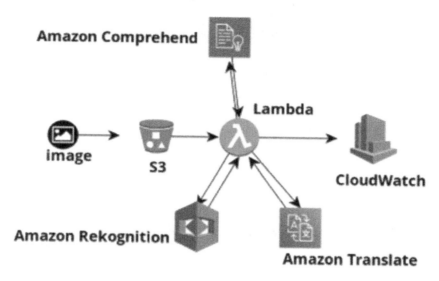

Figure 2.19 – Architecture diagram of the required use case

Let's start by creating an IAM role:

1. Navigate to the IAM console page.

2. Select **Roles** from the left-hand menu.

3. Select **Create role**.

4. Select **Lambda** as the trusted entity.

5. Add the following managed policies:

   - AmazonS3ReadOnlyAccess

   - AmazonRekognitionFullAccess

   - ComprehendFullAccess

   - CloudWatchFullAccess

   - TranslateFullAccess

6. Save the role as `language-translation-from-image`.

7. The next immediate step is to create a Lambda function. Navigate to **Lambda > Functions > Create Function**.

8. Name the function `language-detection-from-image`.

9. Set the runtime to `Python 3.6`.

10. Use an existing role; that is, `language-detection-from-image-role`.

11. Paste the code available at `https://github.com/PacktPublishing/AWS-Certified-Machine-Learning-Specialty-MLS-C01-Certification-Guide/blob/master/Chapter-2/Amazon%20Translate%20Demo/lambda_function/lambda_function.py` and click **Deploy**. We will use the `translate_text` API to translate the input text.

12. The next step is to create a bucket called `language-translation-from-image`.

    Create a folder named `image`. Then, navigate to **Properties > Events> Add notification**.

13. Fill in the required fields, as shown here, and click on **Save** (please make sure you select `.jpg` as the suffix; otherwise, it will trigger the lambda function for any object creation process):

    *   **Name**: *translate-language-image*
    *   **Events**: `All object create events`
    *   **Prefix**: `image/`
    *   **Suffix**: `.jpg`
    *   **Send to**: `Lambda Function`
    *   **Lambda**: `language-translation-from-image`

14. Navigate to **Amazon S3>language-detection-image>input-image**. Upload the `sign-image.jpg` image into the folder. This file is available in this book's GitHub repository: `https://github.com/PacktPublishing/AWS-Certified-Machine-Learning-Specialty-MLS-C01-Certification-Guide/tree/master/Chapter-2/Amazon%20Translate%20Demo/input_image`.

15. Uploading this image will trigger the lambda function. You can monitor the logs by going to **CloudWatch> CloudWatch Logs> Log groups> /aws/lambda/language-translation-from-image**.

16. Click on the streams and select the latest one. It will look as follow:

Figure 2.20 – The logs in CloudWatch for verifying the output

The translation is as follows:

```
Translation of the text from the Image :
{'PREVENCION DEL COVID-19': 'PREVENTION OF COVID-19',
'LAVATE LAS MANOS EVITA EL CONTACTO NO TE TOQUES oJOs,
EVITA': 'WASHE HANDS AVOID CONTACT DO NOT TOUCH EYES',
'60 SEGUNDOS CON CONTAGIADOS NARIZ O BOCA
AGLOMERACIONES': '60 SECONDS WITH CONTAGIOUS NOSE OR
MOUTH AGGLOMERATIONS', 'NO COMPARTAS NO VIAJES A MENOS
SI TE PONES ENFERMO': "DON'T SHARE NOT TRAVEL UNLESS
YOU GET SICK", 'CUBIERTOS NI COMIDA QUE SEA NECESARIO
BUSCA AYUDA MEDICA': 'CUTLERY OR FOOD NEEDED SEEK
MEDICAL HELP'}
```

> **Important note**
>
> For production use cases, it is recommended to use AWS Lambda with AWS Step Function if you have dependent services or a chain of services.
>
> Using the same S3 bucket to store input and output objects is not recommended. Output object creation in the same bucket may trigger recursive Lambda invocation. If you're using same bucket, then we recommend that you use a prefix and suffix to trigger events. Similarly, we recommend using a prefixto store output objects.

In this section, we learned how to combine multiple services and chain their output to achieve a particular use case outcome. We learned how to integrate Amazon Rekognition to detect text in an image. The language can then be detected by using Amazon Comprehend. Then, we used the same input and translated it into English with the help of Amazon Translate. The translated output was then printed on CloudWatch logs for verification. In the next section, we will learn about Amazon Textract, which we can use to extract text from a document.

Extracting text from documents with Amazon Textract

Manually extracting information from documents is slow, expensive, and prone to errors. Traditional optical character recognition software needs a lot of customization, and it will still give erroneous output. To avoid such manual processes and errors, you should use **Amazon Textract**. Generally, we convert the documents into images in order to detect bounding boxes around the texts in images. We then apply character recognition technique to read the text from it. Textract does all this for you, and also extracts text, tables, forms, and other data for you with minimal effort. If you get low-confidence results from Amazon Textract, then Amazon A2I is the best solution.

Textract reduces the manual effort of extracting text from millions of scanned document pages. Once the information has been captured, actions can be taken on the text, such as storing it in different data stores, analyzing sentiments, or searching for keywords. The following diagram shows how Amazon Textract works:

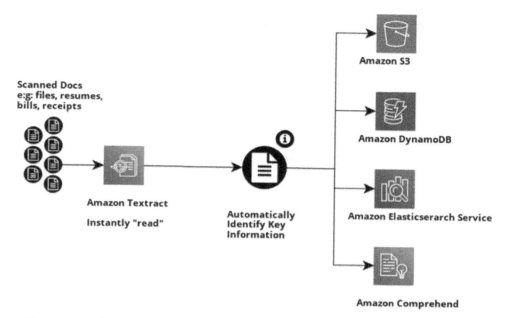

Figure 2.21 – Block diagram representation of Amazon Textract and how it stores its output

Some common uses of Amazon Textract include the following:

- Documenting processing workflows to extract tables or forms.
- Creating search indexes from documents using Amazon Elasticsearch.
- Redacting personally identifiable information in a workflow; Textract identifies data types and form labels automatically.

Next, we'll explore the benefits of Amazon Textract.

Exploring the benefits of Amazon Textract

There are several reasons to use Textract, as follows:

- Zero infrastructure cost.
- Fully managed service (reduced development and management overhead).
- Helps you extract both structured and unstructured data.
- Handwritten reviews can be analyzed.
- Amazon Textract performs better than OCR apps, which use flat bag of words.
- Next, we'll get hands-on with Amazon Textract.

Getting hands-on with Amazon Textract

In this section, we will use the Amazon Textract API to read an image file from our S3 bucket and print the "FORM" details on Cloudwatch. The same can be stored in S3 in your desired format for further use or can be stored in DynamoDB as a key-value pair. Let's get started:

1. First, create an IAM role called `textract-use-case-role` with the following policies. This will allow the Lambda function to execute so that it can read from S3, use Amazon Textract, and print the output in CloudWatch logs:

    *   `CloudWatchFullAccess`
    *   `AmazonTextractFullAccess`
    *   `AmazonS3ReadOnlyAccess`

2. Let's create an S3 bucket called `textract-document-analysis` and upload the `receipt.png` image file. This will be used to contain the FORM details that will be extracted. The image file is available here at `https://github.com/PacktPublishing/AWS-Certified-Machine-Learning-Specialty-MLS-C01-Certification-Guide/tree/master/Chapter-2/Amazon%20Textract%20Demo/input_doc`:

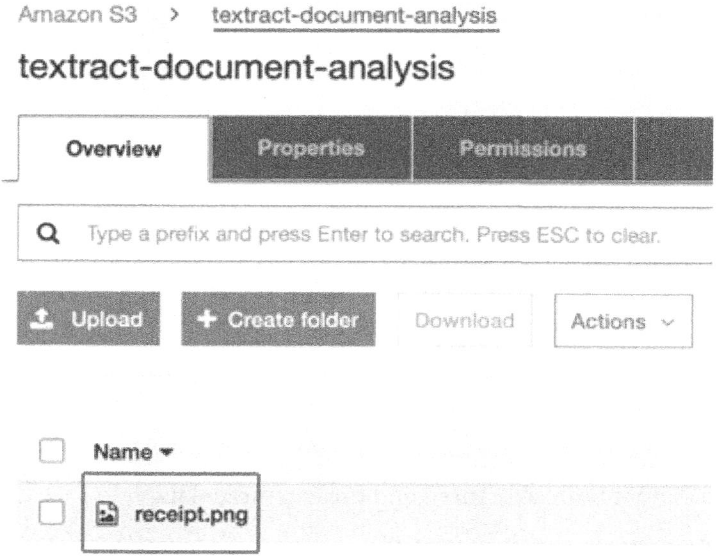

Figure 2.22 – An S3 bucket with an image (.png) file uploaded to the input folder

3. The next step is to create a Lambda function called `read-scanned-doc`, as shown in the following screenshot, with an existing execution role called `textract-use-case-role`:

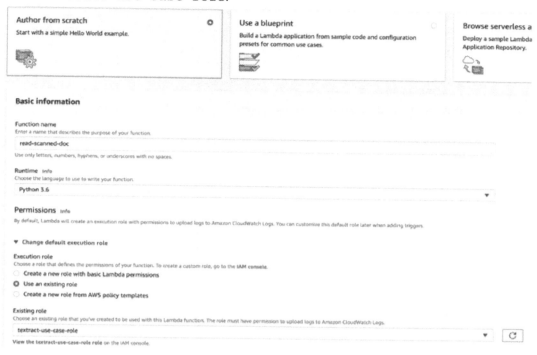

Figure 2.23 – The AWS Lambda Create function dialog

4. Once the function has been created, paste the following code and deploy it. Scroll down to **Basic Settings** to change the default timeout to a higher value (40 secs) to avoid timeout errors. We have used the `analyze_document` API from Amazon Textract to get the `Table and Form` details via the `FeatureTypes` parameter of the API:

```python
import boto3
import time
from trp import Document
textract_client=boto3.client('textract')


def lambda_handler(event, context):
    print("- - - Amazon Textract Demo - - -")
    # read the bucket name from the event
```

```
        name_of_the_bucket=event['Records'][0]['s3']
['bucket']['name']
    # read the object from the event
    name_of_the_doc=event['Records'][0]['s3']['object']
['key']
    print(name_of_the_bucket)
    print(name_of_the_doc)
    response =
textract_client.analyze_document(Document={'S3Object':
{'Bucket': name_of_the_bucket,'Name':
name_of_the_doc}},FeatureTypes=["TABLES","FORMS"])
    print(str(response))
    doc=Document(response)
    for page in doc.pages:
        # Print tables
        for table in page.tables:
            for r, row in enumerate(table.rows):
                for c, cell in enumerate(row.cells):
                    print("Table[{}][{}] =
{}".format(r, c, cell.text))
    for page in doc.pages:
        # Print fields
        print("Fields:")
        for field in page.form.fields:
            print("Key: {}, Value:
{}".format(field.key, field.value))
```

Unlike the previous examples, we will create a test configuration to run our code.

5. Click on the dropdown left of the **Test** button.

6. Select **Configure test events** and choose **Create new test event**.

7. Select **Amazon S3 Put** from the **Event template** dropdown.

8. In the JSON body, change the highlighted values as per our bucket name and key, as shown here:

```
      "x-amz-id-2": "EXAMPLE123/5678abcdefghijklambdaisawesome/
    },
    "s3": {
      "s3SchemaVersion": "1.0",
      "configurationId": "testConfigRule",
      "bucket": {
        "name": "textract-document-analysis",
        "ownerIdentity": {
          "principalId": "EXAMPLE"
        },
        "arn": "arn:aws:s3:::textract-document-analysis"
      },
      "object": {
        "key": "receipt.png",
        "size": 1024,
        "eTag": "0123456789abcdef0123456789abcdef",
        "sequencer": "0A1B2C3D4E5F678901"
      }
    }
```

Figure 2.24 – The Event template for testing the lambda function

9. In the **Event name** field, name the test configuration TextractDemo.

10. Click **Save**.

11. Select your test configuration (TextractDemo) and click on **Test**:

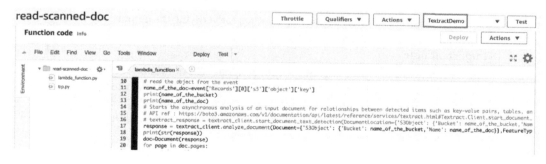

Figure 2.25 – Selecting the test configuration before running your test

12. This will trigger the lambda function. You can monitor the logs from **CloudWatch> CloudWatch Logs> Log groups> /aws/lambda/ read-scanned-doc**.

13. Click on the streams and select the latest one. It will look as follows; the key-value pairs can be seen in the following screenshot:

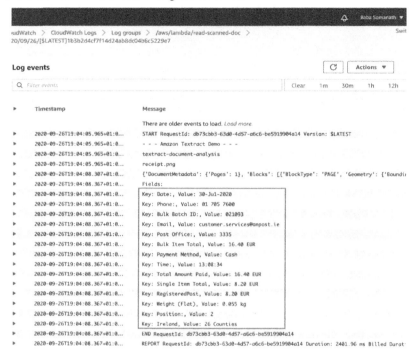

Figure 2.26 – The logs in CloudWatch for verifying the output

---

Important note

The most scalable and cost-effective way to generate S3 Put events for asynchronously invoking downstream AI workflows via Lambda is to generate an AWS Pre-Signed URL, and then provide it to your mobile or web application users. Many users can be served at the same time via this approach, and it may increase performance and throughput.

Considering the same region for your AWS AI services and S3 bucket may improve performance and reduce network latency. AWS VPC endpoints can leverage enhanced security without using the public internet. You can store the AWS AI results in an AWS S3 bucket and encrypt the rest to attain better security.

In this section, we learned how to extract text from a scanned document and print the form data out of it. Unlike the other sections, we used the testing feature of a lambda function by creating a test configuration that includes an event template. In the next section, we will learn about creating a chatbot for organizations and learn how to use it.

Creating chatbots on Amazon Lex

Most of the features that are available in Alexa are powered by **Amazon Lex**. You can easily build a chatbot using Amazon Lex. It uses natural language understanding and automatic speech recognition behind the scenes. Through SLU, Amazon Lex takes natural language speech and text input, understands the intent, and fulfills the intent of the user. An Amazon Lex bot can be created either from the console or via APIs. Its basic requirements are shown in the upcoming diagram.

Some common uses of Amazon Lex include the following:

- Apps that both listen and take input as text.

- Chatbots.

- Conversational AI products to provide a better customer and sales experience.

- Custom business bots for assistance through AWS Lambda functions.

- Voice assistants for your call center, which can speak to a user, schedule a meeting, or request details of your account.

- By integrating with Amazon Cognito, you can control user management, authentication, and sync across all your devices.

Next, we will explore the benefits of Amazon Lex.

Exploring the benefits of Amazon Lex

Some reasons for using Lex include the following:

- Chatbots can be directly built and tested from the AWS management console. These chatbots can be easily integrated into Facebook Messenger, Slack, and Twilio SMS via its rich formatting capabilities.

- Conversation logs can be stored in Amazon CloudWatch for further analysis. You can use them to monitor your bot and derive insights to improve your user experience.

- Amazon Lex can be integrated into other AWS services such as Amazon Cognito, AWS Lambda, Amazon DynamoDB, Amazon CloudWatch, and AWS Mobile Hub to leverage application security, monitoring, user authentication, business logic, storage, and mobile app development in AWS platforms.

- Amazon Lex chatbots can be integrated into your custom web applications too. You just need to build a chatbot widget and integrate it into your UI.

Next, we'll get hands-on with Amazon Lex.

Getting hands-on with Amazon Lex

Let's get started:

1. Log into https://console.aws.amazon.com/lex/.

2. Click on **Get Started** and select **Custom bot**.

3. Fill in the following details and click on **Create**:

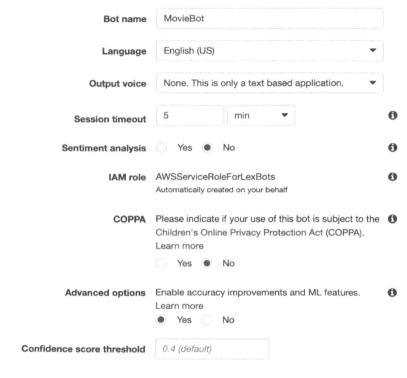

Figure 2.27 – The Create dialog of Amazon Lex

4. Click on **Create Intent**. A dialog will appear. Select **Create Intent**.

5. Name the new intent `MovieIntent` and click on **Add**.

6. Go to the **Slots** section and use the following details:

- Name: `movie_type`

- Slot type: `AMAZON.Genre`

- Prompt: `Which movie do you like?`

7. Click on the + in **Settings**.

Some sample utterances can be seen in the following screenshot. In this example, `movie_type` is my variable:

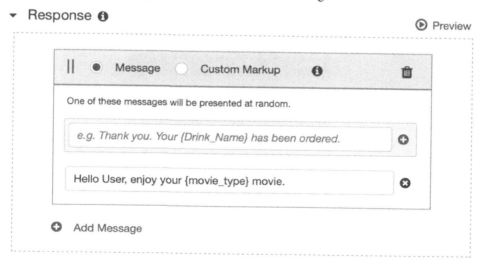

Figure 2.28 – The Sample utterances section

8. Scroll down to the **Response** section to add a message:

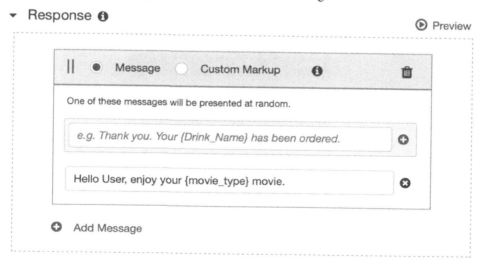

Figure 2.29 – The Response section of Amazon Lex

9. Scroll down to **Save Intent** and click on **Build**. Upon successfully building the prompt, the following success message will appear:

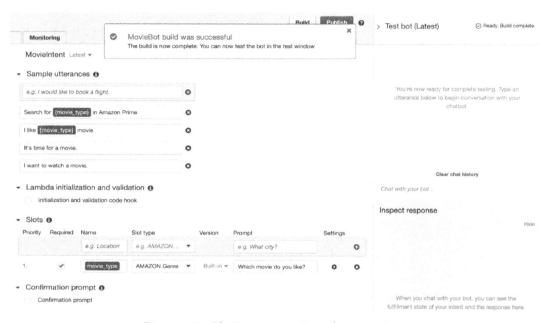

Figure 2.30 – The Response section of Amazon Lex

10. Now, you can test your bot, as shown in the following screenshot:

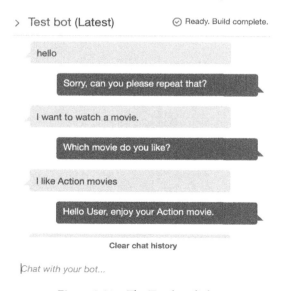

Figure 2.31 – The Test bot dialog

> **Important note**
> Not all Amazon Polly features are available within Alexa – particularly the
> Amazon Polly SSML features – which makes Amazon Polly and Alexa different.

That concludes this chapter's introduction to the various AWS application services that are
available.

Summary

In this chapter, we learned about a few of the AWS AI services that can be used to solve
various problems. We used the Amazon Rekognition service, which detects objects and
faces (including celebrity faces), and can also extract text from images. For text to speech,
we used Amazon Polly, while for speech to text, we used Amazon Transcribe. Toward the
end of this chapter, we built a chatbot in Amazon Lex.

For language detection and translation in an image, we used Amazon Rekognition,
Amazon Comprehend, and Amazon Translate. We learned how to combine all of them
into one Lambda function to solve our problem.

For the certification exam, you don't need to remember all the APIs we used in this
chapter. There may be questions on a few of the best practices that we learned or on the
names of services that solve a specific problem. It is always good to practice using these
AWS AI services as it will enhance your architecting skills.

In the next chapter, we will learn about data preparation and transformation, which is the
most important aspect of machine learning.

Questions

1. Using pre-defined logic and rules to make product recommendations to online
   shoppers is an example of machine learning.

   a. TRUE

   b. FALSE

2. Which level of the ML stack helps you build custom ML models without
   managing infrastructure?

   a. Top level (the AI services)

   b. Middle level (Amazon SageMaker)

   c. Bottom level (ML frameworks and infrastructure)

   d. Your own infrastructure and code level

3. Which of the following can you do with Amazon Textract?

    a. Detect key-value pairs in documents

    b. Build a custom ML model for text extraction

    c. Send text extraction with low confidence scores for human review

    d. Translate the detected text into English

4. With Amazon Comprehend, a new model can be trained to help you extract custom entities from text.

    a. FALSE

    b. TRUE

5. Which of the following is an example of the type of data Amazon Comprehend is designed to analyze?

    a. Social media posts

    b. Data in a table

    c. Log files

    d. GPS data

    > **Answer**
    > For log files, we can use CloudWatch Log Insights.

6. When calling the `DetectKeyPhrases` API, which of the following is not returned by Amazon Comprehend?

    a. The key phrases

    b. The count of each key phrase

    c. The confidence level for each key phrase

    d. The sentiment of each key phrase

    > **Answer**
    > It has nothing to do with sentiment.

7. You want to create a Lex bot that can help you order pizza. Why is it important to add slots as part of intent configuration?

   a. So you can customize your orders with different pizza sizes and toppings.

   b. So you can account for different ways you might convey your intent to order pizza.

   c. So that a lambda function can be automatically set up for you to fulfill the intent.

8. Let's say you're responsible for building a system that analyzes the sentiment of a customer chat. Which service should you integrate with Amazon Lex to do this?

   a. Amazon Transcribe

   b. Amazon Comprehend

   c. Amazon Translate

   d. Amazon Textract

9. In which situation would an Amazon Lex fallback intent help?

   a. When a user orders pizza but, due to background noise, the bot needs the user to repeat what they said.

   b. When a bot has to use a previous exchange with a user to pretend to understand an unclear message from that user.

   c. When a bot is asked a question that is not programmed to answer.

   > **Answer**
   > Fallback intent is meant for those inputs that a bot doesn't expect.

10. Which three of the following options can Amazon Textract handle that traditional OCR methods are not able to?

    a. Extracting words and lines from documents

    b. Extracting forms (key/values) from documents without using any templates

    c. Handling non-textual content such as radio buttons and checkboxes

    d. Preserving the composition of data stored in tables

11. Which of the following is a common use case for integrating Amazon Textract with Amazon A2I (human review)?

    a. You want to identify form labels and values from an image or PDF document.

    b. You are extracting data from a document that requires review due to regulatory requirements or sensitive business decisions.

    c. You have tables in your document, and you need to preserve the composition of the data stored in those tables.

12. You are looking to extract form or table data in a document. You need to do this synchronously because your use is latency-sensitive, such as mobile capture. What API should you use?

    a. AnalyzeDocument

    b. DetectDocumentText

    c. StartDocumentAnalysis

    d. GetDocumentTextDetection

Answers

1. B

2. B

3. A, C

4. B

5. A

6. D

7. A

8. B

9. C

10. B, C, D

11. B

12. A

Section 2: Data Engineering and Exploratory Data Analysis

This section describes how to prepare data for machine learning. It explains different techniques for data manipulation and transformation according to each type of variable. Additionally, it covers the handling of missing data and outliers.

This section contains the following chapters:

- *Chapter 3, Data Preparation and Transformation*
- *Chapter 4, Understanding and Visualizing Data*
- *Chapter 5, AWS Services for Data Storing*
- *Chapter 6, AWS Services for Processing*

3
Data Preparation and Transformation

You have probably heard that data scientists spend most of their time working on data preparation-related activities. It is now time to explain why that happens and which types of activities we are talking about.

In this chapter, you will learn how to deal with categorical and numerical features, as well as applying different techniques to transform your data, such as one-hot encoding, binary encoders, ordinal encoding, binning, and text transformations. You will also learn how to handle missing values and outliers in your data, which are two important tasks you can implement to build good machine learning models.

In this chapter, we will cover the following topics:

- Identifying types of features
- Dealing with categorical features
- Dealing with numerical features
- Understanding data distributions
- Handling missing values
- Dealing with outliers
- Dealing with unbalanced datasets

- Dealing with text data

This is a lengthy chapter, so bear with us! Knowing about these topics in detail will definitely put you in a good position for the AWS Machine Learning Specialty exam.

Identifying types of features

We *cannot* start modeling without knowing what a **feature** is and which type of information it might store. You have already read about different processes that deal with features. For example, you know that feature engineering is related to the task of building and preparing features to your models; you also know that feature selection is related to the task of choosing the best set of features to feed a particular algorithm. These two tasks have one behavior in common: they may vary according to the types of features they are processing.

It is very important to understand this behavior (feature type versus applicable transformations) because it will help you eliminate invalid answers during your exam (and, most importantly, you will become a better data scientist).

When we refer to types of features, we are talking about the data type that a particular feature is supposed to store. The following diagram shows how we could potentially describe the different types of features of a model:

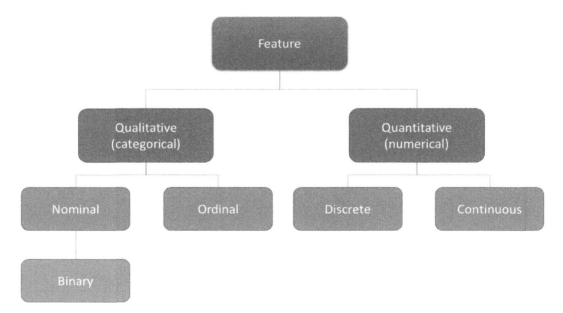

Figure 3.1 – Feature types

In *Chapter 1, Machine Learning Fundamentals*, you were introduced to the feature classification shown in the preceding diagram. Now, let's look at some real examples in order to eliminate any remaining questions you may have:

Feature type	Feature sub-type	Definition	Example
Categorical	Nominal	Labeled variables with no quantitative value	Cloud provider: AWS, MS, Google
Categorical	Ordinal	Adds the sense of order to a labeled variable	Job title: Jr Data Scientist, Sr Data Scientist, Chief Data Scientist
Categorical	Binary	A variable with only two allowed values	Fraud classification: Fraud, Not Fraud
Numerical	Discrete	Individual and countable items	Number of students: 1000
Numerical	Continuous	Infinite number of possible measurements and they often carry decimal points	Total amount: $150.35

Figure 3.2 – Real examples of feature values

Although looking at the values of the variable may help you find its type, you should never rely only on this aspect. The nature of the variable is also very important for making such decisions. For example, someone could encode the cloud provider variable (shown in the preceding table) as follows: 1 (AWS), 2 (MS), 3 (Google). In that case, the variable is still a nominal feature, even if it is now represented by discrete numbers.

If you are building a ML model and you don't tell your algorithm that this variable is not a discrete number, but instead a nominal variable, the algorithm will treat it as a number and the model won't be interpretable anymore.

> **Important note**
> Before feeding any ML algorithm with data, make sure your feature types have been properly identified.

In theory, if you are happy with your features and have properly classified each of them, you should be ready to go into the modeling phase of the CRISP-DM methodology, shouldn't you? Well, maybe not. There are many reasons you may want to spend a little more time on data preparation, even after you have correctly classified your features:

- Some algorithm implementations, such as `scikit-learn`, may not accept string values on your categorical features.
- The data distribution of your variable may not be the most optimal distribution for your algorithm.
- Your ML algorithm may be impacted by the scale of your data.
- Some observations (rows) of your variable may be missing information and you will have to fix it. These are also known as missing values.
- You may find outlier values of your variable that can potentially add bias to your model.
- Your variable may be storing different types of information and you may only be interested in a few of them (for example, a date variable can store the day of the week or the week of the month).
- You might want to find a mathematical representation for a text variable.
- And believe me, this list will never end.

In the following sections, we will understand how to address all these points, starting with categorical features.

Dealing with categorical features

Data transformation methods for categorical features will vary according to the sub-type of your variable. In the upcoming sections, we will understand how to transform nominal and ordinal features.

Transforming nominal features

You may have to create numerical representations of your categorical features before applying ML algorithms to them. Some libraries may have embedded logic to handle that transformation for you, but most of them do not.

The first transformation we will cover is known as **label encoding**. A label encoder is suitable for categorical/nominal variables and it will just associate a number with each distinct label of your variable. The following table shows how a label encoder works:

Country	Label encoding
India	1
Canada	2
Brazil	3
Australia	4
India	1

Figure 3.3 – Label encoder in action

A label encoder will always ensure that a unique number is associated with each distinct label. In the preceding table, although "India" appears twice, the same number was assigned to it.

You now have a numerical representation of each country, but this does not mean you can use that numerical representation in your models! In this particular case, we are transforming a nominal feature, *which does not have an order*.

According to the preceding table, if we pass the encoded version of the *country* variable to a model, it will make assumptions such as "Brazil (3) is greater than Canada (2)", which does not make any sense.

A possible solution for that scenario is applying another type of transformation on top of "*country*": **one-hot encoding**. This transformation will represent all the categories from the original feature as individual features (also known as **dummy variables**), which will store the "presence or absence" of each category. The following table is transforming the same information we looked at in the preceding table, but this time it's applying one-hot encoding:

Country	India	Canada	Brazil	Australia
India	1	0	0	0
Canada	0	1	0	0
Brazil	0	0	1	0
Australia	0	0	0	1
India	1	0	0	0

Figure 3.4 – One-hot encoding in action

We can now use the one-hot encoded version of the *country* variable as a feature of a ML model. However, your work as a skeptical data scientist is never done, and your critical thinking ability will be tested in the AWS Machine Learning Specialty exam.

Let's suppose you have 150 distinct countries in your dataset. How many dummy variables would you come up with? 150, right? Here, we just found a potential issue: apart from adding complexity to your model (which is not a desired characteristic of any model at all), dummy variables also add **sparsity** to your data.

A sparse dataset has a lot of variables filled with zeros. Often, it is hard to fit this type of data structure into memory (you can easily run out of memory) and it is very time-consuming for ML algorithms to process sparse structures.

You can work around the sparsity problem by grouping your original data and reducing the number of categories, and you can even use custom libraries that compress your sparse data and make it easier for manipulation (such as `scipy.sparse.csr_matrix`, from Python).

Therefore, during the exam, remember that one-hot encoding is definitely the right way to go when you need to transform categorical/nominal data to feed ML models; however, take the number of unique categories of your original feature into account and think about if it makes sense to create dummy variables for all of them (maybe it does not make sense, if you have a very large number of unique categories).

Applying binary encoding

For those types of variables with a higher number of unique categories, a potential approach to creating a numerical representation for them is applying **binary encoding**. In this approach, the goal is transforming a categorical column into multiple binary columns, but minimizing the number of new columns.

This process consists of three basic steps:

1. The categorical data is converted into numerical data after being passed through an ordinal encoder.

2. The resulting number is then converted into a binary value.

3. The binary value is split into different columns.

Let's reuse our data from *Figure 3.3* to see how we could use binary encoding in this particular case:

Country	Label encoder	Binary	Col1	Col2	Col3
India	1	001	0	0	1
Canada	2	010	0	1	0
Brazil	3	011	1	1	1
Australia	4	100	1	0	0
India	1	001	0	0	1

Figure 3.5 – Binary encoding in action

As we can see, we now have three columns (Col1, Col2, and Col3) instead of four.

Transforming ordinal features

Ordinal features have a very specific characteristic: *they have an order*. Because they have this quality, it does *not* make sense to apply one-hot encoding to them; if you do so, you will lose the magnitude of order of your feature.

The most common transformation for this type of variable is known as **ordinal encoding**. An ordinal encoder will associate a number with each distinct label of your variable, just like a label encoder does, but this time, it will respect the order of each category. The following table shows how an ordinal encoder works:

Education	Ordinal encoding
Trainee	1
Jr. Data Analyst	2
Sr Data Analyst	3
Chief Data Scientist	4

Figure 3.6 – Ordinal encoding in action

We can now pass the encoded variable to ML models and they will be able to handle this variable properly, with no need to apply one-hot encoding transformations. This time, comparisons such as "Sr Data Analyst is greater than Jr. Data Analyst" make total sense.

Avoiding confusion in our train and test datasets

Do not forget the following statement: encoders are **fitted** on training data and **transformed** on test and production data. This is how your ML pipeline should work.

Let's suppose you have created a one-hot encoder that fits the data from *Figure 3.3* and returns data according to *Figure 3.4*. In this example, we will assume this is our training data. Once you have completed your training process, you may want to apply the same one-hot encoding transformation to your testing data to check the model's results.

In the scenario that we just described (which is a very common situation in modeling pipelines), you *cannot* retrain your encoder on top of the testing data! You should just reuse the previous encoder object that you have created on top of the training data. Technically, we say that you shouldn't use the `fit` method again, and use the `transform` method instead.

You may already know the reasons why you should follow this rule, but let's recap: the testing data was created to extract the performance metrics of your model, so you should not use it to extract any other knowledge. If you do so, your performance metrics will be biased by the testing data and you cannot infer that the same performance (shown in the test data) is likely to happen in production (when new data will come in).

Alright, all good so far. However, what if our testing set has a new category that was not present in the train set? How are we supposed to transform this data? Let's walk through this particular scenario.

Going back to our one-hot encoding example we looked at in *Figures 3.3* (input data) and *Figure 3.4* (output data), our encoder knows how to transform the following countries: Australia, Brazil, Canada, and India. If we had a different country in the testing set, the encoder would not know how to transform it, and that's why we need to define how it will behave in scenarios where there are exceptions.

Most of the ML libraries provide specific parameters for these situations. In our example, we could program the encoder to either raise an error or set all zeros on our dummy variables, as shown in the following table:

Country	India	Canada	Brazil	Australia
India	1	0	0	0
Canada	0	1	0	0
Brazil	0	0	1	0
Australia	0	0	0	1
India	1	0	0	0
Portugal	0	0	0	0

Figure 3.7 – Handling unknown values on one-hot encoding transformations

As we can see, Portugal was not present in the training set (*Figure 3.3*), so during the transformation, we are keeping the same list of known countries and saying that Portugal *IS NOT* any of them (all zeros).

As the very good, skeptical data scientist we know you are becoming, should you be concerned about the fact that you have a particular category that has not been used during training? Well, maybe. This type of analysis really depends on your problem domain.

Handling unknown values is very common and something that you should expect to do in your ML pipeline. However, you should also ask yourself, due to the fact that you did not use that particular category during your training process, if your model can be extrapolated and generalized.

Remember, your testing data must follow the same data distribution as your training data, and you are very likely to find all (or at least most) of the categories (of a categorical feature) either in the training or test sets. Furthermore, if you are facing overfitting issues (doing well in the training, but poorly in the test set) and, at the same time, you realize that your categorical encoders are transforming a lot of unknown values in the test set, guess what? It's likely that your training and testing samples are not following the same distribution, invalidating your model entirely.

As you can see, slowly, we are getting there. We are talking about bias and investigation strategies in fine-grained detail! Now, let's move on and look at performing transformations on numerical features. Yes, each type of data matters and drives your decisions!

Dealing with numerical features

In terms of numerical features (discrete and continuous), we can think of transformations that rely on the training data and others that rely purely on the observation being transformed.

Those that rely on the training data will use the train set to learn the necessary parameters during fit, and then use them to transform any test or new data. The logic is pretty much the same as what we just reviewed for categorical features; however, this time, the encoder will learn different parameters.

On the other hand, those that rely purely on observations do not care about train or test sets. They will simply perform a mathematical computation on top of an individual value. For example, we could apply an exponential transformation to a particular variable by squaring its value. There is no dependency on learned parameters from anywhere – just get the value and square it.

At this point, you might be thinking about dozens of available transformations for numerical features! Indeed, there are so many options that we can't describe all of them here, and you are not supposed to know all of them for the AWS Machine Learning Specialty exam anyway. We will cover the most important ones (for the exam) here, but I don't want to limit your modeling skills: take a moment to think about the unlimited options you have by creating custom transformations according to your use case.

Data normalization

Applying data **normalization** means changing the scale of the data. For example, your feature may store employee salaries that range between 20,000 and 200,000 dollars/year and you want to put this data in the range of 0 and 1, where 20,000 (the minimum observed value) will be transformed into 0 and 200,000 (the maximum observed value) will be transformed into 1.

This type of technique is specifically important when you want to fit your training data on top of certain types of algorithms that are impacted by the scale/magnitude of the underlying data. For instance, we can think about those algorithms that use the dot product of the input variables (such as neural networks or linear regression) and those algorithms that rely on distance measures (such as **k-nearest neighbor** (**KNN**) or **k-means**).

On the other hand, applying data normalization will not result in performance improvements for rule-based algorithms, such as decision trees, since they will be able to check the predictive power of the features (either via **entropy** or **information gain** analysis), regardless of the scale of the data.

> **Important note**
>
> We will learn about these algorithms, along with the appropriate details, in the later chapters of this book. For instance, you can look at entropy and information gain as two types of metrics used by decision trees to check feature importance. Knowing the predictive power of each feature helps the algorithm define the optimal root, intermediaries, and leaf nodes of the tree.

Let's take a moment to understand why data normalization will help those types of algorithms. We already know that the goal of a clustering algorithm is to find groups or clusters in your data, and one of the most used clustering algorithms is known as k-means. We will use k-means to see this problem in action, since it is impacted by data scaling.

The following image shows how different scales of the variable could change the hyper plan's projection:

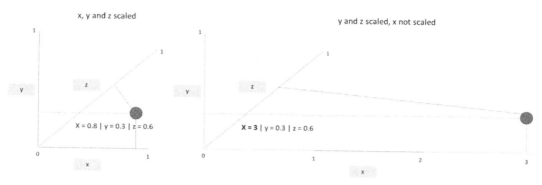

Figure 3.8 – Plotting data of different scales in a hyper plan

On the left-hand side of the preceding image, we can see a single data point plotted in a hyper plan that has three dimensions (x, y, and z). All three dimensions (also known as features) were normalized to the scale of 0 and 1. On the right-hand side, we can see the same data point, but this time, the "x" dimension was *not* normalized. We can clearly see that the hyper plan has changed.

In a real scenario, we would have far more dimensions and data points. The difference in the scale of the data would change the centroids of each clusters and could potentially change the assigned clusters of some points. This same problem will happen on other algorithms that rely on distances calculation, such as KNN.

Other algorithms, such as neural networks and linear regression, will compute weighted sums using your input data. Usually, these types of algorithms will perform operations such as $W1*X1 + W2*X2 + Wi*Xi$, where Xi and Wi refer to a particular feature value and its weight, respectively. Again, we will cover details of neural networks and linear models later, but can you see the data scaling problem by just looking at the calculations that we just described? We can easily come up with very large values if X (feature) and W (weight) are large numbers. That will make the algorithm's optimizations much more complex.

I hope you now have a very good understanding about the reasons you should apply data normalization (and when you should not). Data normalization is often implemented in ML libraries as **Min Max Scaler**. If you find this term in the exam, then remember it is the same as data normalization.

Additionally, data normalization does not necessarily need to transform your feature into a range between 0 and 1. In reality, we can transform the feature into any range we want. The following is how a normalization is formally defined:

$$X_{normalized} = \frac{X - X_{min}}{X_{max} - X_{min}}$$

Figure 3.9 – Normalization formula

Here, X_{min} and X_{max} are the lower and upper values of the range; X is the value of the feature. Apart from data normalization, there is another very important technique regarding numerical transformations that you *must* be aware of, not only for the exam, but also for your data science career. We'll look at this in the next section.

Data standardization

Data **standardization** is another scaling method that transforms the distribution of the data, so that the mean will become zero and the standard deviation will become one. The following image formally describes this scaling technique, where X represents the value to be transformed, μ refers to the mean of X, and σ is the standard deviation of X:

$$X' = \frac{X - \mu}{\sigma}$$

Figure 3.10 – Standardization formula

Unlike normalization, data standardization will *not* result in a predefined range of values. Instead, it will transform your data into a standard **Gaussian distribution**, where your transformed values will represent the number of standard deviations of each value to the mean of the distribution.

> **Important note**
> Gaussian distribution, also known as normal distribution, is one of the most used distribution on statistical models. This is a continuous distribution with two main controlled parameters: μ (mean) and σ (standard deviation). Normal distributions are symmetric around the mean. In other words, most of the values will be close to the mean of the distribution.

Data standardization if often referred to as the **zscore** and is widely used to identify outliers on your variable, which we will see later in this chapter. For the sake of demonstration, the following table simulates the data standardization of a small dataset. The input value is present in the "Age" column, while the scaled value is present in the "Zscore" column:

Age	Mean	Standard Deviation	Zscore
5	31,83	25,47	-1,05
20	31,83	25,47	-0,46
24	31,83	25,47	-0,31
32	31,83	25,47	0,01
30	31,83	25,47	-0,07
80	31,83	25,47	1,89

Figure 3.11 – Data standardization in action

Make sure you are confident when applying normalization and standardization by hand in the AWS Machine Learning Specialty exam. They might provide a list of values, as well as mean and standard deviation, and ask you the scaled value of each element of the list.

Applying binning and discretization

Binning is a technique where you can group a set of values into a bucket or bin; for example, grouping people between 0 and 14 years old into a bucket named "children," another group of people between 15 and 18 years old into a bucket named "teenager," and so on.

Discretization is the process of transforming a continuous variable into discrete or nominal attributes. These continuous values can be discretized by multiple strategies, such as **equal-width** and **equal-frequency**.

An equal-width strategy will split your data across multiple bins of the same width. Equal-frequency will split your data across multiple bins with the same number of frequencies.

Let's look at an example. Suppose we have the following list containing 16 numbers: 10, 11, 12, 13, 14, 15, 16, 17, 18, 19, 20, 21, 22, 23, 24, 90. As we can see, this list ranges between 10 and 90. Assuming we want to create four bins using an equal-width strategy, we would come up with the following bins:

- Bin >= 10 <= 30 > 10, 11, 12, 13, 14, 15, 16, 17, 18, 19, 20, 21, 22, 23, 24

- Bin > 30 <= 50 >

- Bin > 50 <= 70 >

- Bin > 71 <= 90 > 90

In this case, the width of each bin is the same (20 units), but the observations are not equally distributed. Now, let's simulate an equal-frequency strategy:

- Bin >= 10 <= 13 > 10, 11, 12, 13

- Bin > 13 <= 17 > 14, 15, 16, 17

- Bin > 17 <= 21 > 18, 19, 20, 21

- Bin > 21 <= 90 > 22, 23, 24, 90

In this case, all the bins have the same frequency of observations, although they have been built with different bin widths to make that possible.

Once you have computed your bins, you should be wondering what's next, right? Here, you have some options:

- You can name your bins and use them as a nominal feature on your model! Of course, as a nominal variable, you should think about applying one-hot encoding before feeding a ML model with this data.

- You might want to order your bins and use them as an ordinal feature.

- Maybe you want to remove some noise from your feature by averaging the minimum and maximum values of each bin and using that value as your transformed feature.

Take a look at the following table to understand these approaches using our equal-frequency example:

Original value	Bin	Transforming to a nominal feature	Transforming to an ordinal feature	Removing noise
10	Bin >= 10 <= 13	Bin A	1	11,5
11	Bin > 10 <= 13	Bin A	1	11,5
12	Bin > 10 <= 13	Bin A	1	11,5
13	Bin > 10 <= 13	Bin A	1	11,5
14	Bin > 13 <= 17	Bin B	2	15,5
15	Bin > 13 <= 17	Bin B	2	15,5
16	Bin > 13 <= 17	Bin B	2	15,5
17	Bin > 13 <= 17	Bin B	2	15,5
18	Bin > 17 <= 21	Bin C	3	19,5
19	Bin > 17 <= 21	Bin C	3	19,5
20	Bin > 17 <= 21	Bin C	3	19,5
21	Bin > 17 <= 21	Bin C	3	19,5
22	Bin > 21 <= 90	Bin D	4	55,5
23	Bin > 21 <= 90	Bin D	4	55,5
24	Bin > 21 <= 90	Bin D	4	55,5
90	Bin > 21 <= 90	Bin D	4	55,5

Figure 3.12 – Different approaches to working with bins and discretization

Again, playing with different binning strategies will give you different results and you should analyze/test the best approach for your dataset. There is no standard answer here – it is all about data exploration!

Applying other types of numerical transformations

Normalization and standardization rely on your training data to fit their parameters: minimum and maximum values in the case of normalization, and mean and standard deviation in the case of standard scaling. This also means you must fit those parameters using *only* your training data and never the testing data.

However, there are other types of numerical transformations that do not require parameters from training data to be applied. These types of transformations rely purely on mathematical computations. For example, one of these transformations is known as **logarithmic transformation**. This is a very common type of transformation in machine learning models and is especially beneficial for **skewed** features. In case you don't know what a skewed distribution is, take a look at the following diagram:

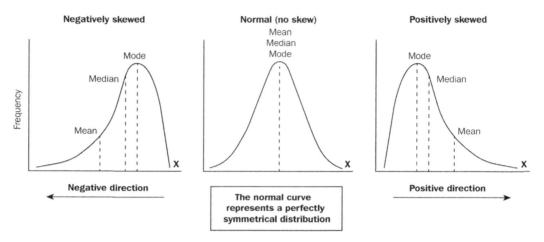

Figure 3.13 – Skewed distributions

In the middle, we have a normal distribution (or Gaussian distribution). On the left- and right-hand sides, we have skewed distributions. In terms of skewed features, there will be some values far away from the mean in one single direction (either left or right). Such behavior will push both the median and mean values of this distribution in the same direction of the long tail we can see in the preceding diagram.

One very clear example of data that used to be skewed is the annual salaries of a particular group of professionals in a given region, such as senior data scientists working in Florida, US. This type of variable usually has most of its values close to the others (because people used to earn an average salary) and just has a few very high values (because a small group of people makes much more money than others).

Hopefully, you can now easily understand why the mean and median values will move to the tail direction, right? The big salaries will push them in that direction.

Alright, but why will a logarithmic transformation be beneficial for this type of feature? The answer to this question can be explained by the math behind it:

$$log(x^n) = nlog(x)$$

Figure 3.14 – Logarithmic properties

Computing the log of a number is the inverse of the exponential function. Log transformation will then reduce the scale of your number according to a given base (such as base 2, base 10, or base e, in the case of a natural logarithm). Looking at our salary's distribution from the previous example, we would bring all those numbers down so that the higher the number, the higher the reduction; however, we would do this in a log scale and not in a linear fashion. Such behavior will remove the outliers of this distribution (making it closer to a normal distribution), which is beneficial for many ML algorithms, such as linear regression. The following table shows you some of the differences when transforming a number in a linear scale versus a log scale:

Original value	Linear scale (normalization)	Log scale (base 10)
10	0.0001	1
1,000	0.01	3
10,000	0.1	4
100,000	1	5

Figure 3.15 – Differences between linear transformation and log transformation

I hope you can see that the linear transformation kept the original magnitude of the data (we can still see outliers, but in another scale), while the log transformation removed those differences of magnitude and still kept the order of the values.

Would you be able to think about another type of mathematical transformation that follows the same behavior of *log* (making the distribution closer to Gaussian)? OK, I can give you another: square root. Take the square root of those numbers shown in the preceding table and see yourself!

Now, pay attention to this: both log and square root belong to a set of transformations known as **power transformations**, and there is very popular method, which is likely to be mentioned on your AWS exam, that can perform a range of power transformations like those we have seen. This method was proposed by George Box and David Cox and its name is **Box-Cox**.

> **Important note**
>
> During your exam, if you see questions around the Box-Cox transformation, remember that it is a method that can perform many power transformations (according to a lambda parameter), and its end goal is making the original distribution closer to a normal distribution (do not forget that).

Just to conclude our discussion regarding why mathematical transformations can really make a difference to ML models, I will give you an intuitive example about **exponential transformations**.

Suppose you have a set of data points, such as those on the left-hand side of *Figure 3.16*. Your goal is to draw a line that will perfectly split blue and red points. Just by looking at the original data (again, on the left-hand side), we know that our best guess for performing this linear task would be the one you can see in the same image. However, the science (not magic) happens on the right-hand side of the image! By squaring those numbers and plotting them in another hyper plan, we can perfectly separate each group of points:

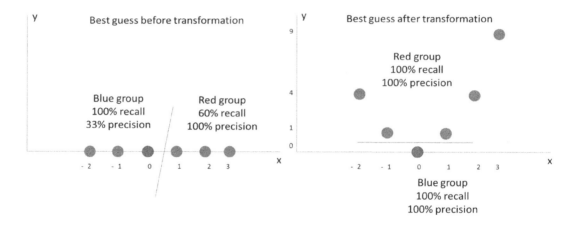

Figure 3.16 – Exponential transformation in action

I know you might be thinking about the infinite ways you can deal with your data. Although this is true, you should always take the business scenario you are working on into account and plan your work accordingly. Remember that model improvements or exploration is always possible, but you have to define your goals (remember the CRISP-DM methodology) and move on.

By the way, data transformation is important, but just one piece of your work as a data scientist. Your modeling journey still has to move to other important topics, such as missing values and outliers handling, which we will look at next. However, before that, you may have noticed that you were introduced to Gaussian distributions during this section, so let's take a moment to discuss them in a bit more detail.

Understanding data distributions

Although the Gaussian distribution is probably the most common distribution for statistical and machine learning models, you should be aware that it is not the only one. There are other types of data distributions, such as the **Bernoulli**, **Binomial**, and **Poisson** distributions.

The Bernoulli distribution is a very simple one, as there are only two types of possible events: success or failure. The success event has a probability "p" of happening, while the failure one has a probability of "1-p".

Some examples that follow a Bernoulli distribution are rolling a six-sided die or flipping a coin. In both cases, you must define the event of success and the event of failure. For example, suppose our events for success and failure in the die example are as follows:

- Success: Getting a number 6
- Failure: Getting any other number

We can then say that we have a p probability of success (1/6 = 0.16 = 16%) and a 1-p probability of failure (1 - 0.16 = 0.84 = 84%).

The Binomial distribution generalizes the Bernoulli distribution. The Bernoulli distribution has only one repetition of an event, while the Binomial distribution allows the event to be repeated many times, and we must count the number of successes. Let's continue with our prior example; that is, counting the number of times we got a 6 out of our 10 dice rolls. Due to the nature of this example, Binomial distribution has two parameters, n and p, where n is the number of repetitions and p is the probability of success in every repetition.

Finally, a Poisson distribution allows us to find a number of events in a time period, given the number of times an event occurs in an interval. It has three parameters: lambda, e, and k, where lambda is the average number of events per interval, e is the Euler number, and k is the number of times an event occurs in an interval.

With all those distributions, including the Gaussian one, it is possible to compute the expected mean value and variance based on their parameters. This information is usually used in hypothesis tests to check whether some sample data follows a given distribution, by comparing the mean and variance **of the sample** against the **expected** mean and variance of the distribution.

I hope you are now more familiar with data distributions generally, not only Gaussian distributions. We will keep talking about data distributions throughout this book. For now, let's move on to missing values and outlier detection.

Handling missing values

As the name suggests, missing values refer to the absence of data. Such absences are usually represented by tokens, which may or may not be implemented in a standard way.

Although using tokens is standard, the way those tokens are displayed may vary across different platforms. For example, relational databases represent missing data with *NULL*, core Python code will use *None*, and some Python libraries will represent missing numbers as (**Not a Number (NaN)**).

> **Important note**
>
> For numerical fields, don't replace those standard missing tokens with *zeros*. By default, zero is not a missing value, but another number. I said "by default" because, in data science, we may face some data quality issues, which we will cover next.

However, in real business scenarios, you may or may not find those standard tokens. For example, a software engineering team might have designed the system to automatically fill missing data with specific tokens, such as "unknown" for strings or "-1" for numbers. In that case, you would have to search by those two tokens to find missing data. People can set anything.

In the previous example, the software engineering team was still kind enough to give us standard tokens. However, there are many cases where legacy systems do not add any data quality layer in front of the user, and you may find an address field filled with "I don't want to share" or a phone number field filled with "Don't call me". This is clearly missing data, but not as standard as the previous example.

There are many more nuances that you will learn regarding missing data, all of which we will cover in this section, but be advised: before you start making decisions about missing values, you should prepare a good data exploration and make sure you find those values. You can either compute data frequencies or use missing plots, but please do something. Never assume that your missing data is represented only by those handy standard tokens.

Why should we care about this type of data? Well, first, because most algorithms (apart from decision trees implemented on very specific ML libraries) will raise errors when they find a missing value. Second (and maybe most importantly), by grouping all the missing data in the same bucket, you are assuming that they are all the same, but in reality, you don't know that.

Such a decision will not only add bias to your model – it will reduce its interpretability, as you will be unable to explain the missing data. Once we know why we want to treat the missing values, we can take a look at our options.

Theoretically, we can classify missing values into two main groups: **MCAR** or **MNAR**. MCAR stands for **Missing Completely at Random** and states that there is no pattern associated with the missing data. On the other hand, MNAR stands for **Missing Not at Random** and means that the underlying process used to generate the data is strictly connected to the missing values.

Let me give you an example of MNAR missing values. Suppose you are collecting user feedback about a particular product in an online survey. Your process of asking questions is dynamic and depends on user answers. When a user specifies an age lower than 18 years old, you never ask his/her marital status. In this case, missing values of marital status are connected to the age of the user (MNAR).

Knowing the class of missing values that you are dealing with will help you understand if you have any control over the underlying process that generates the data. Sometimes, you can come back to the source process and, somehow, complete your missing data.

> **Important note**
>
> Although, in real scenarios, we usually have to treat missing data via exclusion or imputation, never forget that you can always try to look at the source process and check if you can retrieve (or, at least, better understand) the missing data. You may face this option in the exam.

If you don't have an opportunity to recover your missing data from somewhere, then you should move on to other approaches, such as **listwise deletion** and **imputation**.

Listwise deletion refers to the process of discarding some data, which is the downside of this choice. This may happen at the row level or at the column level. For example, suppose you have a DataFrame containing four columns and one of them has 90% of its data missing. In such cases, what usually makes more sense is dropping the entire feature (column), since you don't have that information for the majority of your observations (rows).

From a row perspective, you may have a DataFrame with a small number of observations (rows) containing missing data in one of its features (columns). In such scenarios, instead of removing the entire feature, what makes more sense is removing only those few observations.

The benefit of using this method is the simplicity of dropping a row or a column. Again, the downside is losing information. If you don't want to lose information while handling your missing data, then you should go for an imputation strategy.

Imputation is also known as replacement, where you will replace missing values by substituting a value. The most common approach of imputation is replacing the missing value with the mean of the feature. Please take a note of this approach because it is likely to appear in your exam:

Age
35
30
25
80
75

Figure 3.17 – Replacing missing values with the mean or median

The preceding table shows a very simple dataset with one single feature and five observations, where the third observation has a missing value. If we decide to replace that missing data with the mean value of the feature, we will come up with 49. Sometimes, when we have outliers in the data, the median might be more appropriate (in this case, the median would be 35):

Age	Job status
35	Employee
30	Employee
	Retired
25	Employee
80	Retired
75	Retired

Figure 3.18 – Replacing missing values with the mean or median of the group

If you want to go deeper, you could find the mean or median value according to a given group of features. For example, in the preceding table, we expanded our previous dataset by adding the Job status column. Now, we have clues that help us suspect that our initial approach of changing the missing value by using the overall median (35 years old) is likely to be wrong (since that person is retired).

What you can do now is replace the missing value with the mean or median of the other observations that belong to the same job status. Using this new approach, we can change the missing information to 77.5. Taking into account that the person is retired, 77.5 makes more sense than 35 years old.

> **Important note**
>
> In the case of categorical variables, you can replace the missing data with the value that has the highest occurrence in your dataset. The same logic of grouping the dataset according to specific features is still applicable.

You can also use more sophisticated methods of imputation, including constructing a ML model to predict the value of your missing data. The downside of these imputation approaches (either by averaging or predicting the value) is that you are making inferences on the data, which are not necessarily right and will add bias to the dataset.

To sum this up, the trade-off while dealing with missing data is having a balance between losing data or adding bias to the dataset. Unfortunately, there is no scientific manual that you can follow, whatever your problem. To decide on what you are going to do, you must look to your success criteria, explore your data, run experiments, and then make your decisions.

We will now move to another headache for many ML algorithms, also known as outliers.

Dealing with outliers

We are not on this studying journey just to pass the AWS Machine Learning Specialty exam, but also to become better data scientists. There are many different ways to look at the outlier problem purely from a mathematical perspective; however, the datasets we use are derived from the underlying business process, so we must include a business perspective during an outlier analysis.

An **outlier** is an atypical data point in a set of data. For example, the following chart shows some data points that have been plotted in a two-dimension plan; that is, x and y. The red point is an outlier, since it is an atypical value on this series of data:

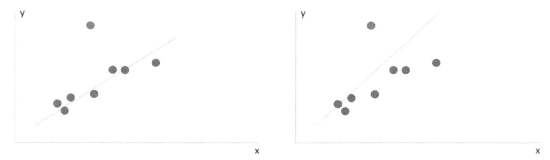

Figure 3.19 – Identifying an outlier

We want to treat outlier values because some statistical methods are impacted by them. Still, in the preceding chart, we can see this behavior in action. On the left-hand side, we drew a line that best fits those data points, ignoring the red point. On the right-hand side, we also drew the best line to fit the data but included the red point.

We can visually conclude that, by ignoring the outlier point, we will come up with a better solution on the plan of the left-hand side of the preceding chart since it was able to pass closer to most of the values. We can also prove this by computing an associated error for each line (which we will discuss later in this book).

It is worth reminding you that you have also seen the outlier issue in action in another situation in this book: specifically, in *Figure 3.17*, when we had to deal with missing values. In that example, we used the median (instead of the mean) to work around the problem. Feel free to go back and read it again, but what should be very clear at this point is that median values are less impacted by outliers than average values.

You now know what outliers are and why you should treat them. You should always consider your business perspective while dealing with outliers, but there are mathematical methods to find them. Now, let's look at these methods of outlier detection.

You have already learned about the most common method: zscore. In *Figure 3.11*, we saw a table containing a set of ages. Refer to it again to refresh your memory. In the last column of that table, we are computing the zscore of each age, according to the equation shown in *Figure 3.10*.

There is no well-defined range for those zscore values; however, in a normal distribution *without* outliers, they will range between -3 and 3. Remember: zscore will give you the number of standard deviations from the mean of the distribution. The following diagram shows some of the properties of a normal distribution:

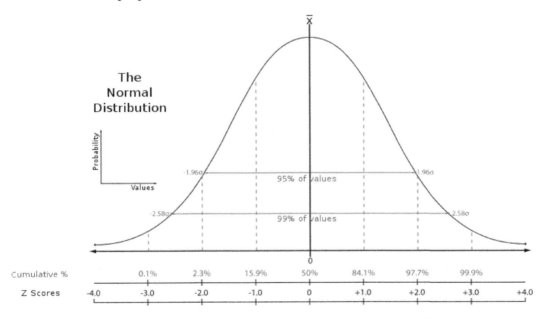

Figure 3.20 – Normal distribution properties. Image adapted from https://pt.wikipedia.org/wiki/
Ficheiro:The_Normal_Distribution.svg

According to the normal distribution properties, 95% of values will belong to the range of -2 and 2 standard deviations from the mean, while 99% of the values will belong to the range of -3 and 3. Coming back to the outlier detection context, we can set thresholds on top of those zscore values to specify whether a data point is an outlier or not!

There is no standard threshold that you can use to classify outliers. Ideally, you should look at your data and see what makes more sense for you… usually (this is not a rule), you will use some number between 2 and 3 standard deviations from the mean to set outliers, since more than 95% of your data will be out of that range. You may remember that there are outliers *below* and *above* the mean value of the distribution, as shown in the following table, where we have flagged outliers with an **absolute** zscore greater than 3 (the value column is hidden for the sake of this demonstration):

Value	Zscore	Is outlier?
...	1.3	NO
...	0.8	NO
...	**3.1**	**YES**
...	-2.9	NO
...	**-3.5**	**YES**
...	1.0	NO
...	1.1	NO

Figure 3.21 – Flagging outliers according to the zscore value

We found two outliers in the preceding table: row number three and row number five. Another way to find outliers in the data is by applying the **box plot** logic. You will learn about box plots in more detail in the next chapter of this book. For now, let's focus on using this method to find outliers.

When we look at a numerical variable, it is possible to extract many descriptive statistics from it, not only the mean, median, minimum, and maximum values, as we have seen previously. Another property that's present in data distributions is known as **quantiles**.

Quantiles are cut-off points that are established at regular intervals from the cumulative distribution function of a random variable. Those regular intervals, also known as *q-quantiles*, will be nearly the same size and will receive special names in some situations; for example:

- The 4-quantiles are called quartiles.
- The 10-quantiles are called deciles.
- The 100-quantiles are called percentiles.

For example, the 20th percentile (of a 100-quantile regular interval) specifies that 20% of the data is below that point. In a box plot, we use regular intervals of 4-quantiles (also known as *quartiles*) to expose the distribution of the data (Q1 and Q3), as shown in the following diagram:

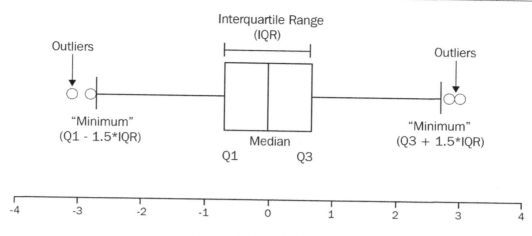

Figure 3.22 – Box plot definition

Q1 is also known as the lower quartile or 25th quartile, and this means that 25% of the data is below that point in the distribution. Q3 is also known as the upper quartile or 75th quartile, and this means that 75% of the data is below that point in the distribution.

Computing the difference between Q1 and Q3 will give you the **interquartile range (IQR)** value, which you can then use to compute the limits of the box plot, shown by the "minimum" and "maximum" labels in the preceding diagram.

After all, we can finally infer that anything below the "minimum" value or above the "maximum" value of the box plot will be flagged as an outlier.

You have now learned about two different ways you can flag outliers on your data: zscore and box plot. You can decide whether you are going to remove these points from your dataset or create another variable to specify that they are, indeed, outliers (as we did in *Figure 3.21*).

Let's continue our journey of data preparation and look at other types of problems we will find in real life. Next, you will learn that several use cases have something known as **rare events**, which makes ML algorithms focus on the wrong side of the problem and propose bad solutions. Luckily, we will learn how to either tune them or prepare the data to make them smarter.

Dealing with unbalanced datasets

At this point, I hope you have realized why data preparation is probably the longest part of our work. We have learned about data transformation, missing data values, and outliers, but the list of problems goes on. Don't worry – bear with me and let's master this topic together!

Another well-known problem with ML models, specifically with binary classification problems, is unbalanced classes. In a binary classification model, we say that a dataset is unbalanced when most of its observations belong to the same class (target variable).

This is very common in fraud identification systems, for example, where most of the events belong to a regular operation, while a very small number of events belong to a fraudulent operation. In this case, we can also say that fraud is a rare event.

There is no strong rule for defining whether a dataset is unbalanced or not, in the sense of it being necessary to worry about it. Most challenge problems will present more than 99% of the observations in the majority class.

The problem with unbalanced datasets is very simple: ML algorithms will try to find the best fit in the training data to maximize their accuracy. In a dataset where 99% of the cases belong to one single class, without any tuning, the algorithm is likely to prioritize the assertiveness of the majority class. In the worst-case scenario, it will classify all the observations as the majority class and ignore the minority one, which is usually our interest when modeling.

To deal with unbalanced datasets, we have two major directions we can follow: tuning the algorithm to handle the issue or resampling the data to make it more balanced.

By tuning the algorithm, you have to specify the weight of each class under classification. This class weight configuration belongs to the algorithm, not to the training data, so it is a hyperparameter setting. It is important to keep in mind that not all algorithms will have that type of configuration, and that not all ML frameworks will expose it, either. As a quick reference, we can mention the `DecisionTreeClassifier` class, from the scikit-learn ML library, as a good example that does implement the class weight hyperparameter.

Another way to work around unbalanced problems is changing the training dataset by applying **undersampling** or **oversampling**. If you decide to apply undersampling, all you have to do is remove some observations from the majority class until you get a more balanced dataset. Of course, the downside of this approach is that you may lose important information about the majority class that you are removing observations from.

The most common approach for undersampling is known as random undersampling, which is a naïve resampling approach where we randomly remove some observations from the training set.

On the other hand, you can decide to go for oversampling, where you will create new observations/samples of the minority class. The simplest approach is the naïve one, where you randomly select observations from the training set (with replacement) for duplication. The downside of this method is the potential issue of overfitting, since you will be duplicating/highlighting the observed pattern of the minority class.

To either underfit or overfit of your model, you should always test the fitted model on your testing set.

> **Important note**
>
> The testing set cannot be under/over sampled: only the training set should pass through these resampling techniques.

You can also oversample the training set by applying synthetic sampling techniques. Random oversample does not add any new information to the training set: it just duplicates the existing ones. By creating synthetic samples, you are deriving those new observations from the existing ones (instead of simply copying them). This is a type of data augmentation technique known as the **Synthetic Minority Oversampling Technique (SMOTE)**.

Technically, what SMOTE does is plot a line in the feature space of the minority class and extract points that are close to that line.

> **Important note**
>
> You may find questions in your exam where the term SMOTE has been used. If that happens, keep the context where this term is applied in mind: oversampling.

Now, let's move on to the next topic regarding data preparation, where we will learn how to prepare text data for machine learning models.

Dealing with text data

We have already learned how to transform categorical features into numerical representations, either using label encoders, ordinal encoders, or one-hot encoding. However, what if we have fields containing long piece of text in our dataset? How are we supposed to provide a mathematical representation for them in order to properly feed ML algorithms? This is a common issue in **natural language processing (NLP)**, a subfield of AI.

NLP models aim to extract knowledge from texts; for example, translating text between languages, identifying entities in a corpus of text (also known as **Name Entity Recognition (NER)**), classifying sentiments from a user review, and many other applications.

Important note

In *Chapter 2, AWS Application Services for AI/ML*, you learned about some AWS application services that apply NLP to their solutions, such as Amazon Translate and Amazon Comprehend. During the exam, you might be asked to think about the fastest or easiest way (with the least development effort) to build certain types of NLP applications. The fastest or easiest way is usually to use those out of the box AWS services, since they offer pre-trained models for some use cases (especially machine translation, sentiment analysis, topic modeling, document classification, and entity recognition).

In a few chapters' time, you will also learn about some built-in AWS algorithms for NLP applications, such as BlazingText, **Latent Dirichlet Allocation (LDA)**, **Neural Topic Modeling**, and the Sequence-to-Sequence algorithm. Those algorithms also let you create the same NLP solutions that are created by those out of box services; however, you have to use them on SageMaker and write your own solution. In other words, they offer more flexibility, but demand more development effort.

Keep that in mind for your exam!

Although AWS offers many out of the box services and built-in algorithms that allow us to create NLP applications, we will not look at those AWS product features now (as we did in *Chapter 2, AWS Application Services for AI/ML*, and will do so again in *Chapter 7, Applying Machine Learning Algorithms*). We will finish this chapter by looking at some data preparation techniques that are extremely important for preparing your data for NLP.

Bag of words

The first one we will cover is known as **bag of words (BoW)**. This is a very common and simple technique, applied to text data, that creates matrix representations to describe the number of words within the text. BoW consists of two main steps: creating a vocabulary and creating a representation of the presence of those known words from the vocabulary in the text. These steps can be seen in the following diagram:

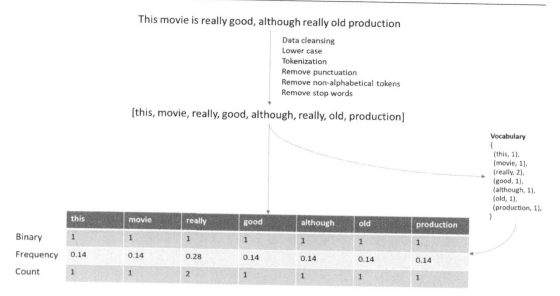

Figure 3.23 – BoW in action

First things first, we usually can't use raw texts to prepare a bag of words representation. There is a data cleansing step where we will lowercase the text; split each work into tokens; remove punctuation, non-alphabetical, and stop words; and, whenever necessary, apply any other custom cleansing technique you may want.

Once you have cleansed your raw text, you can add each word to a global vocabulary. Technically, this is usually a dictionary of tuples, in the form of (word, number of occurrences); for example, {(apple, 10), (watermelon, 20)}. As I mentioned previously, this is a global dictionary, and you should consider all the texts you are analyzing.

Now, with the cleansed text and updated vocabulary, we can build our text representation in the form of a matrix, where each column represents one word from the global vocabulary and each row represents a text you have analyzed. The way you represent those texts on each row may vary according to different strategies, such as binary, frequency, and count. Let's dive into these strategies a little more.

In the preceding diagram, we are processing a single text but trying the three different strategies for bag of words. That's why you can see three rows on that table, instead of just one (in a real scenario, you have to choose one of them for implementation).

In the first row, we have used a binary strategy, which will assign 1 if the word exists in the global vocabulary and 0 if not. Because our vocabulary was built on a single text, all the words from that text belong to the vocabulary (the reason you can only see 1s in the binary strategy).

In the second row, we have used a frequency strategy, which will check the number of occurrences of each word within the text and divide it by the total number of words within the text. For example, the word "this" appears just once (1) and there are seven other words in the text (7), so 1/7 is equal to 0.14.

Finally, in the third row, we have used a count strategy, which is a simple count of occurrences of each word within the text.

> **Important note**
>
> This note is really important – you are likely to find it in your exam. You may have noticed that our BoW matrix contains **unique words** in the *columns* and **each text** representation is in the *rows*. If you have 100 long texts with only 50 unique words across them, your BoW matrix will have 50 columns and 100 rows. During your exam, you are likely to receive a list of texts and be asked to prepare the BoW matrix.

There is one more extremely important concept you should know about BoW, which is the **n-gram** configuration. The term n-gram is used to describe the way you would like to look at your vocabulary, either via single words (uni-gram), groups of two words (bi-gram), groups of three words (tri-gram), or even groups of n words (n-gram). So far, we have seen BoW representations using a uni-gram approach, but more sophisticated representations of BoW may use bi-grams, tri-grams, or n-grams.

The main logic itself does not change, but you need to know how to represent n-grams in BoW. Still using our example from the preceding diagram, a bi-gram approach would combine those words in the following way: [this movie, movie really, really good, good although, although old, old production]. Make sure you understand this before taking the exam.

> **Important note**
>
> The power and simplicity of BoW comes from the fact that you can easily come up with a training set to test your algorithms, or even create a baseline model. If you look at *Figure 3.23*, can you see that having more data and just adding a classification column to that table, such as good or bad review, would allow us to train a binary classification model to predict sentiments?

Alright – you might have noticed that many of the awesome techniques that I have introduced for you come with some downsides. The problem with BoW is the challenge of maintaining its vocabulary. We can easily see that, in a huge corpus of texts, the vocabulary size tends to become bigger and bigger and the matrices' representations tend to be sparse (I know – the sparsity issue again).

One possible way to solve the vocabulary size issue is by using word hashing (also known in ML as the **hashing trick**). Hash functions map data of arbitrary sizes to data of a fixed size. This means you can use the hash trick to represent each text with a fixed number of features (regardless of the vocabulary's size). Technically, this hashing space allows collisions (different texts represented by the same features), so this is something to take into account when you're implementing feature hashing.

TF-IDF

Another problem that comes with BoW, especially when we use the frequency strategy to build the feature space, is that more frequent words will strongly boost their scores due to the high number of occurrences within the document. It turns out that, often, those words with high occurrences are not the key words of the document, but just other words that *also* appear many times in several other documents.

Term Frequency – Inverse Term Frequency (TF-IDF) helps penalize these types of words, by checking how frequent they are in other documents and using that information to rescale the frequency of the words within the document.

At the end of the process, TF-IDF tends to give more importance to words that are unique to the document (document-specific words). Let's look at a concrete example so that you can understand it in depth.

Consider that we have a text corpus containing 100 words and the word "Amazon" appears three times. The **Term Frequency (TF)** of this word would be 3/100, which is equal to 0.03. Now, suppose we have other 1,000 documents and that the word "Amazon" appears in 50 of these. In this case, the **Inverse Term Frequency (IDF)** would be given by the log as 1,000/50, which is equal to 1.30. The TF-IDF score of the word "Amazon", in that specific document under analysis, will be the product of TF * IDF, which is 0.03 * 1.30 (*0.039*).

Let's suppose that instead of 50 documents, the word "Amazon" had also appeared on another 750 documents – in other words, much more frequently than in the prior scenario. In this case, we will not change the TF part of this equation – it is still 0.03. However, the IDF piece will change a little since this time, it will be log 1,000/750, which is equal to *0.0036*. As you can see, this time, the word "Amazon" has much less importance than in the previous example.

Word embedding

Unlike traditional approaches, such as BoW and TD-IDF, modern methods of text representation will take care of the context of the information, as well as the presence or the frequency of words. One very popular and powerful approach that follows this concept is known as **word embedding**. Word embeddings create a dense vector of a fixed length that can store information about the context and meaning of the document.

Each word is represented by a data point in a multidimensional hyper plan, which we call an embedding space. This embedding space will have "n" dimensions, where each of these dimensions refers to a particular position of this dense vector.

Although it may sound confusing, the concept it is actually pretty simple. Let's suppose we have a list of four words, and we want to plot them in an embedding space of five dimensions. The words are king, queen, live, and castle. The following table shows how to do this:

	Dim 1	Dim 2	Dim 3	Dim 4	Dim 5
King	0.22	0.76	0.77	0.44	0.33
Queen	0.98	0.09	0.67	0.89	0.56
Live	0.13	0.99	0.88	0.01	0.55
Castle	0.01	0.89	0.34	0.02	0.90

Figure 3.24 – An embedding space representation

Forget the hypothetical numbers in the preceding table and focus on the data structure; you will see that each word is now represented by "n" dimensions in the embedding space. This process of transforming words into vectors can be performed by many different methods, but the most popular ones are **word2vec** and **GloVe**.

Once you have each word represented as a vector of a fixed length, you can apply many other techniques to do whatever you need. One very common task is plotting those "words" (actually, their dimensions) in a hyper plan and, visually, checking how close they are to each other!

Technically, we don't use this to plot them as-is, since human brains cannot interpret more than three dimensions. Then, we usually apply a dimensionality reduction technique (such as principal component analysis, which you will learn about later) to reduce the number of dimensions to two, and finally plot the words in a cartesian plan. That's why you might have seen pictures like the one at the bottom of the following diagram. Have you ever asked yourself how is it possible to plot words on a graph?

	Dim 1	Dim 2	Dim 3	Dim 4	Dim 5
King	0.22	0.76	0.77	0.44	0.33
Queen	0.98	0.09	0.67	0.89	0.56
Live	0.13	0.99	0.88	0.01	0.55
Castle	0.01	0.89	0.34	0.02	0.90

	PC 1	PC2
King	0.9	0.3
Queen	0.8	0.5
Live	0.33	0.7
Castle	0.28	0.7

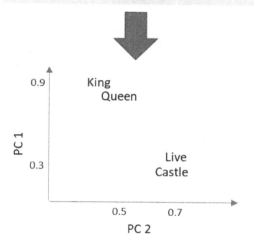

Figure 3.25 – Plotting words

In case you are wondering how we came up with the dimensions shown in *Figure 3.24*, let's dive into it. Again, there are different methods to do this, but let's look at one of the most popular, which uses a co-occurrence matrix with a fixed context window.

First, we have to come up with some logic to represent each word, keeping in mind that we also have to take their context into consideration. To solve the context requirement, we will define a **fixed context window**, which is going to be responsible for specifying how many words will be grouped together for context learning. For instance, let's set this fixed context window to 2.

Next, we will create a **co-occurrence matrix**, which will count the number of occurrences of each pair of words, according to the pre-defined context window. Let's see this in action. Consider the following text: "I will pass this exam, you will see. I will pass it".

The context window of the first word "pass" would be the ones in *bold*: "*I will* pass *this exam*, you will see. I will pass it". Considering this logic, let's see how many times each pair of words appears in the context window:

	I	Will	Pass	This	Exam	You	See	It
I	0	3	...	...	...	...	...	...
Will	3	0	...	...	...	...	...	...
Pass	...	...	0	...	...	...	...	...
This	...	...	...	0	...	...	...	...
Exam	...	...	...	...	0	...	...	...
You	...	...	...	...	...	0	...	...
See	...	...	...	...	...	...	0	...
It	...	...	...	...	...	...	...	0

Figure 3.26 – Co-occurrence matrix

As you can see, the pair of words "I will" appears three times when we use a context window of size 2:

1. *I will* pass this exam, you will see. I will pass it.
2. I will pass this exam, you *will* see. *I* will pass it.
3. I will pass this exam, you will see. *I will* pass it.

Looking at the preceding table, the same logic should be applied to all other pairs of words, replacing "..." with the associated number of occurrences. You now have a numerical representation for each word!

Important note

You should be aware that there many alternatives to co-occurrence matrices with a fixed context window, such as using TD-IDF vectorization or even simpler counters of words per document. The most important message here is that, somehow, you must come up with a numerical representation for each word.

The last step is finally finding those dimensions shown in *Figure 3.24*. You can do this by creating a multilayer model, usually based on neural networks, where the hidden layer will represent your embedding space. The following diagram shows a simplified example where we could potentially compress our words shown in the preceding table into an embedding space of five dimensions:

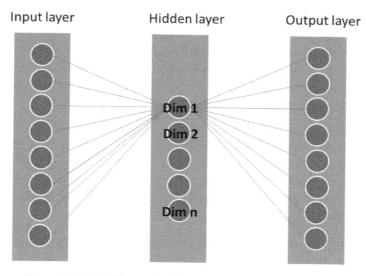

Figure 3.27 – Building embedding spaces with neural networks

We will talk about neural networks in more detail later in this book. For now, understanding where the embedding vector comes from is already an awesome achievement!

Another important thing you should keep in mind while modeling natural language problems is that you can reuse a pre-trained embedding space in your models. Some companies have created modern neural network architectures, trained on billions of documents, which has become the state of the art in this field. For your reference, take a look at **Bidirectional Encoder Representations from Transformers (BERT)**, which was proposed by Google and has been widely used by the data science community and industry.

We have now reached the end of this long – but very important – chapter about data preparation and transformation. Let's take this opportunity to do a quick recap of the awesome things we have learned.

Summary

First, you were introduced to the different types of features that you might have to work with. Identifying the type of variable you'll be working with is very important for defining the types of transformations and techniques that can be applied to each case.

Then, we learned how to deal with categorical features. We saw that, sometimes, categorical variables do have an order (such as the ordinal ones), while other times, they don't (such as the nominal ones). You learned that one-hot encoding (or dummy variables) is probably the most common type of transformation for nominal features; however, depending on the number of unique categories, after applying one-hot encoding, your data might suffer from sparsity issues. Regarding ordinal features, you shouldn't create dummy variables on top of them, since you would be losing the information of order that's been incorporated into the variable. In those cases, ordinal encoding is the most appropriate transformation.

We continued our journey by looking at numerical features, where we learned how to deal with continuous and discrete data. We walked through the most important types of transformations, such as normalization, standardization, binning, and discretization. You saw that some types of transformation rely on the underlying data to find their parameters, so it is very important to avoid using the testing set to learn anything from the data (it must be used strictly for testing).

You have also seen that we can even apply pure math to transform our data; for example, you learned that power transformations can be used to reduce the skewness of your feature and make it more normal.

Next, we looked at missing data and got a sense for how critical this task is. When you are modeling, you *can't* look at the missing values as a simple computational problem, where you just have to replace x with y. This is a much bigger problem where you need to start solving it by exploring your data, and then checking if your missing data was generated at random or not.

When you are making the decision to remove or replace missing data, you must be aware that you are either losing information or adding bias to the data, respectively. Remember to review all the important notes we gave you, since they are likely to be, somehow, present in your exam.

Next, you learned about outlier detection. You looked at different ways to find outliers, such as the zscore and box plot approaches. Most importantly, you learned that you can either flag or smooth them.

At the start, I told you that this chapter would be a long but worthwhile journey about data preparation, which is why I needed to give you a good sense of how to deal with rare events, since this is one the most challenging problems on ML. You learned that, sometimes, your data might be unbalanced, and you must either trick your algorithm (by changing the class weight) or resample your data (applying undersampling and oversampling).

Finally, you learned how to deal with text data for NLP. You should now be able to manually compute bag of words and TF-IDF matrices! We went even deeper and learned how word embedding works. During this subsection, we learned that we can either create our own embedding space (using many different methods) or reuse a pre-trained one, such as BERT.

We are done! I am so glad you made it here and I am sure this chapter is crucial to your success in the exam. Finally, we have prepared some practice questions for you; I hope you enjoy them.

In the next chapter, we will dive into data visualization techniques.

Questions

1. You are working as a data scientist for a healthcare company and are creating a machine learning model to predict fraud, waste, and abuse across the company's claims. One of the features of this model is the number of times a particular drug has been prescribed, to the same patient of the claim, in a period of 2 years. Which type of feature is this?

   a) Discrete

   b) Continuous

   c) Nominal

   d) Ordinal

   > **Answer**
   > a, The feature is counting the number of times that a particular drug has been prescribed. Individual and countable items are classified as discrete data.

2. You are building a ML model for an educational group that owns schools and universities across the globe. Your model aims to predict how likely a particular student is to leave his/her studies. Many factors may contribute to school dropout, but one of your features is the current academic stage of each student: preschool, elementary school, middle school, or high school. Which type of feature is this?

    a) Discrete

    b) Continuous

    c) Nominal

    d) Ordinal

    > **Answer**
    > d, The feature has an implicit order and should be considered a categorical/ordinal variable.

3. You are building a machine learning model for a car insurance company. The company wants to create a binary classification model that aims to predict how likely their insured vehicles are to be stolen. You have considered many features to this model, including the type of vehicle (economy, compact, premium, luxury, van, sport, and convertible). How would you transform the type of vehicle in order to use it in your model?

    a) Applying ordinal encoding

    b) Applying one-hot encoding

    c) No transformation is needed

    d) Options A and B are valid transformations for this problem

    > **Answer**
    > b, In this case, we have a categorical/nominal variable (there is no order among each category). Additionally, the number of unique categories looks pretty manageable; furthermore, one-hot encoding would fit very well for this type of data.

4. You are working as a data scientist for a financial company. The company wants to create a model that aims to classify improper payments. You have decided to use "type of transaction" as one of your features (local, international, pre-approved, and so on). After applying one-hot encoding to this variable, you realize that your dataset has many more variables, and your model is taking a lot of time to train. How could you potentially solve this problem?

a) By applying ordinal encoding instead of one-hot encoding. In this case, we would be creating just one feature.

b) By applying label encoding.

c) By analyzing which types of transactions have the most impact on improper/proper payments. Only apply one-hot encoding to the reduced types of transactions.

d) By porting your model to another programming language that can handle sparse data in a better way.

Answer

c, Your transformation resulted in more features due to the excessive number of categories in the original variable. Although the one-hot encoding approach looks right, since the variable is a nominal feature, the number of levels (unique values) for that feature is probably too high.

In this case, you could do exploratory data analysis to understand the most important types of transactions for your problem. Once you know that information, you can then restrict the transformation to just those specific types (reducing the sparsity of your data). It is worth adding that you would be missing some information during this process because now, your dummy variables would only be focusing only on a subset of categories, but it is a valid approach.

---

5. You are working as a data scientist for a marketing company. Your company is building a clustering model that will be used to segment customers. You decided to normalize the variable "annual income", which ranges from between 50,000 and 300,000.

After applying normalization, what would be the normalized values of a group of customers that earn 50,000, 125,000 and 300,000?

a) 1, 2, and 3

b) 0, 0.5, and 1

c) 0, 0.25, and 1

d) 5, 12, and 30

Answer

b, Applying the normalization formula and assuming the expected range would be 0 and 1, the correct answer is b.

---

6. Consider a dataset that stores the salaries of employees in a particular column. The mean value of salaries on this column is $2,000, while the standard deviation is equal to $300. What is the standard scaled value of someone that earns $3,000?

a) 3.33

b) 6.66

c) 10

d) 1

Answer

a, Remember the standard scale formula: $(X - \mu) / \sigma$, which is $(3,000 - 2,000) / 300$.

---

7. Which type of data transformations can we apply to convert a continuous variable into a binary variable?

a) Binning and one-hot encoding

b) Standardization and binning

c) Normalization and one-hot encoding

d) Standardization and one-hot encoding

Answer

a, In this case, we could discretize a continuous variable by applying binning and then getting the dummy variables.

8. You are a data scientist for a financial company and you have been assigned the task of creating a binary classification model to predict whether a customer will leave the company or not (also known as churn). During your exploratory work, you realize that there is a particular feature (credit utilization amount) with some missing values. This variable is expressed in real numbers; for example, $1,000. What would be the fastest approach to dealing with those missing values, assuming you don't want to lose information?

a) Dropping any missing values.

b) Creating a classification model to predict the credit utilization amount and use it to predict the missing data.

c) Creating a regression model to predict the credit utilization amount and use it to predict the missing data.

d) Replacing the missing data with the mean or median value of the variable.

> **Answer**
>
> d, In this case, almost all the options are valid approaches to deal with missing data for this problem, except option b because predicting the missing data would require you to create a regression model, not a classification model. Option a is a valid approach to deal with missing data, but not to this problem where we don't want to lose information. Option c is also a valid approach, but not the fastest one. Option d is the most appropriate answer for this question.

9. You have to create a machine learning model for a particular client, but you realize that most of the features have more than 50% of data missing. What's our best option on this critical case?

a) Dropping entire columns with more than 50% of missing data

b) Removing all the rows that contains at least one missing information

c) Check with the dataset owner if you can retrieve the missing data from somewhere else

d) Replace the missing information by the mean or median of the feature

Answer

c, This is a very critical case where most of your information is actually missing. You should work with the dataset owner to understand why that problem is occurring and check the process that generates this data. If you decide to drop missing values, you would be losing a lot of information. On the other hand,

if you decide to replace missing values, you would be adding a lot of bias to your data.

10. You are working as a senior data scientist from a human resource company. You are creating a particular machine learning model that uses an algorithm that does not perform well on skewed features, such as the one in the following image:

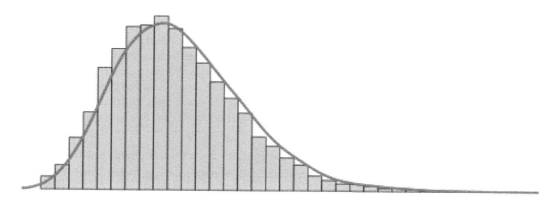

Figure 3.28 – Skewed feature

Which transformations could you apply to this feature to reduce its skewness (choose all the correct answers)?

a) Normalization

b) Log transformation

c) Exponential transformation

d) Box-Cox transformation

> **Answer**
>
> b, d, To reduce skewness, power transformations are the most appropriate. Particularly, you could apply the log transformation or Box-Cox transformation to make this distribution more similar to a Gaussian one.

11. You are working on a fraud identification issue where most of your labeled data belongs to one single class (not fraud). Only 0.1% of the data refers to fraudulent cases. Which modeling techniques would you propose to use on this use case (choose all the correct answers)?

    a) Applying random oversampling to create copies of the fraudulent cases.

    b) Applying random undersampling to remove observations from the not fraudulent cases.

    c) We can't create a classification model on such an unbalanced dataset. The best thing to do would be to ask for more fraudulent cases from the dataset owner.

    d) Applying synthetic oversampling to create copies of the not fraudulent cases.

> **Answer**
>
> a, b, Unbalanced datasets are very common with ML, and there are many different ways to deal with this problem. Option c is definitely not the right one. Pay attention to option d; you should be able to apply synthetic oversampling to your data, but to create more observations of the minority class, not from the majority class. Options a and b are correct.

12. You are preparing text data for machine learning. This time, you want to create a bi-gram BoW matrix on top of the following texts:

    "I will master this certification exam"

    "I will pass this certification exam"

    How many rows and columns would you have on your BoW matrix representation?

    a) 7 rows and 2 columns

    b) 2 rows and 7 columns

    c) 14 rows and 4 columns

    d) 4 columns and 14 rows

Answer

b, Let's compute the matrix in the following table together.

As you can see, the trick is knowing which tokens are common to the two texts. We only have two texts; the number of rows will be also two – one for each of them:

I will	Will master	Master this	This certification	Certification exam	Will pass	Pass this
1	1	1	1	1	0	0
1	0	0	1	1	1	1

Figure 3.29 – Resulting bag of words

13. You are running a survey to check how many years of experience a group of people has on a particular development tool. You came up with the following distribution:

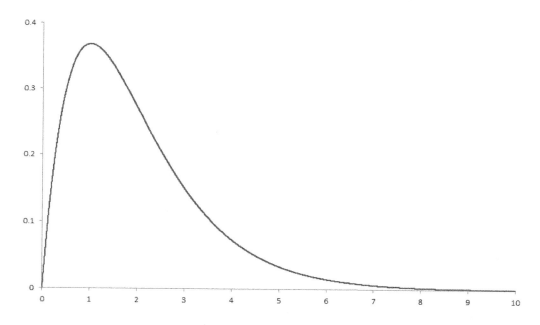

Figure 3.30 – Skewed data distribution

What can you say about the mode, mean, and median of this distribution (choose all the correct answers)?

a) The mean is greater than the median

b) The mean is smaller than the median

c) The median is greater than the mode

d) The median is smaller than the mode

> **Answer**
>
> a, c, This is a skewed distribution (to the right-hand side). This means your mean value will be pushed to the same side of the tail, followed by the median. As result, we will have mode < median < mean.

14. You are working as a data scientist for a retail company. You are building a decision tree-based model for classification purposes. During your evaluation process, you realize that the model's accuracy is not acceptable. Which of the following tasks is *not* a valid approach for increasing the accuracy of your decision tree model?

    a) Tuning the hyperparameters of the model.

    b) Scaling numerical features.

    c) Trying different approaches for transforming categorical features, such as binary encoding, one-hot encoding, and ordinal encoding (whenever applicable).

    d) If the dataset is not balanced, it is worth trying different types of resampling techniques (undersampling and oversampling).

    > **Answer**
    >
    > b, Scaling numerical features is an important task with machine learning models but is not always needed. Particularly on decision tree-based models, changing the scale of the data will not result in better model performance, since this type of model is not impacted by the scale of the data.

15. You are working on a data science project where you must create an NLP model. You have decided to test Word2vec and GloVe during your model development, as an attempt to improve model accuracy. Word2vec and GloVe are two types of what?

a) Pre-trained word embeddings

b) Pre-trained TF-IDF vectors

c) One-hot encoding techniques

d) None of above

Answer

a, Some NPL architectures may include embedding layers. If you are facing this type of project, you can either create your own embedding space by training a specific model for that purpose (using your own corpus of data) or you can use any pre-trained word embedding model, such as the Word2vec model, which is pre-trained by Google.

4
Understanding and Visualizing Data

Data visualization is an art! No matter how much effort you and your team put into data preparation and preliminary analysis for modeling, if you don't know how to show your findings effectively, your audience may not understand the point you are trying to make.

Often, such situations may be even worse when you are dealing with decision-makers. For example, if you choose the wrong set of charts to tell a particular story, people can misinterpret your analysis and make bad decisions.

Understanding the different types of data visualizations and knowing how they fit with each type of analysis will put you in a very good position, in terms of engaging your audience and transmitting the information you want to.

In this chapter, you will learn about some data visualization techniques. We will be covering the following topics:

- Visualizing relationships in your data
- Visualizing comparisons in your data
- Visualizing compositions in your data
- Visualizing distributions in your data

- Building key performance indicators
- Introducing Quick Sight

We already know why we need to master these topics, so let's get started.

Visualizing relationships in your data

When we need to show relationships in our data, we are usually talking about plotting two or more variables in a chart to visualize their level of dependency. A **scatter plot** is probably the most common type of chart to show the relationship between **two** variables. The following is a scatter plot for two variables, **x** and **y**:

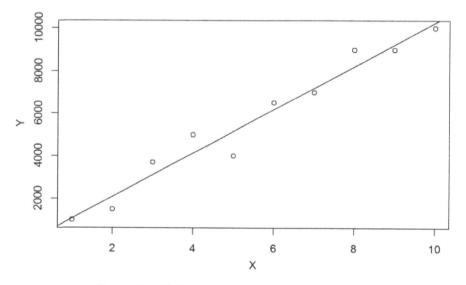

Figure 4.1 – Plotting relationships with a scatter plot

The preceding plot shows a clear relationship between **x** and **y**. As **x** increases, **y** also increases. In this particular case, we can say that there is a linear relationship between both variables. Keep in mind that scatter plots may also catch other types of relationships, not only linear ones. For example, it would also be possible to find an exponential relationship between the two variables.

Another nice chart to make comparisons with is known as a **bubble chart**. Just like a scatter plot, it will also show the relationship between variables; however, here, you can use a third dimension, which will be represented by the size of the point.

The following is a bubble chart that's explaining an investment schema, where **x** is the annual rate, **y** is the investment period, and the size of the bubble is the size of each investment option:

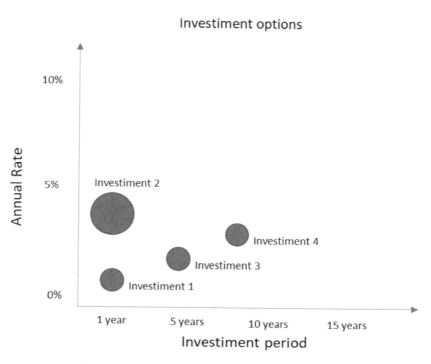

Figure 4.2 – Plotting relationships with a bubble chart

Looking at the preceding chart, we can see two types of relationships: the longer the investment period, the higher your annual rate, and the higher the amount invested, the higher your annual rate. As we can see, this is a very effective way to present this type of analysis. Next, we'll learn how to compare our data.

Visualizing comparisons in your data

Comparisons are very common in data analysis and we have different ways to present them. Let's start with the **bar chart**. I am sure you have seen many reports that have used this type of visualization.

Bar charts can be used to compare one variable among different classes; for example, a car's price across different models or population size per country. In the following graph, we have used a bar chart to present the number of Covid-19 cases per state in India, until June 2020:

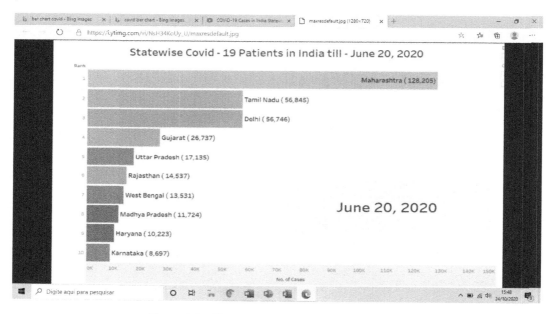

Figure 4.3 – Plotting comparisons with a bar chart

Sometimes, we can also use **stacked column charts** to add another dimension to the data that is being analyzed. For example, in the following graph, we are using a stacked bar chart to show how many people were on board the Titanic, per gender. Additionally, we are breaking down the number of people who survived (positive class) and those who did not (negative class):

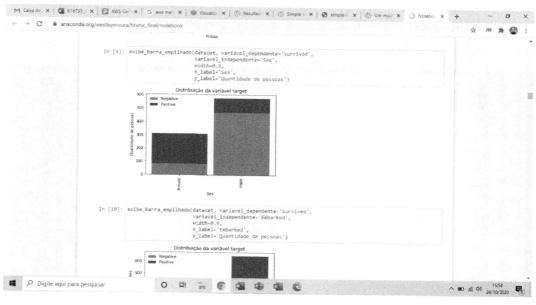

Figure 4.4 – Using a stacked bar chart to analyze the Titanic disaster dataset

As we can see, most of the women survived the disaster, while most of the men did not. The stacked bars help us visualize the difference between genders. Finally, you should know that we can also show percentages on those stacked bars, instead of absolute numbers.

Column charts are also useful If you need to compare one or two variables across different periods. For example, in the following graph, we can see the annual Canadian electronic vehicle sales by province:

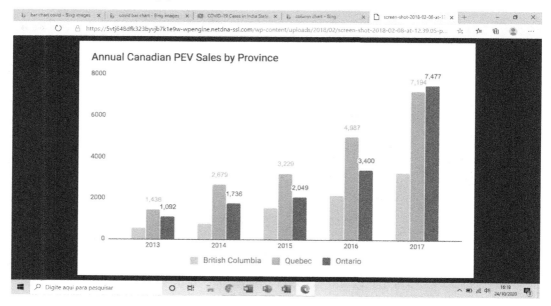

Figure 4.5 – Plotting comparisons with a column chart

Another very effective way to make comparisons across different periods is by using **line charts**. In the following chart, we are showing a pretty interesting example of how we can compare different algorithms' performance, in a particular project, across different release dates.

> **Important note**
>
> Line charts are usually very helpful to show if there is any trend in the data over the period of time under analysis. A very common use case for line charts is **forecasting**, where we usually have to analyze trends and seasonality in time series data.

For example, we can see that the **Classification and Regression Trees (CART)** model used to be the poorest performant model compared to other algorithms, such as **AdaBoost (ADA)**, **Gradient Boosting (GB)**, **Random Forest (RF)**, and **logistic regression (LOGIT)**.

However, in July, the CART model was changed, and it turned out to be the third-best model across all other models. This whole story about the best model for each period can easily be seen in the following chart:

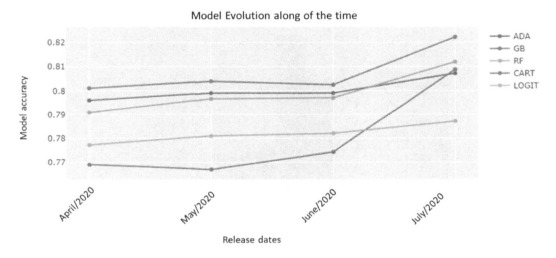

Figure 4.6 – Plotting comparisons with a line chart

Finally, you can also show comparisons of your data using **tables**. Tables are more useful when we have multiple dimensions (usually placed in the rows of the table) and one or multiple metrics to make comparisons against (usually placed in the columns of the table).

In the next section, we will learn about another set of charts that aims to show the distribution of your variables. This set of charts is particularly important for modeling tasks since you must know the distribution of a feature to think about potential data transformations for it. Let's take a look at this!

Visualizing distributions in your data

Exploring the distribution of your feature is very important to understand some key characteristics of it, such as its skewness, mean, median, and quantiles. You can easily visualize skewness by plotting a **histogram**. This type of chart groups your data into **bins** or **buckets** and performs counts on top of them. For example, the following chart shows a histogram for the *age* variable:

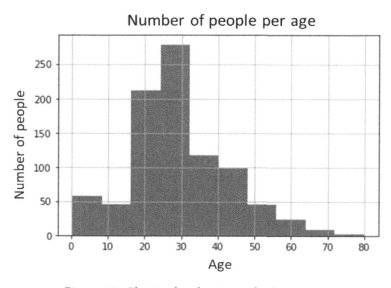

Figure 4.7 – Plotting distributions with a histogram

Looking at the histogram, we can conclude that most of the people are between 20 and 50 years old. We can also see a few people more than 60 years old. Another example of a histogram is shown in the following chart, where we are plotting the distribution of payments from a particular event that has different ticket prices. We want to see how much money people are paying per ticket:

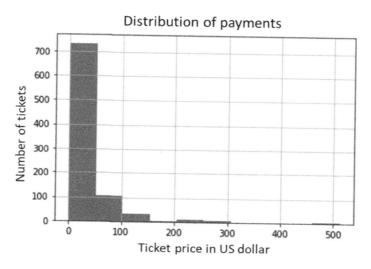

Figure 4.8 – Checking skewness with a histogram

Here, we can see that the majority of the people are paying a maximum of 100 dollars per ticket. That's the reason why we can see a skewed distribution to the right-hand side (the tail side).

If you want to see other characteristics of the distribution, such as its median, quantiles, and outliers, then you should use **box plots**. In the following chart, we are again comparing the performance of different algorithms in a given dataset.

These algorithms were executed many times, in a cross-validation process, which resulted in multiple outputs for the same algorithm; for example, one accuracy metric for each execution of the algorithm on each fold.

Since we have multiple accuracy metrics for each algorithm, we can use a box plot to check how each of those algorithms performed during the cross-validation process:

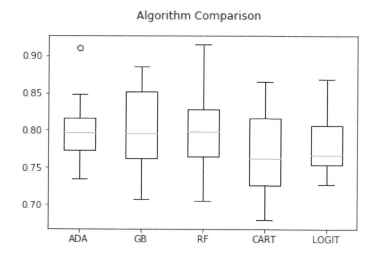

Figure 4.9 – Plotting distributions with a box plot

Here, we can see that box plots can present some information about the distribution of the data, such as its median, lower quartile, upper quartile, and outliers. For a complete understanding of each element of a box plot, take a look at the following diagram:

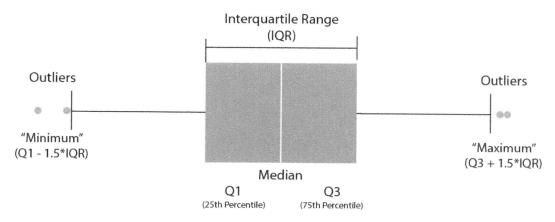

Figure 4.10 – Box plot elements

By analyzing the box plot shown in *Figure 4.9*, we can conclude that the ADA algorithm has presented some outliers during the cross-validation process since one of the executions resulted in a very good model (around 92% accuracy). All the other executions of AdaBoost resulted in less than 85% accuracy, with a median value of around 80%.

Another conclusion we can make after analyzing *Figure 4.9* is that the CART algorithm presented the poorest performance during the cross-validation process (the lowest median and lower quartile).

Before we wrap up this section, note that you can also use a scatter plot to analyze data distributions when you have more than one variable. Now, let's look at another set of charts that is useful for showing compositions in your data.

Visualizing compositions in your data

Sometimes, you want to analyze the various elements that compose your feature; for example, the percentage of sales per region or percentage of queries per channel. In both examples, we are not considering any time dimension; instead, we are just looking at the data as a whole. For these types of compositions, where you don't have the time dimension, you could show your data using **pie charts**, **stacked 100% bar charts**, and **treemaps**.

The following is a pie chart showing the number of queries per customer channel, for a given company, during a pre-defined period of time:

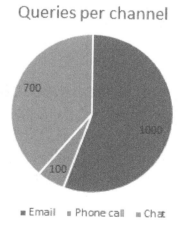

Figure 4.11 – Plotting compositions with a pie chart

If you want to show compositions while considering a time dimension, then your most common options would be a **stacked area chart**, a **stacked 100% area chart**, a **stacked column chart**, or a **stacked 100% column chart**. For reference, take a look at the following chart, which shows the sales per region from 2016 until 2020:

Figure 4.12 – Plotting compositions with a stacked 100% column chart

As we can see, stacked 100% column charts help us understand compositions across different periods.

Building key performance indicators

Before we wrap up these data visualization sections, I want to introduce **key performance indicators**, or **KPIs** for short.

A KPI is usually a single value that describes the results of a business indicator, such as the churn rate, **net promoter score** (**NPS**), **return on investment** (**ROI**), and so on. Although there are some commonly used indicators across different industries, you are free to come up with a number, based on your company's needs.

To be honest, the most complex challenge associated with indicators is not in their visualization aspect itself, but in the way they have been built (the rules used) and the way they will be communicated and used across different levels of the company.

From a visualization perspective, just like any other single value, you can use all those charts that we have learned about to analyze your indicator, depending on your need. However, if you just want to show your KPI, with no time dimension, you can use a **widget**.

Alright, that's all I have to talk about regarding data visualization techniques for the AWS machine learning specialty exam. Now, let's take a look at Quick Sight, an AWS service where you can implement all these visualization techniques you have just learned.

Introducing Quick Sight

Amazon Quick Sight is a cloud-based analytics service that allows you to build data visualizations and ad hoc analysis. Quick Sight supports a variety of data sources, such as Redshift, Aurora, Athena, RDS, and your on-premises database solution.

Other sources of data include S3, where you can retrieve data from Excel, CSV, or log files, and **Software as a Service** (**SaaS**) solutions, where you can retrieve data from Salesforce entities.

Amazon Quick Sight has two versions:

- Standard Edition
- Enterprise Edition

The most important difference between these two versions is the possibility of integration with Microsoft **Active Directory** (**AD**) and encryption at rest. Both features are only provided in the enterprise edition.

> **Important note**
> Keep in mind that AWS services are constantly evolving, so more differences between the standard and enterprise versions may crop up in the future. You should always consult the latest documentation of AWS services to check what's new.

In terms of access management, Quick Sight offers a very simple interface you can use to control user access. In the standard edition, you have pretty much two options for inviting a user to your Quick Sight account:

- You can invite an IAM user.
- You can send an invitation to an email address.

If you invite an IAM user, then they can automatically log into your account and see or edit your visualization, depending on the type of permission you have provided during Quick Sight user creation. If you have invited an email address, then the email owner has to access his/her mailbox to complete this operation.

Removing a user is also pretty straightforward. The only extra information you have to provide while removing a user is whether you want to transfer the orphaned resources to another user into your account, *or* whether you want to delete all the user's resources.

If you are playing with the enterprise edition, this process of authorizing users can be a little different since you have AD working for you. In this case, you can grant access to AD groups, and all the users from that group would be granted access to your account on Quick Sight.

Also, remember that in both versions, all data transfer is encrypted; however, you will only find encryption at rest in the enterprise edition.

When you are bringing data into Quick Sight, you are technically creating what we call **datasets**. Datasets, in turn, are imported in an optimized structure into Quick Sight, known as the **Super-fast, Parallel, In-memory, Calculation Engine** (**SPICE**). That's why Quick Sight can perform data visualization on big data.

We know that Quick Sight offers high availability and durability since the data that's imported into it is replicated.

Something else you should be aware of is that Quick Sight does not only allow you to plot your data but also perform some small data preparation tasks, such as renaming fields, computing new fields, changing data types, preparing queries to retrieve data from the source, and joining tables from the same source.

Let's summarize the main steps for working with Quick Sight:

1. User creation and authorization.
2. Connecting to a **data source**.
3. Bringing data into a **dataset**.
4. Your dataset will be imported into **SPICE**.
5. From a dataset, you can create an **analysis**.
6. Finally, inside your analysis, you can add **visuals**.
7. In case you want to go further, you can create a snapshot of your analysis and place it in a **dashboard**. Alternatively, you can group your analysis into **stories**.

That brings us to the end of this chapter about data visualizations! Now, let's take a look at what we have learned.

Summary

We have reached the end of this chapter about data visualization. Let's take this opportunity to provide a quick recap of what we have learned. We started this chapter by showing you how to visualize relationships in your data. Scatter plots and bubble charts are the most important charts in this category, either to show relationships between two or three variables, respectively.

Then, we moved on to another category of data visualization, which aimed to make comparisons in your data. The most common charts that you can use to show comparisons are bar charts, column charts, and line charts. Tables are also useful to show comparisons.

The next use case that we covered was visualizing data distributions. The most common types of charts that are used to show distributions are histograms and box plots.

Then, we moved on to compositions. We use this set of charts when we want to show the different elements that make up the data. While showing compositions, you must be aware of whether you want to present static data or data that changes over time. For static data, you should use a pie chart, a stacked 100% bar chart, or a treemap. For data that changes over time, you should use a stacked area chart, a stacked 100% area chat, a stacked column chart, or a stacked 100% column chart.

The last section of this chapter was reserved for Quick Sight, which is an AWS service that you can use to visualize your data. You learned about the different versions and features of the service, and you were then introduced to SPICE.

Well done! In the next chapter, you will learn about AWS's data storing services, such as S3, EBS, EFS, and many others. That is going to be a very important chapter for your certification journey, so make sure you're prepared! However, before we jump into that new chapter, let's practice a little more for the exam!

Questions

1. You are working as a data scientist for a fintech company. At the moment, you are working on a regression model that predicts how much money customers will spend on their credit card transactions in the next month. You believe you have created a good model; however, you want to complete your residual analysis to confirm that the model errors are randomly distributed around zero. What is the best chart for performing this residual analysis?

   a) Line chart

   b) Bubble chart

   c) Scatter plot

   d) Stacked bar chart

   > **Answer**
   >
   > C, In this case, you want to show the distribution of the model errors. A scatter plot would be a nice approach to present such an analysis. Having model errors randomly distributed across zero is just more evidence that the model is not suffering from overfitting. Histograms are also nice for performing error analysis.

2. Although you believe that two particular variables are highly correlated, you think this is not a linear correlation. Knowing the type of correlation between these two variables is crucial for determining the type of algorithm that you are going to use in later phases of this project. Which type of chart could you use to show the correlations between these two variables?

   a) Line chart

   b) Bubble chart

   c) Histogram

   d) Scatter plot

   > **Answer**
   >
   > D, Correlation is a type of relationship. In this case, we just have two variables, so a scatter plot would be a good approach to this problem.

3. You are working for a call center company, and the business team wants to see the percentage of calls on each channel of their **interactive voice response device**. You just got those percentages, broken down per month. What's the best way to show this monthly information to your users?

    a) Pie chart

    b) Stacked 100% column chart

    c) Histogram

    d) Scatter plot

    > **Answer**
    >
    > B, In this case, you want to show the composition of your data across different periods. Both a and b could be used to show compositions; however, only option b would be appropriate to show those compositions across each month.

4. You are working as a data scientist for a telecom company. The company offers many different services related to broadband, TV, phone, and mobile. In total, the company offers more than 50 services. You want to see the number of services that each customer usually signs for. What's the most appropriate chart to use to prepare for this visualization?

    a) Pie chart

    b) Stacked 100% column chart

    c) Histogram

    d) Scatter plot

    > **Answer**
    >
    > C, Since the company has so many services and you want to see the distribution of the number of services per customer, the most appropriate chart would be a histogram. Keep in mind that, most of the time, when the goal of the analysis is showing distributions, your most common options are histograms and box plots. Depending on the use case, scatter plots can also be used.

5.　You are working on a sales report for your company and you need to make different types of comparisons regarding your company's sales across different regions. Which of the following types of charts are suitable for presenting comparisons in your data (choose all the correct answers)?

a) Bar chart

b) Column chart

c) Line chart

d) Histogram

> **Answer**
>
> A, B, C, You have multiple options when it comes to using charts to present comparisons on your data. Use bar charts when you have a single variable and no time dimension; use column charts when you have one or two variables changing over time; and use line charts when you have three or more variables changing over time. Finally, remember that it is also possible to show comparisons using tables. This is especially helpful when you have three or more variables.

6.　You are working as a data scientist for a meteorological organization. Your company is measuring the daily temperature of a particular region during the entire summer. The summer is over and it is now time to present a detailed report about the data that has been captured. Which of the following options are not valid types of analysis (choose all correct answers)?

a) Create a box plot to show some statistics about the data; for example, the median temperature, lower and upper quartiles, and outlier points.

b) Create a histogram to show the distribution of the data across all the different days when temperatures have been measured.

c) Create a key performance indicator just to present the average temperature that has been measured during the summer, in that particular region.

d) Create a line chart to show the evolution of the temperature, day after day. That will give you some sense about the increasing and decreasing trends.

Answer

All the answers are valid types of analysis for this particular problem. Box plots and histograms would be very useful to present the distribution of the data; a KPI would provide a straight answer to the question "What was the average temperature?"; and line charts could be used to show the trends in the data during the period of measurement. There are many other types of analysis you could use for this problem. Just as another example, you could think of using a column chart to show the average temperature every month.

7. You are working in a financial company and your team is responsible for the investment portfolio. You have multiple options for investments and the key characteristics of all of them are annual rate, investment period, and investment amount. There is a straight relationship between these three components. You have built a bubble chart to show the relationship among these investment options, but now, you want to compare them and add a few more dimensions, such as level of risk and year after year performance. What is the most appropriate way to present this information in the most compact way?

a) Change the current bubble chart that you created previously, by adding these new dimensions.

b) Create a table to present this information, where each investment option is represented by rows and each metric is represented by columns.

c) Keep the current bubble chart as-is and create a few more visualizations to present the new metrics.

d) Keep the current bubble chart as-is and present the rest of the information in a tabular structure.

Answer

B, You should be aware that, during your exam, you might find questions with multiple correct answers; however, there will be an optimal one. In this case, only one option would be wrong, but all the rest are quite possible. Option b is the most accurate answer since the question is asking about the "most compact way" the present the information. Pay attention to specific keywords in the questions during your exam.

8. You are working as a data scientist for a marketing company. At the moment, you are building a machine learning model to predict churn. One of the features that you are using on your model is *annual salary*. Due to the nature of this variable, you suspect that a log transformation would be beneficial to bring this feature closer to a normal distribution. Which of the following charts would support you to prove that, indeed, a log transformation is a good idea for this feature?

    a) Histogram

    b) Scatter plot

    c) Line chart

    d) Stacked bar chart

    > **Answer**
    >
    > A, Deciding on whether log transformation is a good idea or not will depend on the distribution of the data. If you have a skewed distribution, then log transformation could be beneficial to bringing this data closer to a normal distribution. Depending on the algorithm you are using for modeling, such a transformation can improve the accuracy of your model. The histogram is the right answer to this question since it will present the data distribution that will support your decision.

9. You are working as a data analyst for a tech company. Your company wants to analyze sales across different lines of services, and you've decided to use Quick Sight as a data visualization tool. Which of the following options is *false* about Quick Sight?

    a) Quick Sight imports datasets into SPICE to optimize data processing. With SPICE, your analytical queries process quickly and you don't need to wait for a direct query process.

    b) Although Quick Sight can encrypt data transfers, it does not support encryption at rest.

    c) Quick Sight can connect on Redshift, Aurora, Athena, RDS, on-premises databases, S3, and SaaS.

    d) When access is granted to Active Directory groups, users from that group won't be notified.

Answer

B, All these answers are correct, except option b. Quick Sight does support encryption at rest, but only in the enterprise edition. Another important feature that's only supported in the enterprise edition is integration with AD.

10. You work in a company that uses Quick Sight for data visualization purposes. Which of the following types of analysis are supported by Quick Sight (choose all the correct answers)?

a) Analyzing relationships in the data

b) Analyzing comparisons in the data

c) Analyzing compositions in the data

d) Analyzing data distributions

Answer

Quick Sight is a great tool that supports all the use cases that we have learned about in this chapter. It not only supports these use cases but also optimizes data processing through the use of SPICE.

5
AWS Services for Data Storing

AWS provides a wide range of services to store your data safely and securely. There are various storage options available on AWS such as block storage, file storage, and object storage. It is expensive to manage on-premises data storage due to the higher investment in hardware, admin overheads, and managing system upgrades. With AWS Storage services, you just pay for what you use, and you don't have to manage the hardware. We will also learn about various storage classes offered by Amazon S3 for intelligent access of the data and reducing costs. You can expect questions in the exam on storage classes. As we continue in this chapter, we will master the single-AZ and multi-AZ instances, and **RTO (Recovery Time Objective)** and **RPO (Recovery Point Objective)** concepts of Amazon RDS.

In this chapter, we will learn about storing our data securely for further analytics purposes by means of the following sections:

- Storing data on Amazon S3
- Controlling access on S3 buckets and objects
- Protecting data on Amazon S3
- Securing S3 objects at rest and in transit
- Using other types of data stores

- Relational Database Services (RDSes)

- Managing Failover in Amazon RDS

- Taking automatic backup, RDS snapshots, and restore and read replicas

- Writing to Amazon Aurora with multi-master capabilities

- Storing columnar data on Amazon Redshift

- Amazon DynamoDB for NoSQL databases as a service

Technical requirements

All you will need for this chapter is an AWS account and the AWS CLI configured. The steps to configure the AWS CLI for your account are explained in detail by Amazon here: `https://docs.aws.amazon.com/cli/latest/userguide/cli-chap-configure.html`.

You can download the code examples from Github, here: `https://github.com/PacktPublishing/AWS-Certified-Machine-Learning-Specialty-MLS-C01-Certification-Guide/tree/master/Chapter-5/`.

Storing data on Amazon S3

S3 is Amazon's cloud-based object storage service and it can be accessed from anywhere via the internet. It is an ideal storage option for large datasets. It is region-based, as your data is stored in a particular region until you move the data to a different region. Your data will never leave that region until it is configured. In a particular region, data is replicated in the availability zones of that region; this makes S3 regionally resilient. If any of the availability zones fail in a region, then other availability zones will serve your requests. It can be accessed via the AWS Console UI, AWS CLI, or AWS API requests, or via standard HTTP methods.

S3 has two main components: **buckets** and **objects**.

- Buckets are created in a specific AWS region. Buckets can contain objects, but cannot contain other buckets.

- Objects have two main attributes. One is **Key**, and the other is **Value**. Value is the content being stored, and Key is the name. The maximum size of an object can be 5 TB. As per the Amazon S3 documentation available here, `https://docs.aws.amazon.com/AmazonS3/latest/dev/UsingObjects.html`, objects also have a version ID, metadata, access control information, and subresources.

> **Important note**
>
> As per Amazon's docs, S3 provides read-after-write consistency for PUTS of new objects, which means that if you put a new object or create a new object and you immediately turn around to read the object using its key, then you get the exact data that you just uploaded. However, for overwrites and deletes, it behaves in an **eventually consistent manner**. This means that if you read an object straight after the delete or overwrite operation, then you may read an old copy or a stale version of the object. It takes some time to replicate the content of the object across three availability zones.

A folder structure can be maintained logically by using a prefix. Let's take an example where an image is uploaded into a bucket, `bucket-name-example`, with the prefix `folder-name` and the object name as `my-image.jpg`. The entire structure looks like this: `/bucket-name-example/folder-name/my-image.jpg`.

The content of the object can be read by using the bucket name as `bucket-name-example` and the key as `/folder-name/my-image.jpg`.

There are several storage classes offered by Amazon for the objects being stored in S3:

- **Standard Storage**: This is the storage class for frequently accessed objects and for quick access. S3 Standard has a millisecond first byte latency and objects can be made publicly available.

- **Reduced Redundancy (RR)**: This option provides less redundancy than the Standard Storage class. Non-critical and reproducible data can be stored in this class. AWS S3 documentation suggests not to use this class as the Standard Storage class is more cost-effective.

- **Standard Infrequent Access (IA)**: This option is used when you need data to be returned quickly, but not for frequent access. The object size has to be a minimum of 128 KB. The minimum storage timeframe is 30 days. If the object is deleted before 30 days, you are still charged for 30 days. **Standard IA** objects are resilient to the loss of availability zones.

- **One Zone Infrequent Access**: The object of this storage class is stored in just one availability zone, which makes it cheaper than **Standard IA**. The minimum object size and storage timeframe are the same as **Standard IA**. Objects from this storage class are less available and less resilient. This storage class is used when you have another copy, or if the data can be recreated. A **One Zone IA** storage class should be used for long-lived data that is non-critical and replaceable, and where access is infrequent.

- **Glacier**: This option is used for long-term archiving and backup. It can take anything from minutes to hours to retrieve objects in this storage class. The minimum storage timeframe is 90 days. You cannot use the Amazon Glacier API to access the objects moved from S3 to Glacier as part of object life cycle management.

- **Glacier Deep Archive**: The minimum storage duration of this class is 180 days. This is the least expensive storage class and has a default retrieval time of 12 hours.

- **Intelligent Tiering**: This storage class is designed to reduce operational overheads. Users pay a monitoring fee and AWS selects a storage class between Standard (a frequent access tier) and Standard IA (a lower cost infrequent access tier) based on the access pattern of an object. This option is designed for long-lived data with unknown or unpredictable access patterns.

Through sets of rules, the transition between storage classes and deletion of the objects can be managed easily, and are referred to as **S3 Lifecycle Configurations**. These rules consist of actions. These can be applied to a bucket or a group of objects in that bucket defined by prefixes or tags. Actions can either be **Transition actions** or **Expiration actions**. Transition actions define the storage class transition of the objects following the creation of *a user-defined* number of days. Expiration actions configure the deletion of versioned objects, or the deletion of delete markers or incomplete multipart uploads. This is very useful for managing costs.

An illustration is given in *Figure 5.1*. You can find more details available here: `https://docs.aws.amazon.com/AmazonS3/latest/dev/storage-class-intro.html`:

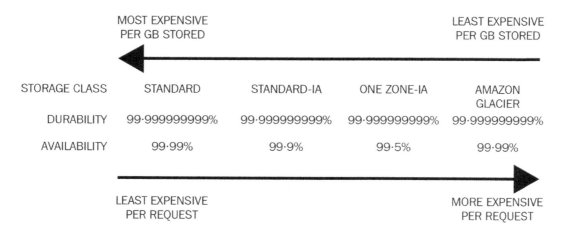

Figure 5.1 – A comparison table of S3 Storage classes

Creating buckets to hold data

Now, let's see how to create a bucket, upload an object, and read the object using the AWS CLI.

1. In the first step, we will check whether we have any buckets created by using the `aws s3 ls` command:

    ```
    $ pwd
    /Users/baba/AWS-Certified-Machine-Learning-Specialty-
    2020-Certification-Guide/Chapter-5/s3demo/demo-files
    $ aws s3 ls
    ```

2. This command returns nothing here. So, we will create a bucket now by using the `mb` argument. Let's say the bucket name is `demo-bucket-baba` in the `us-east-1` region:

    ```
    $ aws s3 mb s3://demo-bucket-baba --region us-east-1
    make_bucket: demo-bucket-baba
    $ aws s3 ls
    2020-11-04 14:39:50 demo-bucket-baba
    ```

3. As we have created a bucket now, our next step is to copy a file to our bucket using the `cp` argument, as shown in the following code:

    ```
    $ aws s3 cp sample-file.txt s3://demo-bucket-baba/
    upload: ./sample-file.txt to s3://demo-bucket-
    baba/sample-file.txt
    ```

4. To validate the file upload operation via the AWS console, please log in to your AWS account and go to the AWS S3 console to see the same. The AWS S3 console lists the result as shown in *Figure 5.2*. The console may have changed by the time you're reading this book!

Figure 5.2 – AWS S3 screenshot to list your files

You can also list the files in your S3 bucket from the command line, as shown here:

```
$ aws s3 ls s3://demo-bucket-baba/
2020-11-04 14:50:02          99 sample-file.txt
```

- If there is a scenario for uploading your filesystem directories and files to the S3 bucket, then `--recursive` will do the job for you:

```
$ aws s3 cp . s3://demo-bucket-baba/ --recursive
upload: folder-1/a.txt to s3://demo-bucket-baba/folder-1/a.txt
upload: folder-2/sample-image.jpg to s3://demo-bucket-baba/folder-2/sample-image.jpg
upload: ./sample-file.txt to s3://demo-bucket-baba/sample-file.txt
$ aws s3 ls s3://demo-bucket-baba/
```

- The contents of one bucket can be copied/moved to another bucket via the `cp` command and the `--recursive` parameter. To achieve this, you will have to create two buckets, `demo-bucket-baba-copied` and `demo-bucket-baba-moved`. The steps are as follows:

```
$ aws s3 mb s3://demo-bucket-baba-copied --region
us-east-2

$ aws s3 mb s3://demo-bucket-baba-moved --region
us-east-2

$ aws s3 cp s3://demo-bucket-baba s3://demo-bucket-baba-
copied/ --recursive

$ aws s3 mv s3://demo-bucket-baba s3://demo-bucket-baba-
moved/ --recursive

$ aws s3 ls
2020-11-04 14:39:50 demo-bucket-baba
2020-11-04 15:44:28 demo-bucket-baba-copied
2020-11-04 15:44:37 demo-bucket-baba-moved
$ aws s3 ls s3://demo-bucket-baba/
```

If all the commands are run successfully, then the original bucket should be empty at the end (as all the files have now been moved).

> **Note**
>
> In the certification exam, you will not find many questions on bucket- and object-level operations. However, it is always better to know the basic operations and the required steps.

5. The buckets must be deleted to avoid costs as soon as the hands-on is finished. The bucket has to be empty before you supply the `rb` command:

```
$ aws s3 rb s3://demo-bucket-baba
$ aws s3 rb s3://demo-bucket-baba-moved
remove_bucket failed: s3://demo-bucket-baba-moved
An error occurred (BucketNotEmpty) when calling the
DeleteBucket operation: The bucket you tried to delete is
not empty
```

6. The `demo-bucket-baba-moved` bucket is not empty, so we couldn't remove the bucket. In such scenarios, use the `--force` parameter to delete the entire bucket and all its contents, as shown here:

```
$ aws s3 rb s3://demo-bucket-baba-moved --force
$ aws s3 rb s3://demo-bucket-baba-copied--force
```

If you want to delete all the content from a specific prefix inside a bucket using the CLI, then it is easy to use the `rm` command with the `--recursive` parameter.

7. Let's take an example of a bucket, `test-bucket`, that has a prefix, `images`. This prefix contains four image files named `animal.jpg`, `draw-house.jpg`, `cat.jpg`, and `human.jpg`.

8. Now, to delete the contents inside the images, the command will be as follows: **aws s3 rm s3://test-bucket/images –recursive**

9. The bucket should now be empty.

In the next section, we are going to learn about object tags and object metadata.

Distinguishing between object tags and object metadata

Let's compare these two terms:

- **Object Tag**: An object tag is a **key-value** pair. AWS S3 object tags can help you filter analytics and metrics, categorize storage, secure objects based on certain categorizations, track costs based on certain categorization of objects, and much more besides. Object tags can be used to create life cycle rules to move objects to cheaper storage tiers. You can have a maximum of 10 tags added to an object and 50 tags to a bucket. A tag key can contain 128 Unicode characters, while a tag value can contain 256 Unicode characters.

- **Object Metadata**: Object metadata is descriptive data describing an object. It consists of **name-value** pairs. Object metadata is returned as HTTP headers on objects. They are of two types: one is **System metadata**, and the other is **User-defined metadata**. User-defined metadata is a custom name-value pair added to an object by the user. The name must begin with **x-amz-meta**. You can change all system metadata such as storage class, versioning, and encryption attributes on an object. Further details are available here: `https://docs.aws.amazon.com/AmazonS3/latest/dev/UsingMetadata.html`.

> **Important note**
> Metadata names are case-insensitive, whereas tag names are case-sensitive.

In the next section, we are going to learn about controlling access to buckets and objects on Amazon S3 through different policies, including the resource policy and the identity policy.

Controlling access to buckets and objects on Amazon S3

Once the object is stored in the bucket, the next major step is to manage access. S3 is private by default, and access is given to other users or groups or resources via several methods. This means that access to the objects can be managed via **Access Control Lists (ACLs)**, **Public Access Settings**, **Identity Policies**, and **Bucket Policies**.

Let's look at some of these in detail.

S3 bucket policy

S3 bucket policy is a resource policy that is attached to a bucket. Resource policies decide who can access that resource. It differs from identity policies in that identity policies can be attached or assigned to the identities inside an account, whereas resource policies can control identities from the same account or different accounts. Resource policies control anonymous principals too, which means an object can be made public through resource policies. The following sample policy allows everyone in the world to read the bucket, because `Principal` is rendered `*`:

```
{
  "Version":"2012-10-17"
  "Statement":[
    {
      "Sid":"AnyoneCanRead",
      "Effect":"Allow",
      "Principal":"*",
      "Action":["s3:GetObject"],
      "Resource":["arn:aws:s3:::my-bucket/*"]
    }
  ]
}
```

By default, everything in S3 is private to the owner. If we want to make a prefix public to the world, then Resource changes to `arn:aws:s3:::my-bucket/some-prefix/*`, and similarly, if it is intended for a specific IAM user or IAM group, then those details go to the principal part in the policy.

There can be conditions added to the bucket policy too. Let's examine a use case where the organization wants to keep a bucket public and whitelist particular IP addresses. The policy would look something like this:

```
{
    "Version":"2012-10-17"
    "Statement":[
        {
            "Sid":"ParticularIPRead",
            "Effect":"Allow",
            "Principal":"*",
            "Action":["s3:GetObject"],
            "Resource":["arn:aws:s3:::my-bucket/*"],
            "Condition":{
                "NotIpAddress":{"aws:SourceIp":"2.3.3.6/32"}
            }
        }
    ]
}
```

More examples are available in the AWS S3 developer guide, which is available here: `https://docs.aws.amazon.com/AmazonS3/latest/dev/example-bucket-policies.html`.

Block public access is a separate setting given to the bucket owner to avoid any kind of mistakes in bucket policy. In a real-world scenario, the bucket can be made public through bucket policy by mistake; to avoid such mistakes, or data leaks, AWS has provided this setting. It provides a further level of security, irrespective of the bucket policy. You can choose this while creating a bucket, or it can be set after creating a bucket.

Identity policies are meant for IAM users and IAM roles. **Identity policies** are validated when an IAM identity (user or role) requests to access a resource. All requests are denied by default. If an identity intends to access any services, resources, or actions, then access must be provided explicitly through **identity policies**. The example policy that follows can be attached to an IAM user and the IAM user will be allowed to have full RDS access within a specific region (`us-east-1` in this example):

```
{
    "Version": "2012-10-17",
    "Statement": [
        {
            "Effect": "Allow",
            "Action": "rds:*",
            "Resource": ["arn:aws:rds:us-east-1:*:*"]
        },
        {
            "Effect": "Allow",
            "Action": ["rds:Describe*"],
            "Resource": ["*"]
        }
    ]
}
```

ACLs are used to grant high-level permissions, typically for granting access to other AWS accounts. ACLs are one of the **Subresources** of a bucket or an object. A bucket or object can be made public quickly via ACLs. AWS doesn't suggest doing this, and you shouldn't expect questions about this on the test. It is good to know about this, but it is not as flexible as the **S3 bucket policy**.

Now, let's learn about the methods to protect our data in the next section.

Protecting data on Amazon S3

In this section, we will learn how to record every version of an object. Along with durability, Amazon provides several techniques to secure the data in S3. Some of those techniques involve enabling versioning and encrypting the objects.

Versioning helps you to roll back to a previous version if there is any problem with the current object during update, delete, or put operations.

Through encryption, you can control the access of an object. You need the appropriate key to read and write an object. We will also learn **Multi Factor Authentication (MFA)** for delete operations. Amazon also allows **Cross-Region Replication (CRR)** to maintain a copy of an object in another region, which can be used for data backup during any disaster, for further redundancy, or for the enhancement of data access speed in different regions.

Applying bucket versioning

Let's now understand how we can enable bucket versioning with the help of some hands-on examples. Bucket versioning can be applied while creating a bucket from the AWS S3 console:

1. To enable versioning on a bucket from the command line, a bucket must be created first and then versioning can be enabled, as shown in the following example. In this example, I have created a bucket, `version-demo-mlpractice`, and enabled versioning through the `put-bucket-versioning` command:

   ```
   $ aws s3 mb s3://version-demo-mlpractice/
   $ aws s3api put-bucket-versioning --bucket version-demo-
   mlpractice --versioning-configuration Status=Enabled
   $ aws s3api get-bucket-versioning --bucket version-demo-
   mlpractice
   {
       "Status": "Enabled"
   }
   ```

2. We have not created this bucket with any kind of encryption. So, if you run `aws s3api get-bucket-encryption --bucket version-demo-mlpractice`, then it will output an error that says the following:

   ```
   The server side encryption configuration was not found
   ```

3. **Server-Side Encryption** (**SSE**) can be applied from the AWS S3 console while creating a bucket. This is called bucket default encryption. You can also apply SSE via the command line using the `put-bucket-encryption` API. The command will look like this:

```
$ aws s3api put-bucket-encryption --bucket version-
demo-mlpractice --server-side-encryption-configuration
'{"Rules":[{"ApplyServerSideEncryptionByDefault":
{"SSEAlgorithm":"AES256"}}]}'
```

4. The same can be verified using the following command: `aws s3api get-bucket-encryption --bucket version-demo-mlpractice`.

We will learn more about encryption in the next section.

Applying encryption to buckets

You also need to understand how enabling versioning on a bucket would help. There are use cases where a file is updated regularly, and versions will be created for the same file. To simulate this scenario, try the following example:

1. In this example, we will create a file with versions written in it. We will overwrite it and retrieve it to check the versions in that file:

```
$ echo "Version-1">version-doc.txt
$ aws s3 cp version-doc.txt s3://version-demo-mlpractice
$ aws s3 cp s3://version-demo-mlpractice/version-doc.txt
check.txt
$ cat check.txt
Version-1
$ echo "Version-2">version-doc.txt
$ aws s3 cp version-doc.txt s3://version-demo-mlpractice
$ aws s3 cp s3://version-demo-mlpractice/version-doc.txt
check.txt
$ cat check.txt
Version-2
```

2. Upon retrieval, we got the latest version of the file, in other words, `Version-2` in this case. To check each of the versions and the latest one of them, S3 provides the `list-object-versions` API, as shown here. From the JSON results, you can deduce the latest version:

```
$ aws s3api list-object-versions
--bucket version-demo-mlpractice
{
    "Versions": [
        {
            "ETag":
"\"b6690f56ca22c410a2782512d24cdc97\"",
            "Size": 10,
            "StorageClass": "STANDARD",
            "Key": "version-doc.txt",
            "VersionId":
"70wbLG6BMBEQhCXmwsriDgQoXafFmgGi",
            "IsLatest": true,
            "LastModified": "2020-11-07T15:57:05+00:00",
            "Owner": {
                "DisplayName": "baba",
                "ID": "XXXXXXXXXXXX"
            }
        },
        {
            "ETag":
"\"5022e6af0dd3d2ea70920438271b21a2\"",
            "Size": 10,
            "StorageClass": "STANDARD",
            "Key": "version-doc.txt",
            "VersionId": "f1iC.9L.MsP00tIb.
sUMnfOEae240sIW",
            "IsLatest": false,
            "LastModified": "2020-11-07T15:56:27+00:00",
            "Owner": {
                "DisplayName": "baba",
                "ID": " XXXXXXXXXXXX"
            }
        }
```

```
        }
    ]
}
```

3. There may be a situation where you have to roll back to the earlier version of the current object. In the preceding example, the latest one is *Version-2*. You can make any desired version the latest or current version by parsing the *VersionId* sub resource to the `get-object` API call and uploading that object again. The other way is to delete the current or latest version by passing `versionId` to the –`version-id` parameter in the `delete-object` API request. More details about the API are available here: `https://docs.aws.amazon.com/cli/latest/reference/s3api/delete-object.html`.

4. When you delete an object in a versioning-enabled bucket, it does not delete the object from the bucket. It just creates a marker called **DeleteMarker**. It looks like this:

```
$ aws s3api delete-object --bucket version-demo-
mlpractice --key version-doc.txt
{
    "DeleteMarker": true,
    "VersionId": "BKv_Cxixtm7V48MWqBO_KUkKbcOaH5JP"
}
```

5. This means that the object is not deleted. You can list it by using this command:

```
aws s3api list-object-versions --bucket version-demo-
mlpractice
```

6. Now the bucket has no objects as `version-doc.txt`, and you can verify this using the `aws s3 ls` command because that marker became the current version of the object with a new ID. If you try to retrieve an object that is deleted, which means a delete marker is serving the current version of the object, then you will get a **404 error**. Hence, the permanent deletion of an object in a versioning-enabled bucket can only be achieved by deleting the object using their version IDs against each version. If a situation arises to get the object back, then the same object can be retrieved by deleting the delete marker, `VersionId`, as shown in the following example commands. A simple delete request **(without the version ID)** will not delete the delete marker and create another delete marker with a unique version ID. So, it's possible to have multiple delete markers for the same object. It is important to note at this point that it will consume your storage and you will be billed for it:

```
$ aws s3 ls s3://version-demo-mlpractice/
$ aws s3api delete-object --bucket version-demo-
mlpractice --key version-doc.txt --version-id BKv_
Cxixtm7V48MWqBO_KUkKbcOaH5JP
{
    "DeleteMarker": true,
    "VersionId": "BKv_Cxixtm7V48MWqBO_KUkKbcOaH5JP"
}
```

7. Upon listing the bucket now, the older objects can be seen:

```
$ aws s3 ls s3://version-demo-mlpractice/
2020-11-07 15:57:05            10 version-doc.txt
```

As we have already covered the exam topics and practiced most of the required concepts, we should delete the objects in the bucket and then delete the bucket to save on costs. This step deletes the versions of the object and, in turn, removes the object permanently.

8. Here, the latest version is deleted by giving the version ID to it, followed by the other version ID:

```
$ aws s3api delete-object --bucket version-demo-
mlpractice --key version-doc.txt --version-id
70wbLG6BMBEQhCXmwsriDgQoXafFmgGi
$ aws s3api delete-object --bucket version-demo-
mlpractice --key version-doc.txt --version-id fliC.9L.
MsP00tIb.sUMnfOEae240sIW
$ aws s3api list-object-versions --bucket version-demo-
mlpractice
```

We can clearly see the empty bucket now.

> **Important note**
> AWS best practices suggest adding another layer of protection through **MFA delete**. Accidental bucket deletions can be prevented, and the security of the objects in the bucket is ensured. MFA delete can be enabled or disabled via the console and CLI. As documented in AWS docs, MFA delete requires two forms of authentication together: your security credentials, and the concatenation of a valid serial number, a space, and the six-digit code displayed on an approved authentication device.

CRR helps you to separate data between different geographical regions. A typical use case can be business-as-usual activities during a disaster. If a region goes down, then another region can support the users if CRR is enabled. This improves the availability of the data. Another use case is to reduce latency if the same data is used by another compute resource, such as EC2 or AWS Lambda being launched in another region. You can also use CRR to copy objects to another AWS account that belongs to a different owner. There are a few important points that are worth noting down for the certification exam:

- In order to use CRR, versioning has to be enabled on both the source and destination bucket.

- Replication is enabled on the source bucket by adding rules. As the source, either an entire bucket, or a prefix, or tags can be replicated.

- Encrypted objects can also be replicated by assigning an appropriate encryption key.

- The destination bucket can be in the same account or in another account. You can change the storage type and ownership of the object in the destination bucket.

- For CRR, an existing role can be chosen or a new IAM role can be created too.

- There can be multiple replication rules on the source bucket, with priority accorded to it. Rules with higher priority override rules with lower priority.

- When you add a replication rule, only new versions an object that are created after the rules are enabled get replicated.

- If versions are deleted from the source bucket, then they are not deleted from the destination bucket.

- When you delete an object from the source bucket, it creates a delete marker in said source bucket. That delete marker is not replicated to the destination bucket by S3.

In the next section, we will cover the concept of securing S3 objects.

Securing S3 objects at rest and in transit

In the previous section, we learned about bucket default encryption, which is completely different from object-level encryption. Buckets are not encrypted, whereas objects are. A question may arise here: *what is bucket default encryption?* We will learn these concepts in this section. Data during transmission can be protected by using **Secure Socket Layer (SSL)** or **Transport Layer Security (TLS)** for the transfer of the HTTPS requests. The next step is to protect the data, where the authorized person can encode and decode the data.

It is possible to have different encryption settings on different objects in the same bucket. S3 supports **Client-Side Encryption (CSE)** and **Server-Side Encryption (SSE)** for objects at rest:

- **Client-Side Encryption**: A client uploads the object to S3 via the S3 endpoint. In CSE, the data is encrypted by the client before uploading to S3. Although the transit between the user and the S3 endpoint happens in an encrypted channel, the data in the channel is already encrypted by the client and can't be seen. In transit, encryption takes place by default through HTTPS. So, AWS S3 stores the encrypted object and cannot read the data in any format at any point in time. In CSE, the client takes care of encrypting the object content. So, control stays with the client in terms of key management and the encryption-decryption process. This leads to a huge amount of CPU usage. S3 is only used for storage.

- **Server-Side Encryption**: A client uploads the object to S3 via the S3 endpoint. Even though the data in transit is through an encrypted channel that uses HTTPS, the objects themselves are not encrypted inside the channel. Once the data hits S3, then it is encrypted by the S3 service. In SSE, you trust S3 to perform encryption-decryption, object storage, and key management. There are three types of SSE techniques available for S3 objects:

  a) SSE-C

  b) SSE-S3

  c) SSE-KMS

- **Server-Side Encryption with Customer-Provided Keys (SSE-C)**: With **SSE-C**, the user is responsible for the key that is used for encryption and decryption. S3 manages the encryption and decryption process. In CSE, the client handles the encryption-decryption process, but in SSE-C, S3 handles the cryptographic operations. This potentially decreases the CPU requirements for these processes. The only overhead here is to manage the keys. Ideally, when a user is doing a PUT operation, the user has to provide a key and an object to S3. S3 encrypts the object using the key provided and attaches the hash (a cipher text) to the object. As soon as the object is stored, S3 discards the encryption key. This generated hash is one-way and cannot be used to generate a new key. When the user provides a GET operation request along with the decryption key, the hash identifies whether the specific key was used for encryption. Then, S3 decrypts and discards the key.

- **Server-Side Encryption with Amazon S3-Managed Keys (SSE-S3)**: With **SSE-S3**, AWS handles both the management of the key and the process of encryption and decryption. When the user uploads an object using a PUT operation, the user just provides the unencrypted object. S3 creates a master key to be used for the encryption process. No one can change anything on this master key as this is created, rotated internally, and managed by S3 end to end. This is a unique key for the object. It uses the AES-256 algorithm by default.

- **Server-Side Encryption with Customer Master Keys stored in AWS Key Management Service (SSE-KMS)**: **AWS Key Management Service (KMS)** manages the **Customer Master Key (CMK)**. AWS S3 collaborates with AWS KMS and generates an AWS-managed CMK. This is the default master key used for **SSE-KMS**. Every time an object is uploaded, S3 uses a dedicated key to encrypt that object and that key is a **Data Encryption Key (DEK)**. The DEK is generated by KMS using the CMK. S3 is provided with both a plain-text version and an encrypted version of the DEK. The plain-text version of DEK is used to encrypt the object and then discarded. The encrypted version of DEK is stored along with the encrypted object. When you're using SSE-KMS, it is not necessary to use the default CMK that is created by S3. You can create and use a customer managed CMK, which means you can control the permission on it as well as the rotation of the key material. So, if you have a regulatory board in your organization that is concerned with rotation of the key or the separation of roles between encryption users and decryption users, then SSE-KMS is the solution. Logging and auditing is also possible on SSE-KMS to track the API calls made against keys.

- **Bucket Default Encryption**: If we set AES-256 while creating a bucket, or we enable it after creating a bucket, then SSE-S3 would be used when you don't set something at object level while performing a PUT operation.

In the next section, we will learn about some of the data stores used with EC2 instances.

Using other types of data stores

Elastic Block Store (EBS) is used to create volumes in an availability zone. The volume can only be attached to an EC2 instance in the same availability zone. Amazon EBS provides both **SSD (Solid State Drive)** and **HDD (Hard Disk Drive)** types of volumes. For SSD-based volumes, the dominant performance attribute is **IOPS (Input Output Per Second)**, and for HDD it is throughput, which is generally measured as MiB/s. The following table shown in *Figure 5.3* provides an overview of the different volumes and types:

Volume Types	Use cases
General Purpose SSD (gp2)	Useful for maintaining balance between price and performance. Good for most workloads, system boot volumes, dev, and test environments.
Provisioned IOPS SSD (io2, io1)	Useful for mission-critical, high-throughput or low-latency workloads. For example, I/O intensive database workloads like MongoDB, Cassandra, Oracle
Throughput Optimized HDD (st1)	Useful for frequently accessed, throughput-intensive workloads. For example, big data processing, data warehouses, log processing
Cold HDD (sc1)	Useful for less frequently accessed workloads.

Figure 5.3 – Different volumes and their use cases

EBS is resilient to an availability zone (AZ). If, for some reason, an AZ fails, then the volume cannot be accessed. To avoid such scenarios, **snapshots** can be created from the EBS volumes and snapshots are stored in S3. Once the snapshot arrives at S3, the data in the snapshot becomes region-resilient. The first snapshot is a full copy of data on the volume and, from then onward, snapshots are incremental. Snapshots can be used to clone a volume. As the snapshot is stored in S3, a volume can be cloned in any AZ in that region. Snapshots can be shared between regions and volumes can be cloned from them during disaster recovery.

AWS KMS manages the CMK. AWS KMS uses an AWS-managed CMK for EBS, or AWS KMS can use a customer-managed CMK. CMK is used by EBS when an encrypted volume is created. CMK is used to create an encrypted DEK, which is stored with the volume on the physical disk. This DEK can only be decrypted using KMS, assuming the entity has access to decrypt. When a snapshot is created from the encrypted volume, the snapshot is encrypted with the same DEK. Any volume created from this snapshot also uses that DEK.

Instance Store volumes are the block storage devices physically connected to the EC2 instance. They provide the highest performance, as the **ephemeral storage** attached to the instance is from the same host where the instance is launched. EBS can be attached to the instance at any time, but the instance store must be attached to the instance at the time of its launch; it cannot be attached later, once the instance is launched. If there is an issue on the underlying host of an EC2 instance, then the same instance will be launched on another host with a new instance store volume and the earlier instance store (ephemeral storage) and older data is lost. The size and capabilities of the attached volumes depend on the instance types and can be found in more detail here: `https://aws.amazon.com/ec2/instance-types/`.

Elastic File System (EFS) provides a network-based filesystem that can be mounted within Linux EC2 instances and can be used by multiple instances at once. It is an implementation of **NFSv4**. It can be used in general-purpose mode, max I/O performance mode (for scientific analysis or parallel computing), bursting mode, and provisioned throughput mode.

As we know, in the case of instance stores, the data is volatile. As soon as the instance is lost, the data is lost from the instance store. That is not the case for EFS. EFS is separate from the EC2 instance storage. EFS is a file store and is accessed by multiple EC2 instances via mount targets inside a VPC. On-premises systems can access EFS storage via hybrid networking to the VPC, such as **VPN** or **Direct Connect**. EFS also supports two types of storage classes: Standard and Infrequent Access. Standard is used for frequently accessed data. Infrequent Access is the cost-effective storage class for long-lived, less frequently accessed data. Life cycle policies can be used for the transition of data between storage classes.

> **Important note**
> An instance store is preferred for max I/O requirements and if the data is replaceable and temporary.

Relational Database Services (RDSes)

This is one of the most commonly featuring exam topics in AWS exams. You should have sufficient knowledge prior to the exam. In this section, we will learn about Amazon's RDS.

AWS provides several relational databases as a service to its users. Users can run their desired database on EC2 instances, too. The biggest drawback is that the instance is only available in one availability zone in a region. The EC2 instance has to be administered and monitored to avoid any kind of failure. Custom scripts will be required to maintain a data backup over time. Any database major or minor version update would result in downtime. Database instances running on an EC2 instance cannot be easily scaled if the load increases on the database as replication is not an easy task.

RDS provides managed database instances that can themselves hold one or more databases. Imagine a database server running on an EC2 instance that you do not have to manage or maintain. You need only access the server and create databases in it. AWS will manage everything else, such as the security of the instance, the operating system running on the instance, the database versions, and high availability of the database server. RDS supports multiple engines such as MySQL, Microsoft SQL Server, MariaDB, Amazon Aurora, Oracle, and PostgreSQL. You can choose any of these based on your requirements.

The foundation of Amazon RDS is a database instance, which can support multiple engines and can have multiple databases created by the user. One database instance can be accessed only by using the database **CNAME** (CNAME is an alias for a canonical name in a domain name system database) of the primary instance. RDS uses standard database engines. So, accessing the database using some sort of tool in a self-managed database server is the same as accessing Amazon RDS.

As we have now understood the requirements of Amazon RDS, let's understand the failover process in Amazon RDS. We will cover what services Amazon offers if something goes wrong with the RDS instance.

Managing failover in Amazon RDS

RDS instances can be **single-AZ** or **multi-AZ**. In multi-AZ, multiple instances work together, similar to an active-passive failover design.

For a single-AZ RDS instance, storage can be allocated for that instance to use. In a nutshell, a single-AZ RDS instance has one attached block store (EBS storage) available in the same availability zone. This makes the databases and the storage of the RDS instance vulnerable to availability zone failure. The storage allocated to the block storage can be SSD (gp2 or io1) or magnetic. To secure the RDS instance, it is advised to use a security group and provide access based on requirements.

Multi-AZ is always the best way to design the architecture to avoid any failure and keep the applications highly available. With multi-AZ features, a standby replica is kept in sync **synchronously** with the primary instance. The standby instance has its own storage in the assigned availability zone. A standby replica cannot be accessed directly, because all RDS access is via a single database CNAME. You can't access the standby unless a failover happens. The standby provides no performance benefit, but it does constitute an improvement in terms of availability of the RDS instance. It can only happen in the same region, another AZ's subnet in the same region inside the VPC. When a multi-AZ RDS instance is online, you can take a backup from the standby replica without affecting the performance. In a single-AZ instance, availability and performance issues can be significant during backup operation.

To understand the workings of multi-AZ, let's take an example of a single-AZ instance and expand it to multi-AZ.

Imagine you have an RDS instance running in availability zone AZ-A of the us-east-1 region inside a VPC named db-vpc. This becomes a primary instance in a single-AZ design of an RDS instance. In this case, there will be storage allocated to the instance in the *AZ-A* availability zone. Once you opt for multi-AZ deployment in another availability zone called *AZ-B*, AWS creates a standby instance in availability zone *AZ-B* of the *us-east-1* region inside the *db-vpc* VPC and allocates storage for the standby instance in *AZ-B* of the *us-east-1* region. Along with that, RDS will enable **synchronous replication** from the primary instance to the standby replica. As we have learned earlier, the only way to access our RDS instance is via the database CNAME, hence, the access request goes to the RDS primary instance. As soon as a write request comes to the endpoint, it writes to the primary instance. Then it writes the data to the hardware, which is the block storage attached to the primary instance. At the same time, the primary instance replicates the same data to the standby instance. Finally, the standby instance commits the data to its block storage.

The primary instance writes the data into the hardware and replicates the data to the standby instance in parallel, so there is a minimal time lag (almost nothing) between the data commit operations in their respective hardware. If an error occurs with the primary instance, then RDS detects this and changes the database endpoint to the standby instance. The clients accessing the database may experience a very short interruption with this. This failover occurs within 60-120 seconds. It does not provide a fault-tolerant system because there will be some impact during the failover operation.

You should now understand failover management on Amazon RDS. Let's now learn about taking automatic RDS backup, using snapshots to restore in the event of any failure, and read replicas in the next section.

Taking automatic backup, RDS snapshots, and restore and read replicas

In this section, we will see how RDS **Automatic Backup** and **Manual Snapshots** work. These features come with Amazon RDS.

Let's consider a database that is scheduled to take a backup at 5 A.M. every day. If the application fails at 11 A.M., then it is possible to restart the application from the backup taken at 11 A.M. with the loss of 6 hours' worth of data. This is called 6 hours **RPO (Recovery Point Objective)**. So, RPO is defined as the time between the most recent backup and the incident and this defines the amount of data loss. If you want to reduce this, then you have to schedule more incremental backups, which increases the cost and backup frequency. If your business demands a lower RPO value, then the business must spend more on meeting the technical solutions.

Now, according to our example, an engineer was assigned this task to bring the system online as soon as the disaster occurred. The engineer managed to bring the database online at 2 P.M. on the same day by adding a few extra hardware components to the current system and installed some updated versions of the software. This is called 3 hours **RTO (Recovery Time Objective)**. So, RTO is determined as the time between the disaster recovery and full recovery. RTO values can be reduced by having spare hardware and documenting the restoration process. If the business demands a lower RTO value, then your business must spend more money on spare hardware and effective system setup to perform the restoration process.

In RDS, RPO and RTO play an important role in the selection of **Automatic Backups** and **Manual Snapshots**. Both of these backup services use AWS-managed S3 buckets, which means it cannot be visible in the user's AWS S3 console. It is region-resilient because the backup is replicated into multiple availability zones in the AWS region. In case of a single-AZ RDS instance, the backup happens from the single available data store, and for a multi-AZ enabled RDS instance, the backup happens from the standby data store (the primary store remains untouched as regards the backup).

The snapshots are manual against RDS instances and these are stored in the AWS-managed S3 bucket. The first snapshot of an RDS instance is a full copy of the data and the onward snapshots are incremental, reflecting the change in the data. In terms of the time taken for the snapshot process, it is higher for the first one and, from then on, the incremental backup is quicker. When any snapshot occurs, it can impact the performance of the single-AZ RDS instance, but not the performance of a multi-AZ RDS instance as this happens on the standby data storage. Manual snapshots do not expire, have to be cleared automatically, and they live past the termination of an RDS instance. When you delete an RDS instance, it suggests making one final snapshot on your behalf and it will contain all the databases inside your RDS instance (there is not just a single database in an RDS instance). When you restore from a manual snapshot, you restore to a single point in time and that affects the RPO.

To automate this entire process, you can choose a time window when these snapshots can be taken. This is called automatic backups. These time windows can be managed wisely to essentially lower the RPO value of the business. Automatic backups have a retention period of 0 to 35 days, with 0 being disabled and the maximum is 35 days. To quote AWS documentation, retained automated backups contain system snapshots and transaction logs from a database instance. They also include database instance properties such as allocated storage and a database instance class, which are required to restore it to an active instance. Databases generate transaction logs, which contain the actual change in data in a particular database. These transaction logs are also written to S3 every 5 minutes by RDS. Transaction logs can also be replayed on top of the snapshots to restore to a point in time of 5 minutes' granularity. Theoretically, the RPO can be a 5-minute point in time.

When you perform a restore, RDS creates a new RDS instance, which means a new database endpoint to access the instance. The applications using the instances have to point to the new address, which significantly affects the RTO. This means that the restoration process is not very fast, which affects the RTO. To minimize the RTO during a failure, you may consider replicating the data. With replicas, there is a high chance of replicating the corrupted data. The only way to overcome this is to have snapshots and an RDS instance can be restored to a particular point in time prior to the corruption. **Amazon RDS Read Replicas** are unlike the multi-AZ replicas. In multi-AZ RDS instances, the standby replicas cannot be used directly for anything unless a primary instance fails, whereas **Read Replicas** can be used directly, but only for read operations. Read replicas have their own database endpoints and read-heavy applications can directly point to this address. They are kept in sync **asynchronously** with the primary instance. Read replicas can be created in the same region as the primary instance or in a different region. Read replicas in other regions are called **Cross-Region Read Replicas** and this improves the global performance of the application.

As per AWS documentation, five direct read replicas are allowed per database instance and this helps to scale out the read performances. Read replicas have a very low RPO value due to asynchronous replication. They can be promoted to a read-write database instance in the case of a primary instance failure. This can be done quickly and it offers a fairly low RTO value.

In the next section, we will learn about Amazon's own database engine, Amazon Aurora.

Writing to Amazon Aurora with multi-master capabilities

Amazon Aurora is the most reliable relational database engine developed by Amazon to deliver speed in a simple and cost-effective manner. Aurora uses a cluster of single primary instances and zero or more replicas. Aurora's replicas can give you the advantage of both read replicas and multi-AZ instances in RDS. Aurora uses a shared cluster volume for storage and is available to all compute instances of the cluster (a maximum of 64 TiB). This allows the Aurora cluster to provision faster and improves availability and performance. Aurora uses SSD-based storage, which provides high IOPS and low latency. Aurora does not ask you to allocate storage, unlike other RDS instances; it is based on the storage that you use.

Aurora clusters have multiple endpoints, including **Cluster Endpoint** and **Reader Endpoint**. If there are zero replicas, then the cluster endpoint is the same as the reader endpoint. If there are replicas available, then the reader endpoint is load balanced across the reader endpoints. Cluster endpoints are used for reading/writing, while reader endpoints are intended for reading from the cluster. If you add more replicas, then AWS manages load balancing under the hood for the new replicas.

When failover occurs, the replicas are promoted to read/write mode and this takes some time. This can be avoided in a **Multi-Master** mode of an Aurora cluster. This allows multiple instances to perform reads and writes at the same time.

Storing columnar data on Amazon Redshift

Amazon Redshift is not used for real-time transaction use, but it is used for data warehouse purposes. It is designed to support huge volumes of data at a petabyte scale. It is a column-based database used for analytics purpose, long-term processing, tending, and aggregation. **Redshift Spectrum** can be used to query data on S3 without loading data to the Redshift cluster (a Redshift cluster is required though). It's not an OLTP, but an OLAP. **AWS QuickSight** can be integrated with Redshift for visualization, with a SQL-like interface that allows you to connect using JDBC/ODBC connections for querying the data.

Redshift uses a clustered architecture in one AZ in a VPC with faster network connectivity between the nodes. It is not high availability by design as it is tightly coupled to the AZ. A Redshift cluster has a **Leader Node**, and this node is responsible for all the communication between the client and the computing nodes of the cluster, query planning, and aggregation. **Compute Nodes** are responsible for running the queries submitted by the leader lode and for storing the data. By default, Redshift uses a public network for communicating with external services or any AWS services. With **Enhanced VPC Routing**, it can be controlled via customized networking settings.

Amazon DynamoDB for NoSQL database as a service

Amazon DynamoDB is a NoSQL database-as-a-service product within AWS. It's a fully managed key/value and document database. Accessing DynamoDB is easy via its endpoint. The input and output throughputs can be managed or scaled manually or in automatic fashion. It also supports data backup, point-in-time recovery, and data encryption. We will not cover the DynamoDB table structure or key structure in this chapter as this is not required for the certification exam. However, it is good to have a basic knowledge of them. For more details, please refer to the AWS docs available here: `https://docs.aws.amazon.com/amazondynamodb/latest/developerguide/SQLtoNoSQL.html`.

Summary

In this chapter, we learned about various data storage services from Amazon, and how to secure data through various policies and use these services. If you are working on machine learning use cases, then you may encounter such scenarios where you have to choose an effective data storage service for your requirements.

In the next chapter, we will learn about the processing of stored data.

Questions

1. To set the region that an S3 bucket is stored in, you must first create the bucket and then set the region separately.

   A. True

   B. False

2. Is it mandatory to have both the source bucket and destination bucket in the same region in order to copy the contents of S3 buckets?

   A. True

   B. False

3. By default, objects are private in a bucket.

   A. True

   B. False

4. By WS, a S3 object is immutable and you can only perform put and delete. Rename is GET and PUT of the same object with a different name.

   A. True

   B. False

5. If a user has stored an unversioned object and a versioned object in the same bucket, then the user can only delete the unversioned object. Versioned objects cannot be deleted.

   A. True

   B. False

   > **Answer**
   >
   > Versioning applies to a complete bucket and not objects. If versioning is enabled on a bucket, then it can only be suspended; it cannot be disabled.

6. A simple delete request on a delete marker will:

A. Delete the delete marker

B. Create a copy of the delete marker

C. Not delete the delete marker, but it will create another delete marker

D. Delete the original version of the object

7. Scaling and performance can be improved via RDS multi-AZ instances.

A. True

B. False

Answer

An RDS multi-AZ has nothing to do with scaling and performance. It is used for failover.

8. What protocol does EFS use?

A. SMB

B. NFS

C. EBS

D. HTTP

9. Which operating systems does EFS support?

A. Linux only

B. Windows only

C. Both Windows and Linux

D. Neither Windows nor Linux

10. Is EFS a private service?

A. Yes.

B. No, it's a public service.

C. It's both a private and a public service.

D. It's neither a private nor a public service.

11. Which two of the following are correct?

    A. Multi-AZ:Same Region::Read Replica:Multiple Region

    B. Multi-AZ:Multiple Region::Read Replica:Same Region

    C. Multi-AZ:Synchronous Replication::Read Replica:Asynchronous Replication

    D. Multi-AZ:ASynchronous Replication::Read Replica:Synchronous Replication

12. Which of the following is correct?

    A. Read replicas are read-only instances.

    B. Read replicas are read-write instances.

    C. Read replicas are write-only instances.

    D. Read replicas are read-only instances, until promoted to read-write.

13. Where is EFS accessible from?

    A. Inside a VPC only

    B. Via AWS endpoints

    C. Anywhere with a public internet connection

    D. Inside a VPC or any on-premises locations connected to that VPC via
       a hybrid network

14. Which three of the following are true?

    A. Instance store volumes are persistent storage.

    B. Instance store volumes are temporary (ephemeral) storage.

    C. Data stored on instance store volumes can be lost if a hardware failure occurs.

    D. Data stored on instance store volumes can be lost when an EC2 instance restarts.

    E. Data stored on instance store volumes can be lost when an EC2 instance stops
       and starts.

> **Answer**
> Hardware failure can change the underlying host. So, there is no guarantee of
> the instance store volume. When you stop the instance and start it again, the
> instance store volume is lost due to the change of host. Instance restarting is
> different from stop and start; it means an operating system restart.

15. In order to enable encryption at rest using EC2 and EBS, you need to...

    A. Configure encryption when creating the EBS volume.

    B. Configure encryption using the appropriate operating system's filesystem.

    C. Configure encryption using X.509 certificates.

    D. Mount the EBS volume in S3 and then encrypt the bucket using a bucket policy.

16. Which of the following is an action you cannot perform on an EBS snapshot?

    A. Create an image from a snapshot.

    B. Create an EBS volume from a snapshot.

    C. Share a snapshot with another AWS account.

    D. Make an unencrypted copy of an encrypted snapshot.

17. With EBS, you need to do the following (choose two).

    A. Create an encrypted volume from a snapshot of another encrypted volume.

    B. Create an encrypted volume from an encrypted snapshot.

    C. Create an encrypted snapshot from an unencrypted snapshot by creating an encrypted copy of the unencrypted snapshot.

    D. Encrypt an existing volume.

Answer

For more on EBS, visit the following link: `https://docs.aws.`
`amazon.com/AWSEC2/latest/UserGuide/EBSEncryption.`
`html#EBSEncryption_c%20onsiderations.`

Answers

1. B

2. B

3. A

4. A

5. B

6. C

7. B

8. B

9. A

10. B

11. A, C

12. D

13. D

14. B, C, E

15. A

16. D

17. A, C

6
AWS Services for Data Processing

In the previous chapter, we learned about several ways of storing data in AWS. In this chapter, we will explore the techniques for using that data and gaining some insight from the data. There are use cases where you have to process your data or load the data to a hive data warehouse to query and analyze the data. If you are on AWS and your data is in S3, then you have to create a table in hive on AWS EMR to query them. To provide the same as a managed service, AWS has a product called Athena, where you have to create a data catalog and query your data on S3. If you need to transform the data, then AWS Glue is the best option to transform and restore it to S3. Let's imagine a use case where we need to stream the data and create analytical reports on that data. For such scenarios, we can opt for AWS Kinesis Data Streams to stream data and store it in S3. Using Glue, the same data can be copied to Redshift for further analytical utilization. Now, let's learn about them and we will cover the following in brief.

- Using Glue for designing ETL jobs
- Querying S3 data using Athena
- Streaming data through AWS Kinesis Data Streams and storing it using Kinesis Firehose

- Ingesting data from on-premises locations to AWS

- Migrating data to AWS and extending on-premises data centers to AWS

- Processing data on AWS

Technical requirements

You can download the data used in the examples from GitHub, available here: `https://github.com/PacktPublishing/AWS-Certified-Machine-Learning-Specialty-MLS-C01-Certification-Guide/tree/master/Chapter-6`.

Creating ETL jobs on AWS Glue

In a modern data pipeline, there are multiple stages, such as Generate Data, Collect Data, Store Data, Perform ETL, Analyze, and Visualize. In this section, we will cover each of these at a high level and understand the **ETL (extract, transform, load)** part in-depth:

- Data can be generated from several devices, including mobile devices or IoT, weblogs, social media, transactional data, online games, and many more besides.

- This huge amount of generated data can be collected by using polling services or through API gateways integrated with AWS Lambda to collect the data, or via streams such as AWS Kinesis or AWS-managed Kafka or Kinesis Firehose. If you have an on-premises database and you want to collect that data to AWS, then you choose AWS DMS for that. You can sync your on-premises data to Amazon S3, Amazon EFS, or Amazon FSx via AWS DataSync. AWS Snowball is used to collect/transfer data into and out of AWS.

- The next step involves storing data, and we have learned some of the services in the previous chapter, such as AWS S3, EBS, EFS, Amazon RDS, Amazon Redshift, and DynamoDB.

- Once we know our data storage, an ETL job can be designed to extract-transform-load or extract-load-transform our structured or unstructured data into our desired format for further analysis. For example, we can think of AWS Lambda to transform the data on the fly and store the transformed data into S3, or we can run a Spark application on an EMR cluster to transform the data and store it in S3 or Redshift or RDS.

- There are many services available in AWS for performing an analysis on transformed data; for example, Amazon EMR, Amazon Athena, Amazon Redshift, Amazon Redshift Spectrum, and Kinesis Analytics.

- Once the data is analyzed, you can visualize the data using AWS Quicksight to understand the pattern or trend. Data scientists or machine learning professionals would love to apply statistical analysis to understand data distribution in a better way. Business users use it to prepare reports. We have already learned various ways to present and visualize data in *Chapter 4, Understanding and Visualizing Data.*

What we understood from the traditional data pipeline is that ETL is all about coding and maintaining code on the servers to run smoothly. If the data format changes in any way, then the code needs to be changed, and that results in a change to the target schema. If the data source changes, then the code must be able to handle that too and it's an overhead. *Should we write code to recognize these changes in data sources? Should we need a system to adapt to the change and discover the data for us?* The answer is **AWS Glue**. Now, let's understand why AWS Glue is so famous.

Features of AWS Glue

AWS Glue is a completely managed serverless ETL service on AWS. It has the following features:

- It automatically discovers and categorizes your data by connecting to the data sources and generates a data catalog.

- Services such as Amazon Athena, Amazon Redshift, and Amazon EMR can use the data catalog to query the data.

- AWS Glue generates the ETL code, which is an extension to Spark in Python or Scala, which can be modified, too.

- It scales out automatically to match your Spark application requirements for running the ETL job and loading the data into the destination.

AWS Glue has **Data Catalog**, and that's the secret of its success. It helps to discover the data from data sources and lets us understand a bit about it:

- Data Catalog automatically discovers new data and extracts schema definitions. It detects schema changes and version tables. It detects Apache Hive-style partitions on Amazon S3.

- Data Catalog comes with built-in classifiers for popular data types. Custom classifiers can be written using **Grok expressions**. The classifiers help to detect the schema.

- Glue crawlers can be run ad hoc or in a scheduled fashion to update the metadata in Glue Data Catalog. Glue crawlers must be associated with an IAM role with sufficient access to read the data sources, such as Amazon RDS, Amazon Redshift, and Amazon S3.

As we now have a brief idea of AWS Glue, let's run the following example to get our hands dirty.

Getting hands-on with AWS Glue data catalog components

In this example, we will create a job to copy data from S3 to Redshift by using AWS Glue. All my components are created in the `us-east-1` region. Let's start by creating a bucket:

1. Navigate to AWS S3 Console and create a bucket. I have named the bucket `aws-glue-example-01`.

2. Click on **Create Folder** and name it `input-data`.

3. Navigate inside the folder and click on the **Upload** button to upload the `sales-records.csv` dataset. The data is available in the following GitHub location: `https://github.com/PacktPublishing/AWS-Certified-Machine-Learning-Specialty-MLS-C01-Certification-Guide/tree/master/Chapter-6/AWS-Glue-Demo/input-data`.

    As we have the data uploaded in the S3 bucket, let's create a VPC in which we will create our Redshift cluster.

4. Navigate to the VPC console by accessing the `https://console.aws.amazon.com/vpc/home?region=us-east-1#` URL and click on **Endpoints** on the left-hand side menu. Click on **Create Endpoint** and then fill in the fields as shown here:

    a) **Service Category**: `AWS services`

    b) **Select a service**: `com.amazonaws.us-east-1.s3` (Gateway type)

    c) **VPC**: `Select the Default VPC` (we will use this default VPC in which our Redshift cluster will be created)

5. Leave the other fields as-is and click on **Create Endpoint**.

6.   Click on **Security Groups** from the VPC console. Give a name to your security group, such as `redshift-self`, and choose the default VPC drop-down menu. Provide an appropriate description of `Redshift Security Group`. Click on **Create security group**.

7.   Click on the **Actions** dropdown and select **Edit Inbound rules**. Click on the Add rule and complete the fields as shown here:

a) **Type**: `All traffic`

b) **Source**: `Custom`

c) In the search field, select the same security group (`redshift-self`)

8.   Click on **Save Rules**.

Now, let's create our Redshift cluster.

9.   Navigate to the Amazon Redshift console. Click on **Create Cluster** and complete the highlighted fields, as shown in *Figure 6.1*:

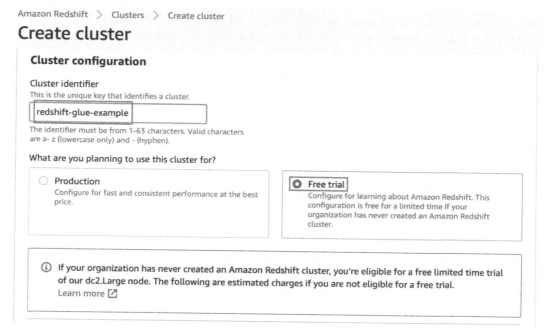

Figure 6.1 – A screenshot of Amazon Redshift's Create cluster

10. Scroll down and fill in the highlighted fields, as shown in *Figure 6.2*:

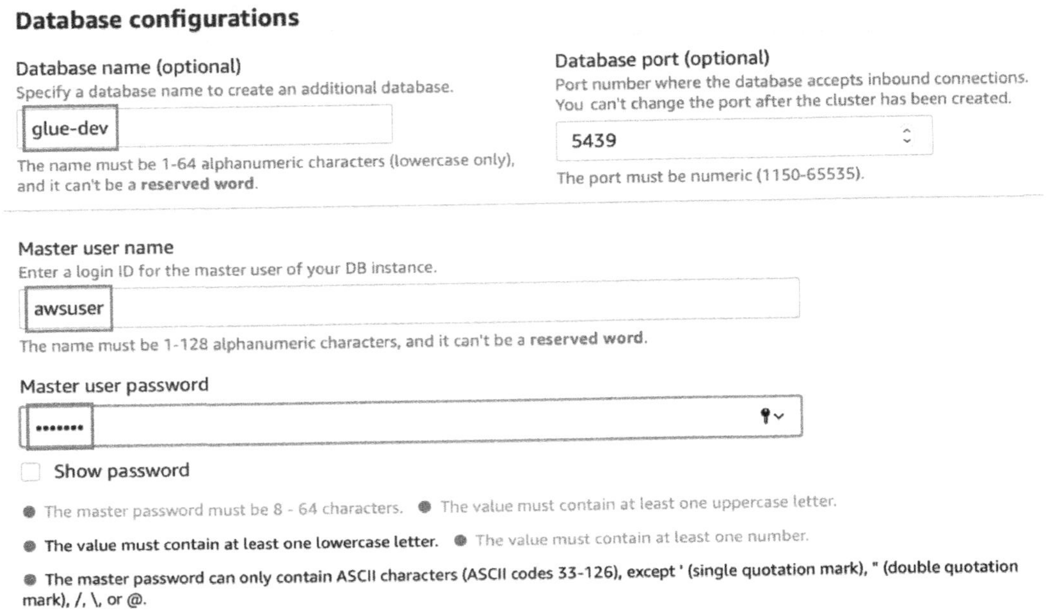

Database configurations

Database name (optional)
Specify a database name to create an additional database.

glue-dev

The name must be 1-64 alphanumeric characters (lowercase only), and it can't be a **reserved word**.

Database port (optional)
Port number where the database accepts inbound connections. You can't change the port after the cluster has been created.

5439	⌄

The port must be numeric (1150-65535).

Master user name
Enter a login ID for the master user of your DB instance.

awsuser

The name must be 1-128 alphanumeric characters, and it can't be a **reserved word**.

Master user password

•••••••	🔑⌄

☐ Show password

● The master password must be 8 - 64 characters.   ● The value must contain at least one uppercase letter.

● **The value must contain at least one lowercase letter.**   ● The value must contain at least one number.

● **The master password can only contain ASCII characters (ASCII codes 33-126), except ' (single quotation mark), " (double quotation mark), /, \, or @.**

Figure 6.2 – A screenshot of Amazon Redshift Cluster's Database configurations section

11. Scroll down and change the **Additional configurations** field, as shown in *Figure 6.3*:

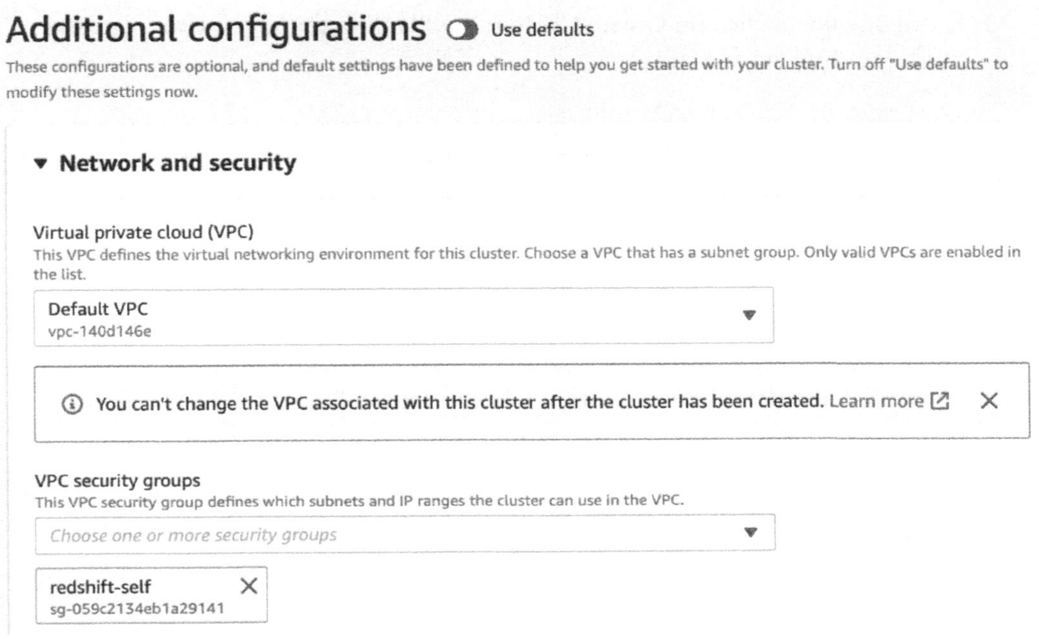

Additional configurations ⬤ Use defaults

These configurations are optional, and default settings have been defined to help you get started with your cluster. Turn off "Use defaults" to modify these settings now.

▼ Network and security

Virtual private cloud (VPC)
This VPC defines the virtual networking environment for this cluster. Choose a VPC that has a subnet group. Only valid VPCs are enabled in the list.

> Default VPC
> vpc-140d146e   ▼

> ⓘ You can't change the VPC associated with this cluster after the cluster has been created. Learn more ↗   ✕

VPC security groups
This VPC security group defines which subnets and IP ranges the cluster can use in the VPC.

> Choose one or more security groups   ▼

> redshift-self   ✕
> sg-059c2134eb1a29141

Figure 6.3 – A screenshot of Amazon Redshift Cluster's Additional configurations section

12. Change the IAM permissions, too, as shown in *Figure 6.4*:

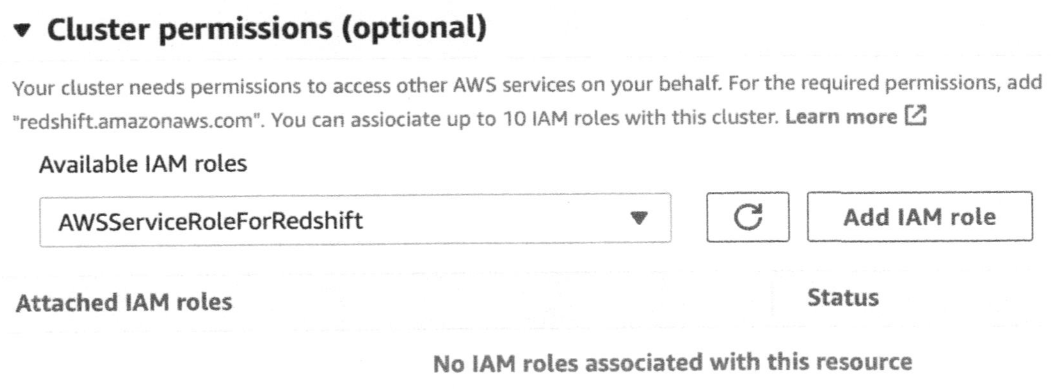

▼ Cluster permissions (optional)

Your cluster needs permissions to access other AWS services on your behalf. For the required permissions, add "redshift.amazonaws.com". You can assiociate up to 10 IAM roles with this cluster. **Learn more** ↗

Available IAM roles

> AWSServiceRoleForRedshift   ▼ | ⟳ | | Add IAM role |

Attached IAM roles   **Status**

No IAM roles associated with this resource

Figure 6.4 – A screenshot of Amazon Redshift Cluster's Cluster permissions section

13. Scroll down and click on **Create Cluster**. It will take a minute or two to get the cluster in the available state.

Next, we will create an IAM role.

14. Navigate to the AWS IAM console and select **Roles** in the **Access Management** section on the screen.

15. Click on the **Create role** button and choose **Glue** from the services. Click on the **Next: permissions** button to navigate to the next page.

16. Search **AmazonS3FullAccess** and select. Then, search **AWSGlueServiceRole** and select. As we are writing our data to Redshift as part of this example, select **AmazonRedshiftFullAccess**. Click on **Next: Tags**, followed by the **Next: Review** button.

17. Provide a name, Glue-IAM-Role, and then click on the **Create role** button. The role appears as shown in *Figure 6.5*:

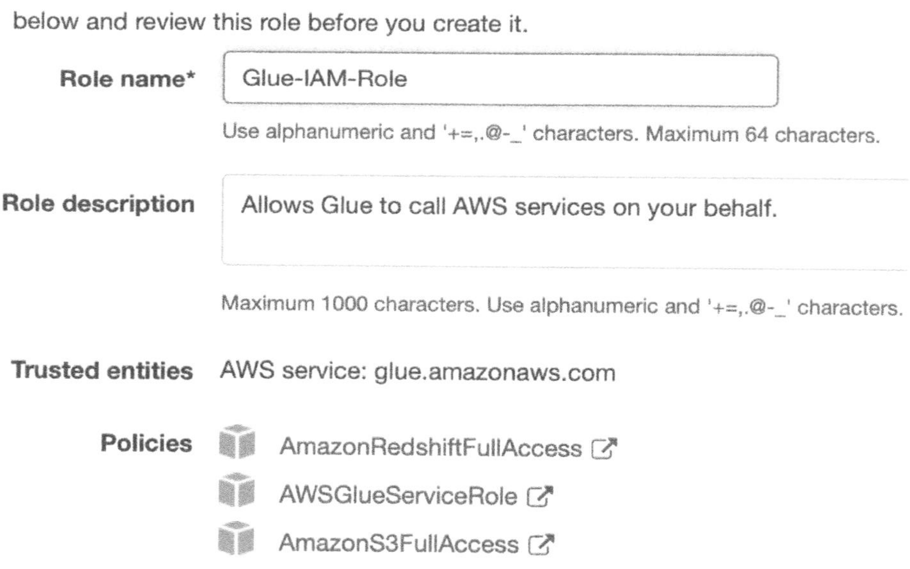

below and review this role before you create it.

Role name*   Glue-IAM-Role

Use alphanumeric and '+=,.@-_' characters. Maximum 64 characters.

Role description   Allows Glue to call AWS services on your behalf.

Maximum 1000 characters. Use alphanumeric and '+=,.@-_' characters.

Trusted entities   AWS service: glue.amazonaws.com

Policies   AmazonRedshiftFullAccess ⤢

AWSGlueServiceRole ⤢

AmazonS3FullAccess ⤢

Figure 6.5 – A screenshot of the IAM role

Now, we have the input data source and the output data storage handy. The next step is to create the Glue crawler from the AWS Glue console.

18. Select **Connections** under **Databases**. Click on the **Add connection** button and complete the fields as shown here:

    a) **Connection name**: `glue-redshift-connection`

    b) **Connection type**: `Amazon Redshift`

19. Click on **Next** and then fill in the fields as shown here:

    a) **Cluster**: `redshift-glue-example`

    b) **Database name**: `glue-dev`

    c) **Username**: `awsuser`

    d) **Password**: ✱✱✱✱✱✱✱✱ (enter the value as created in *step 10*)

20. Click on **Next** and then **Finish**. To verify the working, click on **Test Connection**, select `Glue-IAM-Role` for the IAM role section, and then click **Test Connection**.

21. Go to **Crawler** and select **Add Crawler**. Provide a name for the crawler, `s3-glue-crawler`, and then click **Next**. In the **Specify crawler source type** page, leave everything as their default settings and then click **Next**.

22. On **the Add a data store** page, choose **Include path**: `s3://aws-glue-example-01/input-data/sales-records.csv`.

23. Click **Next**.

24. **Add another datastore**: No. Click **Next**.

25. **Choose an existing IAM Role**: `Glue-IAM-Role`. Then click **Next**.

26. **Frequency**: `Run on demand`. Click **Next**.

27. There's no database created, so click on **Add database**, provide a name, `s3-data`, click **Next**, and then click **Finish**.

28. Select the crawler, `s3-glue-crawler`, and then click on **Run Crawler**. Once the run is complete, you can see that there is a `1` in the **Tables Added** column. This means that a database, `s3-data`, has been created, as mentioned in the previous step, and a table is added. Click on **Tables** and select the newly created table, `sales_records_csv`. You can see that the schema has been discovered now. You can change the data type if the inferred data type does not meet your requirements.

In this hands-on section, we learned about database tables, database connections, crawlers on S3, and creation of the Redshift cluster. In the next hands-on section, we will learn about creating ETL jobs using Glue.

Getting hands-on with AWS Glue ETL components

In this section, we will use the Data Catalog components created earlier to build our job. Let's start by creating jobs:

1. Navigate to the AWS Glue console and click on **Jobs** under the **ETL** section.

2. Click on the **Add Job** button and complete the fields as shown here:

   - **Name**: s3-glue-redshift
   - **IAM role**: Glue-IAM-Role (this is the same role we created in the previous section)
   - **Type**: Spark
   - **Glue version**: Spark 2.4, Python 3 with improved job start up times (Glue version 2.0)

3. Leave the other fields as they are and then click on **Next**.

4. Select sales_records_csv and click on **Next**.

5. Select **Change Schema** by default and then click **Next** (at the time of writing this book, machine learning transformations are not supported for Glue 2.0).

6. Select **Create tables in your data target**. Choose JDBC as the data store and glue-redshift-connection as the connection. Provide glue-dev as the database name (as created in the previous section) and then click **Next**.

7. Next comes the **Output Schema Definition** page, where you can choose the desired columns to be removed from the target schema. Scroll down and click on **Save job and edit script**.

8. You can now see the pipeline being created on the left-hand side of the screen and the suggested code on the right-hand side, as shown in *Figure 6.6*. You can modify the code based on your requirements. Click on the **Run job** button. A pop-up window appears, asking you to edit any details that you wish to change. This is optional. Then, click on the **Run job** button:

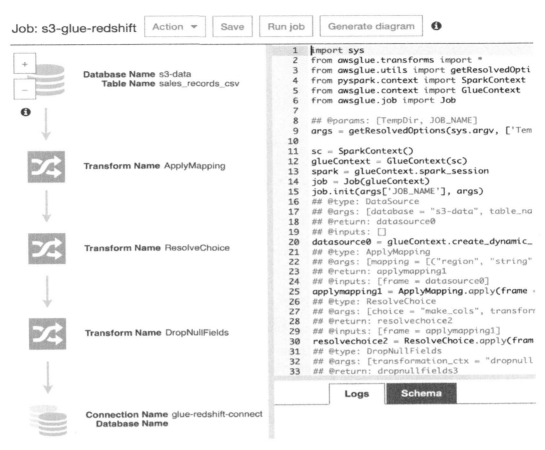

Figure 6.6 – A screenshot of the AWS Glue ETL job

9. Once the job is successful, navigate to Amazon Redshift and click on **Query editor**.

10. Set the database name as `glue-dev` and then provide the username and password to create a connection.

11. Select the `public` schema and now you can query the table to see the records, as shown in *Figure 6.7*:

Figure 6.7 – A screenshot of Amazon Redshift's Query editor

We now understand how to create an ETL job using AWS Glue to copy the data from the S3 bucket to Amazon Redshift. We also queried the data in Amazon Redshift using the query editor from the UI console. It is recommended to delete the Redshift cluster and AWS Glue job if you have completed the steps successfully. AWS creates two buckets in your account to store the AWS Glue scripts and AWS Glue temporary results. Therefore, delete these as well to save costs. We will use the data catalog created on S3 data in the next section.

In the following section, we will learn about querying the S3 data using Athena.

Querying S3 data using Athena

Athena is a serverless service designed for querying data stored in S3. It is serverless because the client doesn't manage the servers that are used for computation:

- Athena uses a schema to present the results against the query on the data stored in S3. You define how you want your data to appear in the form of a schema and Athena reads the raw data from S3 to show the results as per the defined schema.

- The output can be used by other services for visualization, storing, or various analytics purposes. The source data in S3 can be in any of the following structured, semi-structured, and unstructured data formats, including XML, JSON, CSV/TSV, AVRO, Parquet, ORC, and more. CloudTrail, ELB Logs, and VPC flow logs can also be stored in S3 and analyzed by Athena.

- This follows the schema-on-read technique. Unlike traditional techniques, tables are defined in advance in a data catalog, and data is projected when it reads. SQL-like queries are allowed on data without transforming the source data.

Now, let's understand this with the help of an example, where we will use **AWSDataCatlog** created in AWS Glue on the S3 data and query them using Athena:

1. Navigate to the AWS Athena console. Select `AWSDataCatalog` from **Data source** (if you're doing this for the first time, then a `sampledb` database will be created with a table, `elb_logs`, in the AWS Glue data catalog).

2. Select `s3-data` as the database.

3. Click on **Settings** from the top-right corner and fill in the details as shown in *Figure 6.8* (I have used the same bucket as in the previous example and a different folder):

Figure 6.8 – A screenshot of Amazon Athena's settings

4. The next step is to write your query in the query editor and execute it. Once your execution is complete, please delete your S3 buckets and AWS Glue data catalogs. This will save you money.

In this section, we learned about querying S3 data using Amazon Athena through the AWS data catalog. You can also create your schema and query the data from S3. In the next section, we will learn about Amazon Kinesis Data Streams.

Processing real-time data using Kinesis data streams

Kinesis is Amazon's streaming service and can be scaled based on requirements. It is highly available in a region. It has a level of persistence that retains data for 24 hours by default or optionally up to 365 days. Kinesis data streams are used for large-scale data ingestion, analytics, and monitoring:

- Kinesis can be ingested by multiple producers and multiple consumers can also read data from the stream. Let's understand this by means of an example in real time. Suppose you have a producer ingesting data to a Kinesis stream and the default retention period is 24 hours, which means the data ingested at 05:00:00 A.M. today will be available in the stream until 04:59:59 A.M. tomorrow. This data won't be available beyond that point and ideally, this should be consumed before it expires or can be stored somewhere if it's critical. The retention period can be extended to a maximum of 365 days at an extra cost.

- Kinesis can be used for real-time analytics or dashboard visualization. Producers can be imagined as a piece of code pushing data into the Kinesis stream, and it can be an EC2 instance running the code, a Lambda function, an IoT device, on-premises servers, mobile applications or devices, and so on.

- Similarly, the consumer can also be a piece of code running on an EC2 instance, Lambda function, or on-premises servers that know how to connect to a kinesis stream, read the data, and apply some action to the data. AWS provides triggers to invoke a lambda consumer as soon as data arrives at the kinesis stream.

- Kinesis is scalable due to its shard architecture, which is the fundamental throughput unit of a kinesis stream. *What is a shard?* A shard is a logical structure that partitions the data based on a partition key. A shard supports a writing capacity of *1 MB/sec* and a reading capacity of *2 MB/sec*. *1,000* PUT records per second are supported by a single shard. If you have created a stream with *3 shards*, then *3 MB/ sec write throughput* and *6 MB/sec read throughput* can be achieved and this allows *3,000* PUT records. So, with more shards, you have to pay an extra amount to get higher performance.

- The data in a shard is stored via a Kinesis data record and can be a maximum of 1 MB. Kinesis data records are stored across the shard based on the partition key. It also has a sequence number. A sequence number is assigned by kinesis as soon as a `putRecord` or `putRecords` API operation is performed so as to uniquely identify a record. The partition key is specified by the producer while adding the data to the Kinesis data stream, and the partition key is responsible for segregating and routing the record to different shards in the stream to balance the load.

- There are two ways to encrypt the data in a kinesis stream: server-side encryption and client-side encryption. Client-side encryption is hard to implement and manage the keys because the client has to encrypt the data before putting it into the stream and decrypt the data after reading from the stream. With server-side encryption enabled via **AWS/KMS**, the data is automatically encrypted and decrypted as you put the data and get it from a stream.

> **Note**
>
> Amazon Kinesis shouldn't be confused with Amazon SQS. Amazon SQS supports one production group and one consumption group. If your use case demands multiple users sending data and receiving data, then Kinesis is the solution.
>
> For decoupling and asynchronous communications, SQS is the solution, because the sender and receiver do not need to be aware of one another.
>
> In SQS, there is no concept of persistence. Once the message is read, the next step is deletion. There's no concept of the retention time window for Amazon SQS. If your use case demands large-scale ingestion, then Kinesis should be used.

In the next section, we will learn about storing the streamed data for further analysis.

Storing and transforming real-time data using Kinesis Data Firehose

There are a lot of use cases demanding the data to be streamed and stored for future analytics purposes. To overcome such problems, you can write a kinesis consumer to read the Kinesis stream and store the data in S3. This solution needs an instance or a machine to run the code with the required access to read from the stream and write to S3. The other possible option would be to run a Lambda function that gets triggered on the putRecord or putRecords API made to the stream and reads the data from the stream to store in the S3 bucket:

- To make this easy, Amazon provides a separate service called Kinesis Data Firehose. This can easily be plugged into a Kinesis data stream and it will require essential IAM roles to write data into S3. This is a fully managed service to reduce the load of managing servers and code. It also supports loading the streamed data into Amazon Redshift, Amazon Elasticsearch Service, and Splunk. Kinesis Data Firehose scales automatically to match the throughput of the data.

- Data can be transformed via an AWS Lambda function before storing or delivering it to the destination. If you want to build a raw data lake with the untransformed data, then by enabling source record backup, you can store it in another S3 bucket prior to the transformation.

- With the help of AWS/KMS, data can be encrypted following delivery to the S3 bucket. It has to be enabled while creating the delivery stream. Data can also be compressed in supported formats such as GZIP, ZIP, and SNAPPY compression formats.

In the next section, we will learn about different AWS services used for ingesting data from on-premises servers to AWS.

Different ways of ingesting data from on-premises into AWS

With the increasing demand for data-driven use cases, managing data on on-premises servers is pretty tough at the moment. Taking backups is not easy when you deal with a huge amount of data. This data in data lakes is being used to build deep neural networks, to create a data warehouse to extract meaningful information from it, to run analytics, and to generate reports.

Now, if we look at the available options to migrate data into AWS, then it comes with various challenges, too. For example, if you want to send data to S3, then you have to write a few lines of code to send your data to AWS. You will have to manage the code and servers to run the code. It has to be ensured that the data is commuting via the HTTPS network. You need to verify whether the data transfer was successful. This adds complexity as well as time and effort challenges to the process. To avoid such scenarios, AWS provides services to match or solve your use cases by designing hybrid infrastructure that allows data sharing between the on-premises data centers and AWS. Let's learn about these in the following sections.

AWS Storage Gateway

Storage Gateway is a hybrid storage virtual appliance. It can run in three different modes – **File Gateway**, **Tape Gateway**, and **Volume Gateway**. It can be used for extension, migration, and backups of the on-premises data center to AWS:

- In Tape Gateway mode, the storage gateway stores virtual tapes on S3, and when ejected and archived, the tapes are moved from S3 to Glacier. Active tapes are stored in S3 for storage and retrieval. Archived or exported tapes are stored in **Virtual Tape Shelf** (**VTS**) in Glacier. Virtual tapes can be created and can range in size from 100 GiB to 5 TiB. A total of 1 petabyte of storage can be configured locally and an unlimited number of tapes can be archived to Glacier. This is ideal for an existing backup system on tape and where there is a need to migrate backup data into AWS. You can decommission the physical tape hardware later.

- In File Gateway mode, the storage gateway maps files onto S3 objects, which can be stored using one of the available storage classes. This helps you to extend the data center into AWS. You can load more files to your File Gateway and these are stored as S3 objects. It can run on your on-premises virtual server, which connects to various devices using **Server Message Block (SMB)** or **Network File System (NFS)**. The File Gateway connects to AWS using an HTTPS public endpoint to store the data on S3 objects. Life cycle policies can be applied to those S3 objects. You can easily integrate your **Active Directory** (**AD**) with File Gateway to control access to the files on the file share.

- In Volume Gateway mode, the storage gateway presents block storage. There are two ways of using this, one is **Gateway Cached**, and the other is **Gateway Stored**:

- **Gateway Stored** is a volume storage gateway running locally on-premises and it has local storage and an upload buffer. A total of 32 volumes can be created and each volume can be up to 16 TB in size for a total capacity of 512 TB. Primary data is stored on-premises and backup data is asynchronously replicated to AWS in the background. Volumes are made available via **Internet Small Computer Systems Interface (iSCSI)** for network-based servers to access. It connects to **Storage Gateway Endpoint** via an HTTPS public endpoint and creates EBS snapshots from backup data. These snapshots can be used to create standard EBS volumes. This option is ideal for migration to AWS or disaster recovery or business continuity. The local system will still use the local volume, but the EBS snapshots are in AWS, which can be used instead of backups. It's not the best option for data center extension because you require a huge amount of local storage.

- **Gateway Cached** is a volume storage gateway running locally on-premises and it has cache storage and an upload buffer. The difference is that the data that is added to the storage gateway is not local but uploaded to AWS. Primary data is stored in AWS. Frequently accessed data is cached locally. This is an ideal option for extending the on-premises data center to AWS. It connects to **Storage Gateway Endpoint** via an HTTPS public endpoint and creates **S3 Backed Volume (AWS-managed bucket)** snapshots that are stored as standard EBS snapshots.

Snowball, Snowball Edge, and Snowmobile

They belong to the same product clan for the physical transfer of data between business operating locations and AWS. For moving a large amount of data into and out of AWS, you can use any of the three:

- **Snowball**: This can be ordered from AWS by logging a job. AWS delivers the device to load your data and send it back. Data in Snowball is encrypted using KMS. It comes with two capacity ranges, one 50 TB and the other 80 TB. It is economical to order one or more Snowball devices for data between 10 TB and 10 PB. The device can be sent to different premises. It does not have any compute capability; it only comes with storage capability.

- **Snowball Edge**: This is like Snowball, but it comes with both storage and computes capability. It has a larger capacity than Snowball. It offers fastened networking, such as 10 Gbps over RJ45, 10/25 Gb over SFP28, and 40/100 Gb+ over QSFP+ copper. This is ideal for the secure and quick transfer of terabytes to petabytes of data into AWS.

- **Snowmobile**: This is a portable data center within a shipping container on a truck. This allows you to move exabytes of data from on-premises to AWS. If your data size exceeds 10 PB, then Snowmobile is preferred. Essentially, upon requesting Snowmobile, a truck is driven to your location, you plug your data center into the truck, and transfer the data. If you have multiple sites, choosing Snowmobile for data transfer is not an ideal option.

AWS DataSync

AWS DataSync is designed to move data from on-premises storage to AWS, or vice versa:

- It is an ideal product from AWS for data processing transfers, archival or cost-effective storage, disaster recovery, business continuity, and data migrations.

- It has a special data validation feature that verifies the original data with the data in AWS, as soon as the data arrives in AWS. In other words, it checks the integrity of the data.

- Let's understand this product in depth by considering an example of an on-premises data center that has SAN/NAS storage. When we run the AWS DataSync agent on a VMWare platform, this agent is capable of communicating with the NAS/SAN storage via an NFS/SMB protocol. Once it is on, it communicates with the AWS DataSync endpoint and, from there, it can connect with several different types of location, including various S3 storage classes or VPC-based resources, such as the **Elastic File System** (**EFS**) and FSx for Windows Server.

- It allows you to schedule data transfers during specific periods. By configuring the built-in bandwidth throttle, you can limit the amount of network bandwidth that DataSync uses.

Processing stored data on AWS

There are several services for processing the data stored in AWS. We will go through AWS Batch and AWS EMR (Elastic MapReduce) in this section. EMR is a product from AWS that primarily runs MapReduce jobs and Spark applications in a managed way. AWS Batch is used for long-running, compute-heavy workloads.

AWS EMR

EMR is a managed implementation of Apache Hadoop provided as a service by AWS. It includes other components of the Hadoop ecosystem, such as Spark, HBase, Flink, Presto, Hive, Pig, and many more. We will not cover these in detail for the certification exam:

- EMR clusters can be launched from the AWS console or via the AWS CLI with a specific number of nodes. The cluster can be a long-term cluster or an ad hoc cluster. If you have a long-running traditional cluster, then you have to configure the machines and manage them yourself. If you have jobs to be executed faster, then you need to manually add a cluster. In the case of EMR, these admin overheads are gone. You can request any number of nodes to EMR and it manages and launches the nodes for you. If you have autoscaling enabled on the cluster, then with the increased requirement, EMR launches new nodes in the cluster and decommissions the nodes once the load is reduced.

- EMR uses EC2 instances in the background and runs in one availability zone in a VPC. This enables faster network speeds between the nodes. AWS Glue uses EMR clusters in the background, where users do not need to worry about the operational understanding of AWS EMR.

- From a use case standpoint, EMR can be used for processing or transforming the data stored in S3 and outputs data to be stored in S3. EMR uses nodes (EC2 instances) as the computing units for data processing. EMR nodes come in different variants, including Master node, Core node, and Task node.

- The EMR master node acts as a Hadoop namenode and manages the cluster and its health. It is responsible for distributing the job workload among the other core nodes and task nodes. If you have SSH enabled, then you can connect to the master node instance and access the cluster.

- The EMR cluster can have one or more core nodes. If you relate to the Hadoop ecosystem, then core nodes are similar to Hadoop data nodes for HDFS and they are responsible for running tasks therein.

- Task nodes are optional and they don't have HDFS storage. They are responsible for running tasks. If a task node fails for some reason, then this does not impact HDFS storage, but a core node failure causes HDFS storage interruptions.

- EMR has its filesystem called EMRFS. It is backed by S3 and this feature makes it regionally resilient. If a core node fails, the data is still safe in S3. HDFS is efficient in terms of I/O and faster than EMRFS.

In the following section, we will learn about AWS Batch, which is a managed batch processing compute service that can be used for long-running services.

AWS Batch

This is a managed batch processing product. If you are using AWS Batch, then jobs can be run without end user interaction or can be scheduled to run:

- Imagine an event-driven application that launches a Lambda function to process the data stored in S3. If the processing time goes beyond 15 minutes, then Lambda has the execution time limit. For such scenarios, AWS Batch is a better solution, where computation-heavy workloads can be scheduled or driven through API events.

- AWS Batch is a good fit for use cases where a longer processing time is required or more computation resources are needed.

- AWS Batch runs a job that can be a script or an executable. One job can depend on another job. A job needs a definition, such as who can run a job (with IAM permissions), where the job can be run (resources to be used), mount points, and other metadata.

- Jobs are submitted to queues where they wait for compute environment capacity. These queues are associated with one or more compute environments.

- Compute environments do the actual work of executing the jobs. These can be ECS or EC2 instances, or any computing resources. You can define their sizes and capacities too.

- Environments receive jobs from the queues based on their priority and execute the jobs. They can be managed or unmanaged compute environments.

- AWS Batch can store the metadata in DynamoDB for further use and can also store the output to the S3 bucket.

> **Note**
>
> If you get a question in exams on an event-style workload that requires flexible compute, a higher disk space, no time limit (more than 15 minutes), or an effective resource limit, then choose AWS Batch.

Summary

In this chapter, we learned about different ways of processing data in AWS. We also learned the capabilities in terms of extending our data centers to AWS, migrating data to AWS, and the ingestion process. We also learned the various ways of using the data to process it and make it ready for analysis in our way. We understood the magic of having a data catalog that helps us to query our data via AWS Glue and Athena.

In the next chapter, we will learn about various machine learning algorithms and their usages.

Questions

1. If you have a large number of IoT devices sending data to AWS to be consumed by a large number of mobile devices, which of the following should you choose?

    A. SQS standard queue

    B. SQS FIFO queue

    C. Kinesis stream

2. If you have a requirement to decouple a high-volume application, which of the following should you choose?

    A. SQS standard queue

    B. SQS FIFO queue

    C. Kinesis stream

3. Which of the following do I need to change to improve the performance of a Kinesis stream?

    A. The read capacity unit of a stream

    B. The write capacity unit of a stream

    C. Shards of a stream

    D. The region of a stream

4. Which of the following ensures data integrity?

    A. AWS Kinesis

    B. AWS DataSync

    C. AWS EMR

    D. Snowmobile

5. Which storage gateway mode can replace a tape drive with S3 storage?

   A. Volume Gateway Stored

   B. Volume Gateway Cached

   C. File

   D. VTL

6. Which storage gateway mode can be used to present storage over SMB to clients?

   A. Volume Gateway Stored

   B. Volume Gateway Cached

   C. File

   D. VTL

7. Which storage gateway mode is ideal for data center extension to AWS?

   A. Volume Gateway Stored

   B. Volume Gateway Cached

   C. File

   D. VTL

8. What storage product in AWS can be used for Windows environments for shared storage?

   A. S3

   B. FSx

   C. EBS

   D. EFS

9. Which node within an EMR cluster handles operations?

   A. Master node

   B. Core node

   C. Task node

   D. Primary node

10. Which nodes in an EMR cluster are good for spot instances?

    A. Master node

    B. Core node

    C. Task node

    D. Primary node

11. If you have large quantities of streaming data and add it to Redshift, which services would you use (choose three)?

    A. Kinesis Data Streams

    B. Kinesis Data Firehose

    C. S3

    D. SQS

    E. Kinesis Analytics

12. Kinesis Firehose supports data transformation using Lambda.

    A. True

    B. False

13. Which of the following are valid destinations for Kinesis Data Firehose (choose five)?

    A. HTTP

    B. Splunk

    C. Redshift

    D. S3

    E. Elastic Search

    F. EC2

    G. SQS

Answers

1. C

2. A

3. C

4. B

5. D

6. C

7. B

8. B

9. A

10. C

11. A, B, C

12. A

13. A, B, C, D, E

Section 3: Data Modeling

This section summarizes the most common machine learning algorithms. It describes the logic of each algorithm, when to use each of them, and how to tune their hyperparameters.

This section contains the following chapters:

7

Applying Machine Learning Algorithms

In the previous chapter, we studied AWS services for data processing, including Glue, Athena, and Kinesis! It is now time to move on to the modeling phase and study machine learning algorithms. I am sure that, during the earlier chapters, you have realized that building machine learning models requires a lot of knowledge about AWS services, data engineering, data exploratory, data architecture, and much more. This time, we will go deeper into the algorithms that we have been talking about so far and many others.

Having a good sense of the different types of algorithms and machine learning approaches will put you in a very good position to make decisions during your projects. Of course, this type of knowledge is also crucial to the AWS machine learning specialty exam.

Bear in mind that there are thousands of algorithms out there and, by the way, you can even propose your own algorithm for a particular problem. Furthermore, we will cover the most relevant ones and, hopefully, the ones that you will probably face in the exam.

The main topics of this chapter are as follows:

- Storing the training data
- A word about ensemble models
- Regression models
- Classification models
- Forecasting models
- Object2Vec
- Clustering
- Anomaly detection
- Dimensionality reduction
- IP Insights
- Natural language processing
- Reinforcement learning

Alright, let's do it!

Introducing this chapter

During this chapter, we will talk about several algorithms, modeling concepts, and learning strategies. We think all these topics will be beneficial for you during the exam and your data scientist career.

We have structured this chapter in a way so that it covers not only the necessary topics of the exam but also gives you a good sense of the most important learning strategies out there. For example, the exam will check your knowledge regarding the basic concepts of K-means; however, we will cover it on a much deeper level, since this is an important topic for your career as a data scientist.

We will follow this approach, looking deeper into the logic of the algorithm, for some types of models that we feel every data scientist should master. So, keep that in mind: sometimes, we might go deeper than expected in the exam, but that will be extremely important for you.

Many times, during this chapter, we will use the term **built-in algorithms**. We will use this term when we want to refer to the list of algorithms that's implemented by AWS on their SageMaker SDK.

Let me give you a concrete example: you can use scikit-learn's KNN algorithm (if you don't remember what scikit-learn is, refresh your memory by going back to *Chapter 1, Machine Learning Fundamentals*) to create a classification model and deploy it to SageMaker. However, AWS also offers its own implementation of the KNN algorithm on their SDK, which is optimized to run in the AWS environment. Here, KNN is an example of a built-in algorithm.

As you can see, the possibilities on AWS are endless, because you can either take advantage of built-in algorithms or bring in your own algorithm to create models on SageMaker. Finally, just to make this very clear, here is an example of how to import a built-in algorithm from the AWS SDK:

```
import sagemaker
knn = sagemaker.estimator.Estimator(get_image_uri(boto3.
Session().region_name, "knn"),
        get_execution_role(),
        train_instance_count=1,
        train_instance_type='ml.m5.2xlarge',
        output_path=output_path,
        sagemaker_session=sagemaker.Session())
knn.set_hyperparameters(**hyperparams)
```

You will learn how to create models on SageMaker in *Chapter 9, Amazon SageMaker Modeling*. For now, just understand that AWS has its own set of libraries where those built-in algorithms are implemented.

To train and evaluate a model, you need training and testing data. After instantiating your estimator, you should then feed it with those datasets. I don't want to spoil *Chapter 9, Amazon SageMaker Modeling*, but you should know the concepts of **data channels** in advance.

Data channels are configurations related to input data that you can pass to SageMaker when you're creating a training job. You should set these configurations just to inform SageMaker of how your input data is formatted.

In *Chapter 9, Amazon SageMaker Modeling*, you will learn how to create training jobs and how to set data channels. As of now, you should know that, while configuring data channels, you can set **content types (ContentType)** and an **input mode (TrainingInputMode)**. Let's take a closer look at how and where the training data should be stored so that it can be integrated properly with AWS's built-in algorithms.

Storing the training data

First of all, you can use multiple AWS services to prepare data for machine learning, such as EMR, Redshift, Glue, and so on. After preprocessing the training data, you should store it in S3, in a format expected by the algorithm you are using. The following table shows the list of acceptable data formats per algorithm:

Data format	Algorithm
application/x-image	Object Detection Algorithm, Semantic Segmentation
application/x-recordio	Object Detection Algorithm
application/x-recordio-protobuf	Factorization Machines, K-means, KNN, Latent Dirichlet Allocation, Linear Learner, NTM, PCA, RCF, Sequence-to-Sequence
application/jsonlines	BlazingText, DeepAR
image/.jpeg	Object Detection Algorithm, Semantic Segmentation
image/.png	Object Detection Algorithm, Semantic Segmentation
text/.csv	IP Insights, K-means, KNN, Latent Dirichlet Allocation, Linear Learner, NTM, PCA, RCF, XGBoost
text/.libsvm	XGBoost

Figure 7.1 – Data formats that are acceptable per AWS algorithm

As we can see, many algorithms accept text/.csv format. Keep in mind that you should follow these rules if you want to use that format:

- Your CSV file *can't* have a header record.
- For supervised learning, the target variable must be in the first column.
- While configuring the training pipeline, set the input data channel as content_type equal to text/csv.
- For unsupervised learning, set the label_size within the **content_type** to 'content_type=text/csv;label_size=0'.

Although text/.csv format is fine for many use cases, most of the time, AWS's built-in algorithms work better with **recordIO-protobuf**. This is an optimized data format that's used to train AWS's built-in algorithms, where SageMaker converts each observation in the dataset into a binary representation that's a set of 4-byte floats.

RecordIO-protobuf accepts two types of input mode: **pipe mode** and **file mode**. In pipe mode, the data will be streamed directly from S3, which helps optimize storage. In file mode, the data is copied from S3 to the training instance's store volume.

We are almost ready! Now, let's have a quick look at some modeling definitions that will help you understand some more advanced algorithms.

A word about ensemble models

Before we start diving into the algorithms, there is an important modeling concept that you should be aware of, known as **ensemble**. The term ensemble is used to describe methods that use multiple algorithms to create a model.

For example, instead of creating just one model to predict fraudulent transactions, you could create multiple models that do the same thing and, using a vote sort of system, select the predicted outcome. The following table illustrates this simple example:

Transaction	Model A	Model B	Model C	Prediction
1	Fraud	Fraud	Not Fraud	Fraud
2	Not Fraud	Not Fraud	Not Fraud	Not Fraud
3	Fraud	Fraud	Fraud	Fraud
4	Not Fraud	Not Fraud	Fraud	Not Fraud

Figure 7.2 – An example of a voting system on ensemble methods

The same approach works for regression problems, where, instead of voting, we could average the results of each model and use that as the final outcome.

Voting and averaging are just two examples of ensemble approaches. Other powerful techniques include **blending** and **stacking**, where you can create multiple models and use the outcome of each model as features for a main model. Looking back at the preceding table, columns "Model A," "Model B," and "Model C" would be used as features to predict the final outcome.

It turns out that many machine learning algorithms use ensemble methods while training, in an embedded way. These algorithms can be classified into two main categories:

- **Bootstrapping Aggregation** or **Bagging**: With this approach, several models are trained on top of different samples of the data. Then, predictions are made through the voting or averaging system. The main algorithm from this category is known as **Random Forest**.

- **Boosting**: With this approach, several models are trained on top of different samples of the data. Then, one model tries to correct the error of the next model by penalizing incorrect predictions. The main algorithms from this category are known as **Stochastic Gradient Boosting** and **AdaBoost**.

Now that you know what ensemble models are, let's move on and study some machine learning algorithms that are likely to be present in your exam. Not all of them use ensemble approaches, but I trust it is going to be easier for you to recognize that.

We will split the next few sections up based on AWS algorithm categories:

- Supervised learning
- Unsupervised learning
- Textual analysis
- Image processing

Finally, we will provide an overview of reinforcement learning in AWS.

Supervised learning

AWS provides supervised learning algorithms for general purposes (regression and classification tasks) and for more specific purposes (forecasting and vectorization). The list of built-in algorithms that can be found in these sub-categories is as follows:

- Linear learner algorithm
- Factorization machines algorithm
- XGBoost algorithm
- K-Nearest Neighbor algorithm
- Object2Vec algorithm
- DeepAR Forecasting algorithm

Let's start with regression models and the linear learner algorithm.

Working with regression models

Okay; I know that real problems usually aren't linear nor simple. However, looking into **linear regression** models is a nice way to figure out what's going on inside **regression models** in general (yes, regression models can be linear and non-linear). This is mandatory knowledge for every data scientist and can help you solve real challenges as well. We'll take a closer look at this in the following subsections.

Introducing regression algorithms

Linear regression models aim to predict a numeric value (Y) according to one or more variables (X). Mathematically, we can define such a relationship as Y = f(X), where Y is known as the **dependent variable** and X is known as the **independent variable**.

With regression models, the component that we want to predict (Y) is always a continuous number; for example, the price of houses or the number of transactions. We saw that in *Chapter 1, Machine Learning Fundamentals, Table 2,* when we were choosing the right type of supervised learning algorithm, given the target variable. Please, feel free to go back and review it.

When we use just one variable to predict Y, we refer to this problem as **simple linear regression**. On the other hand, when we use *more than one variable to predict Y,* we say that we have a **multiple linear regression** problem.

There is also another class of regression models, known as **non-linear regression**. However, let's put that aside for a moment and understand what simple linear regression means.

Regression models belong to the supervised side of machine learning (the other side is non-supervised) because algorithms try to predict values according to existing correlations between independent and dependent variables.

But what does "f" mean in Y=f(X)? "f" is the regression function responsible for predicting Y based on X. In other words, this is the function that we want to figure out! When we start talking about simple linear regression, pay attention to the next three questions and answers:

1. What is the shape of "f" in linear regression?

   Linear, sure!

2. How can we represent a linear relationship?

   Using a *straight* line (you will understand why in a few minutes).

3. So, what's the function that defines a line?

   ax + b (just check any *mathematics* book).

That's it! Linear regression models are given by **y = ax + b**. Once we are trying to predict Y given X, we just need to find out the values of "a" and "b". We can adopt the same logic to figure out what's going on inside other kinds of regression.

And believe me, finding out the values of "a" and "b" isn't the only thing we're going to do. It's nice to know that "a" is also known as the **alpha coefficient**, or **slope**, and represents the line's inclination, while "b" is also known as the **beta coefficient**, or **y-intercept**, and represents the place where the line crosses the y-axis (into a two-dimensional plan consisting of x and y). You will see these two terms in the next subsection.

It's also nice to know that there is an error associated with every predictor that we don't have control. Let's name it "e" and formally define simple linear regression as **y = ax + b + e**. Mathematically, this error is expressed by the difference between the prediction and the real value.

Alright, let's find alpha and beta and give this section a happy ending!

Least square method

There are different ways to find the slope and y-intercept of a line, but the most used method is known as the **least square method**. The principle behind this method is simple: we have to find the *best line that reduces the sum of squared error*.

In the following graph, we can see a Cartesian plane with multiple points and lines in it. "Line a" represents the best fit for this data – in other words, that would be the best linear regression function for those points. But how do I know that? It's simple: if we compute the error associated with each point (like the one we've zoomed in on in the following graph), we will realize that "line a" contains the least sum of square errors:

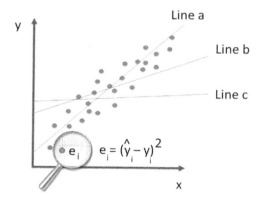

Figure 7.3 – Visualizing the principle of the least square method

It is worth understanding linear regression from scratch, not only for the certification exam but mainly for your career as a data scientist. To provide you with a complete example, we have developed a spreadsheet containing all the calculations that we are going to see, step by step! We encourage you to jump on this support material and perform some simulations. Let's see this in action.

Creating a linear regression model from scratch

We are going to use a very simple dataset, with only two variables:

- X: Represents the person's number of years of work experience

- Y: Represents the person's average salary

We want to understand the relationship between X and Y and, if possible, predict the salary (Y) based on years of experience (X). As I mentioned previously, often, real problems have far more independent variables and are not necessarily linear. However, I am sure this example will give you the baseline knowledge to master more complex algorithms.

To find out what the alpha and beta coefficients are (or slope and y-intercept, if you prefer), we need to find some statistics related to the dataset, so let's take a look at the data and the auxiliary statistics shown here:

X (INDEPENDENT)	Y (DEPENDENT)	X MEAN	Y MEAN	COVARIANCE (X,Y)	X VARIANCE	Y VARIANCE
1	1,000			21,015	20	21,808,900
2	1,500			14,595	12	17,388,900
3	3,700			4,925	6	3,880,900
4	5,000			1,005	2	448,900
5	4,000			895	0	2,788,900
6	6,500			145	0	688,900
7	7,000			1,995	2	1,768,900
8	9,000			8,325	6	11,088,900
9	9,000			11,655	12	11,088,900
10	10,000			19,485	20	18, 748,900
COUNT	10	550	567,000	842,500	825	897,010,000

Figure 7.4 – Dataset to predict average salary based on amount of work experience

As we can see, there is an almost perfect linear relationship between X and Y. As the amount of work experience increases, so does the salary. In addition to X and Y, we need to compute the following statistics: the number of records, the mean of X, the mean of Y, the covariance of X and Y, the variance of X, and the variance of Y. The following formulas provide a mathematical representation of variance and covariance (respectively), where *x bar*, *y bar*, and *n* represent the mean of X, the mean of Y, and the number of records, respectively:

$$s^2 = \frac{\sum (x_i - \bar{x})}{n}$$

$$Cov(X, Y) = \frac{\sum_{i=1}^{n} (x_i - \bar{x})(y_i - \bar{y})}{n}$$

If you want to check the calculation details of the formulas for each of those auxiliary statistics in *Table 7.2*, please refer to the support material provided along with this book. There, you will find those formulas already implemented for you.

These statistics are important because they will be used to compute our alpha and beta coefficients. The following image explains how we are going to compute both coefficients, along with the correlation coefficients **R** and **R squared**. These last two metrics will give us an idea about the quality of the model, where the closer the model is to 1, the better the model is:

Line inclination | Angular coefficient (A, Alfa)
A = cov(x,y) / var(x)

Interceptor (B, Beta)
B = Mean Y - (Alfa * Mean X)

Correlation coefficient R
R = cov(x,y) / sqrt (variance x * variance y)

R adjusted
R adjusted = R^2

Error (variability not explained)
Ei=Yi - yi

Equation
Y = A.X + B + Ei

Figure 7.5 – Equations to calculate coefficients for simple linear regression

After applying these formulas, we will come up with the results shown here:

Cofficient	Description	Value
Alpha	Line inclination	1,021,212,121
Beta	Interceptor	53
R	Correlation	0,979,364,354
R^2	Determination	0,959,154,538

Figure 7.6 – Finding regression coefficients

The preceding table already contains all the information that we need to make predictions on top of the new data. If we replace the coefficients in the original equation, **y = ax + b + e**, we will find the regression formula to be as follows:

Y = 1021,212 * X + 53,3

From this point on, to make predictions, all we have to do is replace X with the number of years of experience. As a result, we will find Y, which is the projected salary. We can see the model fit in the following graph and some model predictions in *Figure 7.8*:

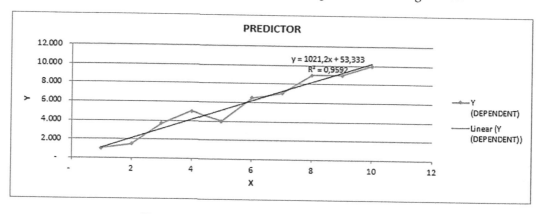

Figure 7.7 – Fitting data in the regression equation

We see the prediction values here:

INPUT	PREDICTION	ERROR
1	1,075	75
2	2,096	596
3	3,117	- 583
4	4,138	- 862
4	5,159	1,159
5	6,181	- 319
6	7,202	202
7	8,223	- 777
8	9,244	244
9	10,265	265
10	11,287	
11	12,308	
12	13,329	
13	14,350	
14	15,372	
15	16,393	
16	17,414	
17	18,435	
18	19,456	
19	20,478	

Figure 7.8 – Model predictions

While you are analyzing regression models, you should be able to understand whether your model is of a good quality or not. We talked about many modeling issues (such as overfitting) in *Chapter 1, Machine Learning Fundamentals*, and you already know that you always have to check model performance.

A good approach to regression models is performing what is called **residual analysis**. This is where we plot the errors of the model in a scatter plot and check if they are randomly distributed (as expected) or not. If the errors are *not* randomly distributed, this means that your model was unable to generalize the data. The following graph shows a residual analysis of our example:

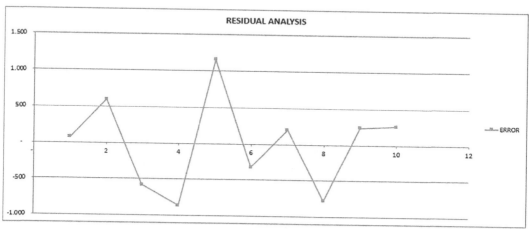

Figure 7.9 – Residual analysis

The takeaway here is that the errors are randomly distributed. Such evidence, along with a high R squared rating, can be used as arguments to support the use of this model.

> **Important note**
>
> In *Chapter 8, Evaluating and Optimizing Models*, we will learn about evaluation metrics. For instance, we will learn that each type of model may have its own set of evaluation metrics. Regression models are commonly evaluated with **Mean Square Error** (**MSE**) and **Root Mean Square Error** (**RMSE**). In other words, apart from R, R squared, and residual analysis, ideally, you will execute your model on test sets to extract other performance metrics. You can even use a cross-validation system to check model performance, as we learned in *Chapter 1, Machine Learning Fundamentals*.

Very often, when the model residuals *do* present a pattern and are *not* randomly distributed, it's because the existing relationship in the data is not linear, but non-linear, so another modeling technique must be applied. Now, let's take a look at how we can interpret a model's results.

Interpreting regression models

It is also good to know how to interpret a linear regression model. Sometimes, we use linear regression not necessarily to create a predictive model but to do a regression analysis, where we can understand the relationship between the independent and dependent variables.

Looking back at our regression equation (Y = 1021,212 * X + 53,3), we can see our two terms: alpha or slope (1021.2) and beta or y-intercept (53.3). We can interpret this model as follows: *for each additional year of working experience, you will increase your salary by $1,021.3 dollars*. Also, note that when "years of experience" is equal to zero, the expected salary is going to be $53.3 dollars (this is the point where our straight line crosses the y-axis).

From a generic perspective, your regression analysis should answer the following question: for each extra unit that's added to the independent variable (slope), what is the average change in the dependent variable? Please take notes and make sure you know how to interpret simple linear regression models – this is a very important thing to do as one of your daily activities as a data scientist! Let's move on and take a look at some final considerations about linear regression.

Checking R squared adjusted

At this point, I hope you have a much better idea of regression models! There is just another very important topic that you should be aware of, regardless of whether it will come up in the exam or not, which is the parsimony aspect of your model.

We have talked about parsimony already, in *Chapter 1, Machine Learning Fundamentals*. This is your ability to prioritize simple models over complex models. Looking into regression models, you might have to use more than one feature to predict your outcome. This is also known as a multiple regression model.

When that's the case, the R and R squared coefficients tend to reward more complex models that have more features. In other words, if you keep adding new features to a multiple regression model, you will come up with higher R and R squared coefficients. That's why you *can't* anchor your decisions *only* based on those two metrics.

Another additional metric that you could use (apart from R, R squared, MSE, and RMSE) is known as **R squared adjusted**. This metric is penalized when we add extra features to the model that do not bring any real gain. In the following table, we have illustrated a hypothetical example just to show you when you are starting to lose parsimony:

Number of Features	R Squared	R Squared Adjusted
1	81	79
2	83	82
3	88	87
4	90	86
5	92	85

Figure 7.10 – Comparing R squared and R squared adjusted

Here, we can conclude that maintaining three variables in the model is better than maintaining four or five variables. Adding four or five variables to that model will increase R squared (as expected), but decrease R squared adjusted.

Alright; at this point, you should have a very good understanding of regression models. Now, let's check what AWS offers in terms of built-in algorithms for this class of models. That is going to be important for your exam, so let's take a look.

Regression modeling on AWS

AWS has a built-in algorithm known as **linear learner**, where we can implement linear regression models. The built-in linear learner uses **Stochastic Gradient Descent (SGD)** to train the model.

> **Important note**
> We will learn more about SGD when we talk about neural networks. For now, we can look at SGD as an alternative to the popular least square error method that we just dissected.

The linear learn built-in algorithm provides a hyperparameter that can apply normalization to the data, prior to the training process. The name of this hyperparameter is `normalize_data`. This is very helpful since linear models are sensitive to the scale of the data and usually take advantage of data normalization.

> **Important note**
> We talked about data normalization in *Chapter 3, Data Preparation and Transformation*. Please review that chapter if you need to.

Some other important hyperparameters of the linear learner algorithm are **L1** and **wd**, which play the roles of **L1 regularization** and **L2 regularization**, respectively.

L1 and L2 regularization help the linear learner (or any other regression algorithm implementation) avoid overfitting. Conventionally, we call regression models that implement L1 regularization **Lasso Regression** models, while for regression models with L2 regularization, we call them **Ridge Regression** models.

Although it might sound complex, it is not! Actually, the regression model equation is still the same; that is, **y = ax + b + e**. The change is in the loss function, which is used to find the coefficients that best minimize the error. If you look back at *Figure 7.3*, you will see that we have defined the error function as **e = (ŷ - y)2**, where **ŷ** is the regression function value and **y** is the real value.

L1 and L2 regularization add a penalty term to the loss function, as shown in the following formulas (note that we are replacing ŷ with ax + b):

$$L_1 = (\ ax + b - y)^2 + \lambda |\ a|$$

$$L_2 = (\ ax + b - y)^2 + \lambda\ a^2$$

The λ (lambda) parameter must be greater than 0 and manually tuned. A very high lambda value may result in an underfitting issue, while a very low lambda may not result in expressive changes in the final results (if your model is overfitted, it will stay overfitted).

In practical terms, the main difference between L1 and L2 regularization is that L1 will shrink the less important coefficients to zero, which will force the feature to be dropped (acting as a feature selector). In other words, if your model is overfitting due to it having a high number of features, L1 regularization should help you solve this problem.

> **Important note**
> During your exam, remember the basis of L1 and L2 regularization, especially the key difference between them, where L1 works well as a feature selector.

Last but not least, many built-in algorithms can serve multiple modeling purposes. The linear learner algorithm can be used for regression, binary classification, and multi-classification. Make sure you remember this during your exam (it is *not only* about regression models).

Still going in that direction, AWS has other built-in algorithms that work for regression and classification problems; that is, **Factorization Machines, K-Nearest Neighbor (KNN)** and the **XGBoost** algorithm. Since these algorithms can also be used for classification purposes, we'll cover them in the section about classification algorithms.

> **Important note**
> You just got a very important tip to remember during the exam: linear learner, Factorization Machines, K-Nearest Neighbor, and XGBoost are suitable for both regression and classification problems. These algorithms are often known as algorithms for general purposes.

With that, we have reached the end of this section on regression models. I hope you have enjoyed it; remember to check out our support material before you take your exam. By the way, you can use that reference material when you're working on your daily activities! Now, let's move on to another classical example of a machine learning problem: classification models.

Working with classification models

You have been learning what classification models are throughout this book. However, now, we are going to discuss some algorithms that are suitable for classification problems. Keep in mind that there are hundreds of classification algorithms out there, but since we are preparing for the AWS machine learning specialty exam, we will cover the ones that have been pre-built by AWS.

We already know what the linear learner does (and we know that it is suitable for both regression and classification tasks), so let's take a look at the other built-in algorithms for general purposes (which includes classification tasks).

We will start with **Factorization Machines**. Factorization machines are considered an extension of the linear learner, optimized to find the relationship between features within high-dimensional sparse datasets.

> **Important note**
> A very traditional use case for Factorization machines is *recommendation systems*, where we usually have a high level of sparsity in the data. During the exam, if you are faced with a general-purpose problem (either a regression or binary classification task) where the underlying datasets are sparse, then Factorization Machines are probably the best answer from an algorithm perspective.

When we use Factorization Machines in a regression model, the **Root Mean Square Error (RMSE)** will be used to evaluate the model. On the other hand, in binary classification mode, the algorithm will use Log Loss, Accuracy, and F1 score to evaluate results. We will have a deeper discussion about evaluation metrics in *Chapter 8, Evaluating and Optimizing Models*.

You should be aware that Factorization Machines only accept input data in **recordIO-protobuf** format. This is because of the data sparsity issue, in which recordIO-protobuf is supposed to do a better job on data processing than text/.csv format.

The next built-in algorithm suitable for classification problems is known as K-Nearest Neighbors, or KNN for short. As the name suggests, this algorithm will try to find the *K* closest points to the input data and return either of the following predictions:

- The most repeated class of the k closest points, if it's a classification task
- The average value of the label of the k closest points, if it's a regression task

We say that KNN is an **index-based algorithm** because it computes distances between points, assigns indexes for these points, and then stores the sorted distances and their indexes. With that type of data structure, KNN can easily select the top K closest points to make the final prediction.

Note that K is a hyperparameter of KNN and should be optimized during the modeling process.

The other AWS built-in algorithm available for general purposes, including classification, is known as **eXtreme Gradient Boosting**, or **XGBoost** for short. This is an ensemble, decision tree-based model.

XGBoost uses a set of **weaker** models (decision trees) to predict the target variable, which can be a regression task, binary class, or multi-class. This is a very popular algorithm and has been used in machine learning competitions by the top performers.

XGBoost uses a boosting learning strategy when one model tries to correct the error of the prior model. It carries the name "gradient" because it uses the gradient descent algorithm to minimize the loss when adding new trees.

Important note
The term weaker is used in this context to describe very simple decision trees.

Although XGBoost is much more robust than a single decision tree, it is important to go into the exam with a clear understanding of what decision trees are and their main configurations. By the way, they are the base model of many ensemble algorithms, such as AdaBoost, Random Forest, Gradient Boost, and XGBoost.

Decision trees are rule-based algorithms that organize decisions in the form of a tree, as shown in the following diagram:

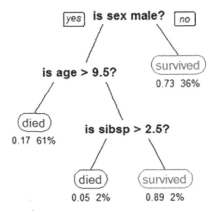

Figure 7.11 – Example of what a decision tree model looks like

They are formed by a root node (at the very top of the tree), intermediary or decision nodes (in the middle of the tree), and leaf nodes (bottom nodes with no splits). The depth of the tree is given by the difference between the root node and the very last leaf node. For example, in the preceding diagram, the depth of the tree is 3.

The depth of the tree is one of the most important hyperparameters of this type of model and it is often known as the **max depth**. In other words, max depth controls the maximum depth that a decision tree can reach.

Another very important hyperparameter of decision tree models is known as the minimum number of samples/observations in the leaf nodes. It is also used to control the growth of the tree.

Decision trees have many other types of hyperparameters, but these two are especially important for controlling how the model overfits. Decision trees with a high depth or very small number of observations in the leaf nodes are likely to face issues during extrapolation/prediction.

The reason for this is simple: decision trees use data from the leaf nodes to make predictions, based on the proportion (for classification tasks) or average value (for regression tasks) of each observation/target variable that belongs to that node. Thus, the node should have enough data to make good predictions outside the training set.

In case you face the term **CART** during the exam, you should know that it stands for **Classification and Regression Trees**, since decision trees can be used for classification and regression tasks.

To select the best variables to split the data in the tree, the model will choose the ones that maximize the separation of the target variables across the nodes. This task can be performed by different methods, such as **Gini** and **Information Gain**.

Forecasting models

Time series, or **TS** for short, refers to data points that are collected on a regular basis with an ordered dependency. Time series have a measure, a fact, and a time unit, as shown in the following image:

Figure 7.12 – Time series statement

Additionally, time series can be classified as **univariate** or **multivariate**. Univariate time series have just one variable connected across a period of time, while a multivariate time series have two or more variables connected across a period of time. The following graph shows the univariate time series we showed in the preceding image:

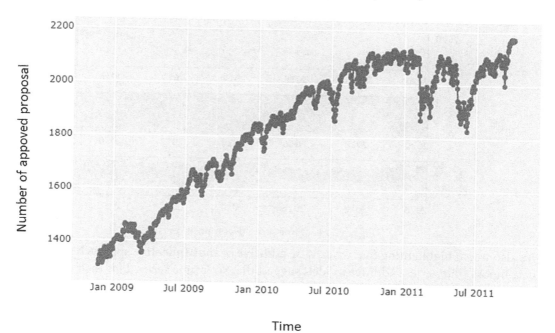

Figure 7.13 – Time series example

Time series can be decomposed as follows:

- **Observed** or **level**: The average values of the series

- **Trend**: Increasing, decreasing pattern (sometimes, there is no trend)

- **Seasonality**: Regular peaks at specific periods of time (sometimes, there is no seasonality)

- **Noise**: Something we cannot explain

Sometimes, we can also find isolated peaks in the series that cannot be captured in a forecasting model. In such cases, we might want to consider those peaks as outliers. The following is a decomposition of the time series shown in the preceding graph:

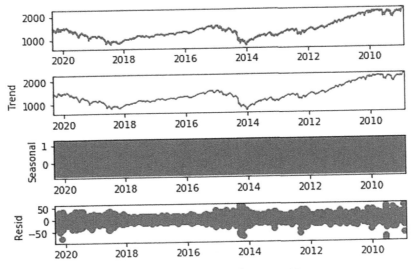

Figure 7.14 – Time series decomposition

It's also worth highlighting that we can use **additive** or **multiplicative** approaches to decompose time series. Additive models suggest that your time series *adds* each component to explain the target variable; that is, **y(t) = level + trend + seasonality + noise**.

Multiplicative models, on the other hand, suggest that your time series *multiplies* each component to explain the target variable; that is, **y(t) = level * trend * seasonality * noise**.

In the next section, we will have a closer look at time series components.

Checking the stationarity of time series

Decomposing time series and understanding how their components interact with additive and multiplicative models is a great achievement! However, the more we learn, the more we question ourselves. Maybe you have realized that time series without trend and seasonality are easier to predict than the ones with all those components!

That is naturally right. If you don't have to understand trend and seasonality, and if you don't have control over the noise, all you have to do is explore the observed values and find their regression relationship.

We refer to time series with constant mean and variance across a period of time as **stationary**. In general, time series *with* trend and seasonality are *not* stationary. It is possible to apply data transformations to the series to transform it into a stationary time series so that the modeling task tends to be easier. This type of transformation is known as **differentiation**.

While you are exploring a time series, you can check stationarity by applying hypothesis tests, such as **Dickey-Fuller**, **KPSS**, and **Philips-Perron**, just to mention a few. If you find it non-stationary, then you can apply differentiation to make it a stationary time series. Some algorithms already have that capability embedded.

Exploring, exploring, and exploring

At this point, I am sure I don't have to remind you that exploration tasks happen all the time in data science. Nothing is different here. While you are building time series models, you might want to have a look at the data and check if it is suitable for this type of modeling.

Autocorrelation plots are one of the tools that you can use for time series analysis. Autocorrelation plots allow you to check the correlations between lags in the time series. The following graph shows an example of this type of visualization:

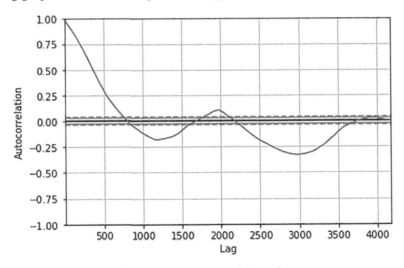

Figure 7.15 – Autocorrelation plot

Remember, if you're playing with univariate time series, your time series just has one variable, so finding autocorrelation across the lags of your unique variable is crucial to understanding whether you can build a good model or not.

And yes, it turns out that, sometimes, it might happen that you don't have a time series in front of you. Furthermore, no matter your efforts, you will not be able to model this data as a time series. This type of data is often known as **white noise**.

Another type of series that we cannot predict is known as **random walk**. Random walks are random by nature, but they have a dependency on the previous time step. For example, the next point of a random walk could be a random number between 0 and 1, and also the last point of the series.

> **Important note**
> Be careful if you come across those terms in the exam and remember to relate them to randomness in time series.

With that, we have covered the main theory about time series modeling. You should also be aware that the most popular algorithms out there for working with time series are known as **Auto-Regressive Integrated Moving Average (ARIMA)** and **Exponential Smoothing (ETS)**. We will not look at the details of these two models. Instead, we will see what AWS can offer us in terms of time series modeling.

Understanding DeepAR

The **DeepAR** forecasting algorithm is a built-in SageMaker algorithm that's used to forecast a one-dimensional time series using a **Recurrent Neural Network (RNN)**.

Traditional time series algorithms, such as ARIMA and ETS, are designed to fit one model per time series. For example, if you want to forecast sales per region, you might have to create one model per region, since each region might have its own sales behaviors. DeepAR, on the other hand, allows you to operate more than one time series in a single model, which seems to be a huge advantage for more complex use cases.

The input data for DeepAR, as expected, is one *or more* time series. Each of these time series can be associated with the following:

- A vector of static (time-independent) categorical features, controlled by the `cat` field
- a vector of dynamic (time-dependent) time series, controlled by `dynamic_feat`

> **Important note**
> Note that the ability to train and make predictions on top of multiple time series is strictly related to the vector of static categorical features. While defining the time series that DeepAR will train on, you can set categorical variables to specify which group each time series belongs to.

Two of the main hyperparameters of DeepAR are `context_length`, which is used to control how far in the past the model can see during the training process, and `prediction_length`, which is used to control how far in the future the model will output predictions.

DeepAR can also handle missing values, which, in this case, refers to existing gaps in the time series. A very interesting functionality of DeepAR is its ability to create derived features from time series. These derived features, which are created from basic time frequencies, help the algorithm learn time-dependent patterns. The following table shows all the derived features created by DeepAR, according to each type of time series that it is trained on:

Frequency of the Time Series	Derived Features
Minute	Minute-of-hour, hour-of-day, day-of-week, day-of-month, day-of-year
Hour	Hour-of-day, day-of-week, day-of-month, day-of-year
Day	Day-of-week, day-of-month, day-of-year
Week	Day-of-month, week-of-year
Month	Month-of-year

Figure 7.16 – DeepAR derived features per frequency of time series

We have now completed this section about forecasting models. Next, we will have a look at the last algorithm regarding supervised learning; that is, the **Object2Vec** algorithm.

Object2Vec

Object2Vec is a built-in SageMaker algorithm that generalizes the well-known **word2vec** algorithm. Object2Vec is used to create **embedding spaces** for high multidimensional objects. These embedding spaces are, per the definition, compressed representatiosn of the original object and can be used for multiple purposes, such as feature engineering or object comparison:

Figure 7.17 – A visual example of an embedding space

The preceding diagram illustrates what we mean by an embedding space. The first and the last layers of the neural network model just map the input data with itself (represented by the same vector size).

As we move on to the internal layers of the model, the data is compressed more and more until it hits the layer in the middle of this architecture, known as the embedding layer. On that particular layer, we have a smaller vector, which aims to be an accurate and compressed representation of the high-dimensional original vector from the first layer.

With this, we just completed our first section about machine learning algorithms in AWS. Coming up next, we will have a look at some unsupervised algorithms.

Unsupervised learning

AWS provides several unsupervised learning algorithms for the following tasks:

- Clustering:
  - K-means algorithm
- Dimension reduction:
  - **Principal Component Analysis (PCA)**
- Pattern recognition:
  - IP Insights
- Anomaly detection:
  - **Random Cut Forest Algorithm (RCF)**

Let's start by talking about clustering and how the most popular clustering algorithm works: K-means.

Clustering

Clustering algorithms are very popular in data science. Basically, they aim to identify groups in a given dataset. Technically, we call these findings or groups **clusters**. Clustering algorithms belong to the field of non-supervised learning, which means that they don't need a label or response variable to be trained.

This is just fantastic because labeled data used to be scarce. However, it comes with some limitations. The main one is that clustering algorithms provide clusters for you, but not the meaning of each cluster. Thus, someone, as a subject matter expert, has to analyze the properties of each cluster to define their meanings.

There are many types of clustering approaches, such as hierarchical clustering and partitional clustering. Inside each approach, we will find several algorithms. However, **K-Means** is probably the most popular clustering algorithm and you are likely to come across it in your exam, so let's take a closer look at it.

When we are playing with K-means, somehow, we have to specify the number of clusters that we want to create. Then, we have to allocate the data points across each cluster so that each data point will belong to a single cluster. This is exactly what we expect as a result at the end of the clustering process!

You, as a user, have to specify the number of clusters you want to create and pass this number to K-means. Then, the algorithm will randomly initiate the central point of each cluster, which is also known as **centroid** initialization.

Once we have the centroids of each cluster, all we need to do is assign a cluster to each data point. To do that, we have to use a proximity or distance metric! Let's adopt the term distance metric.

The **distance metric** is responsible for calculating the distance between data points and centroids. The data point will belong to the closer cluster centroid, according to the distance metric!

The most well-known and used distance metric is called **Euclidean distance** and the math behind it is really simple: imagine that the points of your dataset are composed of two dimensions, X and Y. So, we could consider points a and b as follows:

- a (X=1, Y=1)
- b (X=2, Y=5)

The Euclidean distance between points a and b is given by the following formula, where X1 and Y1 refer to the values of point a and X2 and Y2 refer to the values of point b:

$$\text{Dist} = \sqrt{(x_1 - x_2)^2 + (y_1 - y_2)^2}$$

The same function can be generalized by the following equation: $\sqrt{\sum_{i=1}^{n}(x_i - y_i)^2}$

Once we have completed this process and assigned a cluster with each data point, we have to recalculate the cluster centroids. This process can be done by different methods, such as **single link**, **average link**, and **complete link**.

Due to this centroid refreshment, we will have to keep checking the closest cluster for each data point and keep refreshing the centroids. We have to reexecute steps 1 and 2 **iteratively**, until the cluster centroids converge or the maximum number of allowed iterations is reached.

Alright; let's recap the components that compose the K-means method:

- Centroid initialization, cluster assignment, centroid refreshment, and then redo the last two steps until it converges.

- The algorithm itself:

- A distance metric to assign data points to each cluster:

- We have selected Euclidian distance here.

- And a linkage method to recalculate the cluster centroids:

- For the sake of our demonstration, we'll select the average linkage.

With these definitions, we are ready to walk through our real example, step by step. As with our regression models, some support material is also available for your reference.

Computing K-means step by step

In this example, we will simulate K-means in a very small dataset, with only two columns (x and y) and six data points (A, B, C, D, E, F), as defined in the following table:

Iteration input		
Point	x	y
A	1	1
B	2	2
C	5	5
D	5	6
E	1	5
F	2	6
Cluster 1	1	1
Cluster 2	2	2
Cluster 3	5	5

Figure 7.18 – Input data for K-means

In the preceding table, we created three clusters with the following centroids: (1,1), (2,2), (5,5). The number of clusters (3) was defined *a priori* and the centroid for each cluster was randomly defined. The following graph shows the stage of the algorithm we are at right now:

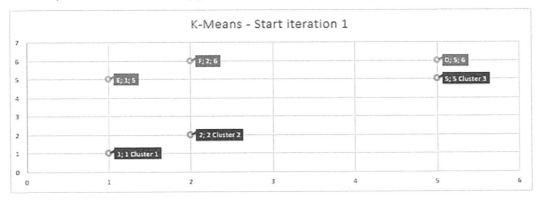

Figure 7.19 – Plotting the K-means results before completing the first iteration

Here, you can't see points A, B, and C since they overlap with cluster centroids, but don't worry – they will appear soon. What we have to do now is compute the distance of each data point to each cluster centroid. Then, we need to choose the cluster that is the closest to each point:

Iteration processing

xc1	yc1	xc2	yc2	xc3	yc3	distance-c1	distance-c2	distance-c3	Cluster
1	1	2	2	5	5	0,0	1,4	5,7	Cluster 1
1	1	2	2	5	5	1,4	0,0	4,2	Cluster 2
1	1	2	2	5	5	5,7	4,2	0,0	Cluster 3
1	1	2	2	5	5	6,4	5,0	1,0	Cluster 3
1	1	2	2	5	5	4,0	3,2	4,0	Cluster 2
1	1	2	2	5	5	5,1	4,0	3,2	Cluster 3

Legend
xc1 = x value of cluster 1
yc1 = y value of cluster 1

Figure 7.20 – Processing iteration 1

In the preceding table, we have the following elements:

- Each row represents a data point.

- The first six columns represent the centroid axis (x and y) of each cluster.

- The next three columns represent the distance of each data point to each cluster centroid.

- The last column represents the clusters that are the closest to each data point.

Looking at data point A (first row), we can see that it was assigned to cluster 1 because the distance from data point A to cluster 1 is 0 (remember when I told you they were overlapping?). The same calculation happens to all other data points to define a cluster for each data point.

Before we move on, you might want to see how we computed those distances between the clusters and the data points. As we stated previously, we have used the Euclidian distance, so let's see that in action. For demonstration purposes, let's check out how we came up with the distance between data point A and cluster 3 (the first row in *Figure 7.20*, column `distance-c3`, value 5,7).

First of all, we applied the same equation from the following formula:

$$Dist = \sqrt{((x_1 - x_2)^2 + (y_1 - y_2)^2)}$$

Here, we have the following:

- X1 = X of data point A = 1
- Y1 = Y of data point A = 1
- X2 = X of cluster 3 = 5
- Y2 = Y of cluster 3 = 5

Applying the formula step by step, we will come up with the following results:

$$Dist = \sqrt{(1 - 5)^2 + (1 - 5)^2)}$$
$$\sqrt{(4)^2 + (4)^2}$$
$$\sqrt{16 + 16}$$
$$\sqrt{32}$$
$$5,656 \text{ or } \sim 5,7$$

Figure 7.21 – Computing the Euclidian distance step by step

That is just fantastic, isn't it? We have almost completed the first iteration of K-means. In the very last step of iteration 1, we have to refresh the cluster centroids. Remember: initially, we randomly defined those centroids, but now, we have just assigned some data points to each cluster, which means we should be able to identify where the central point of the cluster is.

In this example, we have defined that we are going to use the **average linkage** method to refresh the cluster centroids. This is a very simple step, and the results are present in the following table:

Iteration output		
Point	x	y
A	1	1
B	2	2
C	5	5
D	5	6
E	1	5
F	2	6
Cluster 1	1	1
Cluster 2	1,5	3,5
Cluster 3	4	5,7

Figure 7.22 – K-means results after iteration 1

The preceding table shows the same data points that we are dealing with (by the way, they will never change), and the centroids of clusters 1, 2, and 3. Those centroids are quite different from what they were initially, as shown in *Figure 7.18*. This is because they were refreshed using average linkage! The method got the average value of all the x and y values of the data points of each cluster. For example, let's see how we came up with (1.5, 3.5) as centroids of cluster 2.

If you look at *Figure 7.20*, you will see that cluster 2 only has two data points assigned to it: B and E. These are the second and fifth rows in that image. If we take the average values of the x-axis of each point, then we'll have **(2 + 1) / 2 = 1.5** and **(2 + 5) / 2 = 3.5**.

With that, we are done with iteration 1 of K-means and we can view the results:

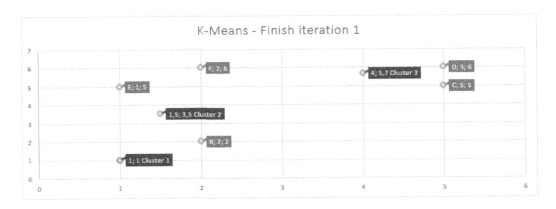

Figure 7.23 – Plotting the K-means results after the first iteration

Now, we can see almost all the data points, except for data point A because it is still overlapping with the centroid of cluster 1. Moving on, we have to redo the following steps:

- Recalculate the distance between each data point and each cluster centroid and reassign clusters, if needed
- Recalculate the cluster centroids

We do those two tasks many times until the cluster centroids converge and they don't change anymore *or* we reach the maximum number of allowed iterations, which can be set as a hyperparameter of K-means. For demonstration purposes, after four iterations, our clusters will look as follows:

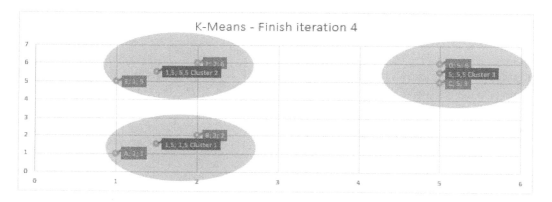

Figure 7.24 – Plotting the K-means results after the fourth iteration

On the fourth iteration, our cluster centroids look pretty consistent, and we can clearly see that we can group our six data points according to their proximity.

> **Important note**
>
> In this example, we have only set two dimensions for each data point (dimension x and y). In real use cases, we can see far more dimensions, and that's why clustering algorithms play a very important role in identifying groups in the data in a more automated fashion.

I hope you have enjoyed how to compute K-means from scratch! I am sure this knowledge will be beneficial for your exam and for your career as a data scientist. By the way, I have told you many times that data scientists must be skeptical and curious, so you might be wondering why we defined three clusters in this example and not two or four. You may also be wondering how we measure the quality of the clusters.

You didn't think I wouldn't explain this to you, did you? In the next section, we will clarify those points together.

Defining the number of clusters and measuring cluster quality

Although K-means is a great algorithm for finding patterns in your data, it will not provide the meaning of each cluster, nor the number of clusters you have to create to maximize cluster quality.

In clustering, cluster quality means that we want to create groups with a high homogeneity among the elements of the same cluster, and a high heterogeneity among the elements of different clusters. In other words, the elements of the same clusters should be close/similar, whereas the elements of different clusters should be well separated.

One way to compute the cluster's homogeneity is by using a metric known as **Sum of Square Errors**, or **SSE** for short. This metric will compute the sum of squared differences between each data point and its cluster centroid. For example, when all the data points are located at the same point where the cluster centroid is, then SSE will be 0. In other words, we want to minimize SSE. The following equation formally defines SSE:

$$SSE = \sum_{i=1}^{n} (x_i - \bar{x})^2$$

Now that we know how to check cluster quality, it is easier to understand how to define the number of appropriated clusters for a given dataset. All we have to do is find several clusters that minimize SSE. A very popular method that works around that logic is known as the **Elbow method**.

The Elbow method proposes executing the clustering algorithm many times. In each execution, we will test a different number of clusters, k. After each execution, we compute the SSE related to that k number of cluster clusters. Finally, we can plot these results and select the number of k where the SSE stops to drastically decrease.

> **Important note**
> Adding more clusters will naturally decrease the SSE. In the Elbow method, we want to find the point where that change becomes smoother.

In the previous example, we decided to create three clusters. The following graph shows the Elbow analysis that supports this decision:

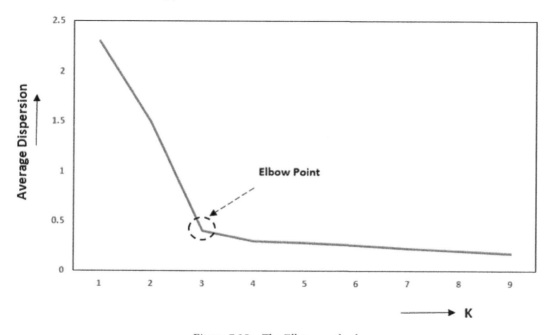

Figure 7.25 – The Elbow method

We can conclude that adding more than three or four clusters will add unnecessary complexity to the clustering process.

Of course, you should always consider the business background while defining the number of clusters. For example, if you are creating a customer segmentation model and your company has prepared the commercial team and business processes to support four segments of customers, considering the preceding graph, there is no harm in setting four clusters instead of three.

Finally, you should know that AWS has implemented K-means as part of their list of built-in algorithms. In other words, you don't have to use external libraries or bring your own algorithm to play with K-means on AWS.

Conclusion

That was a really good accomplishment: you just mastered the basics of clustering algorithms and you should now be able to drive your own projects and research about this topic! For the exam, remember that clustering belongs to the unsupervised field of machine learning, so there is no need to have labeled data.

Also, make sure that you know how the most popular algorithm of this field works; that is, K-means. Although clustering algorithms do not provide the meaning of each group, they are very powerful for finding patterns in the data, either to model a particular problem or just to explore the data.

Coming up next, we'll keep studying unsupervised algorithms and see how AWS has built one of the most powerful algorithms out there for anomaly detection, known as **Random Cut Forest (RCF)**.

Anomaly detection

Finding anomalies in data is very common in modeling and data exploratory analysis. Sometimes, you might want to find anomalies in the data just to remove them before fitting a regression model, while other times, you might want to create a model that identifies anomalies as an end goal, for example, in fraud detection systems.

Again, we can use many different methods to find anomalies in the data. With some creativity, the possibilities are endless. However, there is a particular algorithm that works around this problem that you should definitely be aware of for your exam: **Random Cut Forest (RCF)**.

RCF is an unsupervised decision tree-based algorithm that creates multiple decision trees (forests) using random subsamples of the training data. Technically, it randomizes the data and then creates samples according to the number of trees. Finally, these samples are distributed across each tree.

These sets of trees are used to assign an anomaly score tp the data points. This anomaly score is defined as the expected change in the complexity of the tree as a result of adding that point to the tree.

The most important hyperparameters of RCF are `num_trees` and `num_samples_per_tree`, which are the number of trees in the forest and the number of samples per tree, respectively.

Dimensionality reduction

Another unsupervised algorithm that's implemented by AWS in their list of built-in algorithms is known as **Principal Component Analysis**, or **PCA** for short. PCA is a technique that's used to reduce the number of variables/dimensions in a given dataset.

The main idea behind PCA is plotting the data points to another set of coordinates, known as **principal components (PC)**, which aims to explain the most variance in the data. By definition, the first component will capture more variance than the second component, then the second component will capture more variance than the third one, and so on.

You can set up as many principal components as you need as long as it does not surpass the number of variables in your dataset. The following graph shows how these principal components are drawn:

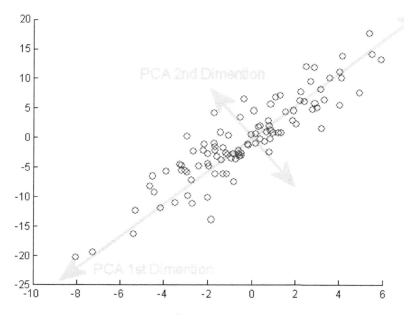

Figure 7.26 – Finding principal components in PCA

As we mentioned previously, the first principal component will be drawn in such a way that it will capture most of the variance in the data. That's why it passes close to the majority of the data points in the preceding graph.

Then, the second principal component will be perpendicular to the first one, so that it will be the second component that explains the variance in the data. If you want to create more components (consequentially, capturing more variance), you just have to follow the same rule of adding perpendicular components. **Eigenvectors** and **eigenvalues** are the linear algebra concepts associated with PCA that compute the principal components.

So, what's the story with dimension reduction here? In case it is not clear yet, these principal components can be used to replace your original variables. For example, let's say you have 10 variables in your dataset and you want to reduce this dataset to three variables that best represent the others. A potential solution for that would be applying PCA and extracting the first three principal components!

Do these three components explain 100% of your dataset? Probably not, but ideally, they will explain most of the variance. Adding more principal components will explain more variance, but at the cost of you adding extra dimensions.

Using AWS's built-in algorithm for PCA

In AWS, PCA works in two different modes:

- **Regular**: For datasets with a moderate number of observations and features
- **Randomized**: For datasets with a large number of observations and features

The difference is that, in randomized mode, it is used an approximation algorithm.

Of course, the main hyperparameter of PCA is the number of components that you want to extract, known as num_components.

IP Insights

IP Insights is an unsupervised algorithm that's used for pattern recognition. Essentially, it learns the usage pattern of IPv4 addresses.

The modus operandi of this algorithm is very intuitive: it is trained on top of pairs of events in the format of entity and IPv4 address so that it can understand the pattern of each entity that it was trained on.

> **Important note**
> For instance, we can understand "entity" as user IDs or account numbers.

Then, to make predictions, it receives a pair of events with the same data structure (entity, IPv4 address) and returns an anomaly score for that particular IP address regarding the input entity.

> **Important note**
> This anomaly score that's returned by IP Insight infers how anomalous the pattern of the event is.

We might come across many applications with IP Insights. For example, you can create an IP Insights model that was trained on top of your application login events (this is your entity). You should be able to expose this model through an API endpoint to make predictions in real time.

Then, during the authentication process of your application, you could call your endpoint and pass the IP address that is trying to log in. If you got a high score (meaning this pattern of logging in looks anomalous), you can request extra information before authorizing access (even if the password was right).

This is just one of the many applications of IP Insights you could think about. Next, we will discuss textual analysis.

Textual analysis

Modern applications use **Natural Language Processing (NLP)** for several purposes, such as **text translation**, **document classifications**, **web search**, **named entity recognition (NER)**, and many others.

AWS offers a suite of algorithms for most NLP use cases. In the next few subsections, we will have a look at these built-in algorithms for textual analysis.

Blazing Text algorithm

Blazing Text does two different types of tasks: text classification, which is a supervised learning approach that extends the **fastText** text classifier, and **word2vec**, which is an unsupervised learning algorithm.

The Blazing Text's implementations of these two algorithms are optimized to run on large datasets. For example, you can train a model on top of billions of words in a few minutes.

This scalability aspect of Blazing Text is possible due to the following:

- Its ability to use multi-core CPUs and a single GPU to accelerate text classification

- Its ability to use multi-core CPUs or GPUs, with custom CUDA kernels for GPU acceleration, when playing with the word2vec algorithm

The word2vec option supports a **batch_skipgram** mode, which allows Blazing Text to do distributed training across multiple CPUs.

> **Important note**
> The distributed training that's performed by Blazing Text uses a mini-batching approach to convert **level-1 BLAS** operations into **level-3 BLAS** operations. If you see these terms during your exam, you should know that they are related to Blazing Text in terms of word2vec.

Still in word2vec mode, Blazing Text supports both the **skip-gram** and **continuous bag of words (CBOW)** architectures.

Last but not least, note the following configurations of Blazing Text, since they are likely to be present in your exam:

- In word2vec mode, only the train channel is available.

- Blazing Text expects a single text file with space-separated tokens. Each line of the file must contain a single sentence. This means you usually have to pre-process your corpus of data before using Blazing Text.

Sequence-to-sequence algorithm

This is a supervised algorithm that transforms an input sequence into an output sequence. This sequence can be a text sentence or even an audio recording.

The most common use cases for sequence-to-sequence are machine translation, text summarization, and speech-to-text. Anything that you think is a sequence-to-sequence problem can be approached by this algorithm.

Technically, AWS SageMaker's Seq2Seq uses two types of neural networks to create models: a **Recurrent Neural Network** (**RNN**) and a **Convolutional Neural Network** (**CNN**) with an attention mechanism.

Latent Dirichlet Allocation, or **LDA** for short, is used for topic modeling. Topic modeling is a textual analysis technique where you can extract a set of topics from a corpus of text data. LDA learns these topics based on the probability distribution of the words in the corpus of text.

Since this is an unsupervised algorithm, there is no need to set a target variable. Also, the number of topics must be specified up-front and you will have to analyze each topic to find their domain meaning.

Neural Topic Model (NTM) algorithm

Just like the LDA algorithm, the **Neural Topic Model** (**NTM**) also aims to extract topics from a corpus of data. However, the difference between LDA and NTM is their learning logic. While LDA learns from probability distributions of the words in the documents, NTM is built on top of neural networks.

The NTM network architecture has a bottleneck layer, which creates an embedding representation of the documents. This bottleneck layer contains all the necessary information to predict document composition, and its coefficients can be considered topics.

With that, we have completed this section on textual analysis. In the next section, we will learn about image processing algorithms.

Image processing

Image processing is a very popular topic in machine learning. The idea is pretty self-explanatory: creating models that can analyze images and make inferences on top of them. By inference, you can understand this as detecting objects in an image, classifying images, and so on.

AWS offers a set of built-in algorithms we can use to train image processing models. In the next few sections, we will have a look at those algorithms.

Image classification algorithm

As the name suggests, the image classification algorithm is used to classify images using supervised learning. In other words, it needs a label within each image. It supports multi-label classification.

The way it operates is simple: during training, it receives an image and its associated labels. During inference, it receives an image and returns all the predicted labels. The image classification algorithm uses a CNN (**ResNet**) for training. It can either train the model from scratch or take advantage of transfer learning to pre-load the first few layers of the neural network.

According to AWS's documentation, the .jpg and .png file formats are supported, but the recommended format is **MXNet RecordIO**.

Semantic segmentation algorithm

The semantic segmentation algorithm provides a pixel-level capability for creating computer vision applications. It tags each pixel of the image with a class, which is an important feature for complex applications such as self-driving and medical image diagnostics.

In terms of its implementation, the semantic segmentation algorithm uses the **MXNet Gluon framework** and the **Gluon CV toolkit**. You can choose any of the following algorithms to train a model:

- **Fully convolutional network (FCN)**
- **Pyramid scene parsing (PSP)**
- DeepLabV3

All these options work as an **encoder-decoder** neural network architecture. The output of the network is known as a **segmentation mask**.

Object detection algorithm

Just like the image classification algorithm, the main goal of the object detection algorithm is also self-explanatory: it detects and classifies objects in images. It uses a supervised approach to train a deep neural network.

During the inference process, this algorithm returns the identified objects and a score of confidence regarding the prediction. The object detection algorithm uses a **Single Shot MultiBox Detector (SSD)** and supports two types of network architecture: **VGG** and **ResNet**.

Summary

That was such a journey! Let's take a moment to highlight what we have just learned. We broke this chapter into four main sections: supervised learning, unsupervised learning, textual analysis, and image processing. Everything that we have learned fits those subfields of machine learning.

The list of supervised learning algorithms that we have studied includes the following:

- Linear learner algorithm
- Factorization machines algorithm
- XGBoost algorithm
- K-Nearest Neighbors algorithm
- Object2Vec algorithm
- DeepAR forecasting algorithm

Remember that you can use linear learner, factorization machines, XGBoost, and KNN for multiple purposes, including to solve regression and classification problems. Linear learner is probably the simplest algorithm out of these four; factorization machines extend linear learner and are good for sparse datasets, XGBoost uses an ensemble method based on decision trees, and KNN is an index-based algorithm.

The other two algorithms, Object2Vec and DeepAR, are used for specific purposes. Object2Vec is used to create vector representations of the data, while DeepAR is used to create forecast models.

The list of unsupervised learning algorithms that we have studied includes the following:

- K-means algorithm
- **Principal Component Analysis (PCA)**
- IP Insights
- **Random Cut Forest (RCF)** algorithm

K-means is a very popular algorithm that's used for clustering. PCA is used for dimensionality reduction, IP Insights is used for pattern recognition, and RCF is used for anomaly detection.

We then looked at regression models and K-means in more detail. We did this because, as a data scientist, we think you should at least master these two very popular algorithms so that you can go deeper into other algorithms by yourself.

Then, we moved on to the second half of this chapter, where we talked about textual analysis and the following algorithms:

- Blazing Text algorithm
- Sequence-to-sequence algorithm
- **Latent Dirichlet Allocation (LDA)** algorithm
- **Neural Topic Model (NTM)** algorithm

Finally, we talked about image processing and looked at the following:

- Image classification algorithm
- Semantic segmentation algorithm
- Object detection algorithm

Since this is a very important chapter regarding the AWS machine learning specialty exam, we encourage you to jump onto the AWS website and search for machine learning algorithms. There, you will find the most recent information about the algorithms that we have just covered.

That brings us to the end of this quick refresher and the end of this chapter. In the next chapter, we will have a look at the existing mechanisms provided by AWS that we can use to optimize these algorithms.

Questions

1. You are working as a lead data scientist for a retail company. Your team is building a regression model and using the linear learner built-in algorithm to predict the optimal price of a particular product. The model is clearly overfitting to the training data and you suspect that this is due to the excessive number of variables being used. Which of the following approaches would best suit a solution that addresses your suspicion?

   a) Implementing a cross-validation process to reduce overfitting during the training process.

   b) Applying L1 regularization and changing the wd hyperparameter of the linear learner algorithm.

   c) Applying L2 regularization and changing the wd hyperparameter of the linear learner algorithm.

   d) Applying L1 and L2 regularization.

   > **Answers**
   >
   > C, This question prompts about to the problem of overfitting due an excessive number of features being used. L2 regularization, which is available in linear learner through the wd hyperparameter, will work as a feature selector. Some less important features will be penalized by receiving very low weights, which will, in practical terms, eliminate the variable.

2. RecordIO-protobuf is an optimized data format that's used to train AWS, built-in algorithms, where SageMaker converts each observation in the dataset into a binary representation as a set of 4-byte floats. RecordIO-protobuf can operate in two modes: pipe and file mode. What is the difference between them?

   a) Pipe mode accepts encryption at rest, while file mode does not.

   b) In pipe mode, the data will be streamed directly from S3, which helps optimize storage. In file mode, the data is copied from S3 to the training instance's store volume.

   c) In pipe mode, the data is copied from S3 to the training instance store volume. In file mode, the data will be streamed directly from S3, which helps optimize storage.

   d) In pipe mode, the data will be streamed directly from S3, which helps optimize storage. In file mode, the data is copied from S3 to another temporary S3 bucket.

> **Answers**
> B, Remember that RecordIO-protobuf has a pipe mode, which allows us to stream data directly from S3.

3. You are the cloud administrator of your company. You have done great work creating and managing user access and you have fine-grained control of daily activities in the cloud. However, you want to add an extra layer of security by identifying accounts that are attempting to create cloud resources from an unusual IP address. What would be the fastest solution to address this use case (choose all the correct answers)?

   a) Create an IP Insights model to identity anomalous accesses.

   b) Create a clustering model to identify anomalies in the application connections.

   c) Integrate your IP Insights with existing rules from Amazon Guard Duty.

   d) Integrate your anomaly detection model with existing rules from Amazon Guard Duty.

> **Answers**
> A,C, Remember: You can always come up with different approaches to solve problems. However, taking advantage of SageMaker's built-in algorithms is usually the fastest way to do things.

4. You are working as a data scientist for a large company. One of your internal clients has requested that you improve a regression model that they have implemented in production. You have added a few features to the model and now you want to know if the model's performance has improved due to this change. Which of the following options best describes the evaluation metrics that you should use to evaluate your change?

   a) Check if the R squared of the new model is better than the R squared of the current model in production.

   b) Check if the R squared adjusted of the new model is better than the R squared of the current model in production.

   c) Check if the R squared and the RMSE of the new model are better than the R squared of the current model in production.

   d) Check if the R squared adjusted RMSE of the new model is better than the R squared of the current model in production.

Answers

D, In this case, you have been exposed to a particular behavior of regression model evaluation, where, by adding new features, you will always increase R squared. You should use R squared adjusted to understand if the new features are adding value to the model or not. Additionally, RMSE will give you a business perspective of the model's performance. Although option b is correct, option d best describes the optimal decision you should make.

5. Which of the following algorithms is optimized to work with sparse data?

a) Factorization machines

b) XGBoost

c) Linear Learner

d) KNN

Answers

A, Factorization machines is a general-purpose algorithm that is optimized for sparse data.

6. Which of the following algorithms uses an ensemble method based on decision trees during the training process?

a) Factorization machines

b) XGBoost

c) Linear learner

d) KNN

Answers

B, XGBoost is a very popular algorithm that uses an ensemble of decision trees to train the model. XGBoost uses a boosting approach, where decision trees try to correct the error of the prior model.

7. Which of the following options is considered an index-based algorithm?

a) Factorization machines

b) XGBoost

c) Linear learner

d) KNN

> **Answers**
>
> D, We say that KNN is an index-based algorithm because it has to compute distances between points, assign indexes for these points, and then store the sorted distances and their indexes. With that type of data structure, KNN can easily select the top K closest points to make the final prediction.

8. You are a data scientist in a big retail company that wants to predict their sales per region on a monthly basis. You have done some exploratory work and discovered that the sales pattern per region is different. Your team has decided to approach this project as a time series model, and now, you have to select the best approach to create a solution. Which of the following options would potentially give you a good solution with the least effort?

    a) Approach this problem using the ARIMA algorithm. Since each region might have different sales behavior, you would have to create one independent model per region.

    b) Approach this problem with the RNN algorithm. Since neural networks are robust, you could create one single model to predict sales in any region.

    c) Develop a DeepAR model and set the region, associated with each time series, as a vector of static categorical features. You can use the **cat** field to set up this option.

    d) Develop a DeepAR model and set the region, associated with each time series, as a vector of static categorical features. You can use the **dynamic_feat** field to set this option.

> **Answers**
>
> C, Options a and c are potentially right. However, the problem states that we want the solution with the least effort. In this case, setting up a DeepAR model and separating the time series by region would be the expected solution (option c). We can set up that type of configuration by passing a vector of static categorical features into the cat field of the DeepAR class model.

9. You are working on a dataset that contains nine numerical variables. You want to create a scatter plot to see if those variables could be potentially grouped on clusters of high similarity. How could you achieve this goal?

a) Execute the K-means algorithm.

b) Compute the two **principal components (PCs)** using PCA. Then, plot PC1 and PC2 in the scatter plot.

c) Execute the KNN algorithm.

d) Compute the three **principal components (PCs)** using PCA. Then, plot PC1, PC2, and PC3 in the scatter plot.

> **Answers**
> B, Using K-means or KNN will not solve this question. You have to apply PCA to reduce the number of features and then plot the results in a scatter plot. Since scatter plots only accept two variables, option b is the right one.

10. How should you preprocess your data in order to train a Blazing Text model on top of 100 text files?

a) You should create a text file with space-separated tokens. Each line of the file must contain a single sentence. If you have multiple files for training, you should concatenate all of them into a single one.

b) You should create a text file with space-separated tokens. Each line of the file must contain a single sentence. If you have multiple files for training, you should apply the same transformation to each one.

c) You should create a text file with comma-separated tokens. Each line of the file must contain a single sentence. If you have multiple files for training, you should concatenate all of them into a single one.

d) You should create a text file with comma-separated tokens. Each line of the file must contain a single sentence. If you have multiple files for training, you should apply the same transformation to each one.

> **Answers**
> Option a is the right one. You should provide just a single file to Blazing Text with space-separated tokens, where each line of the file must contain a single sentence.

8

Evaluating and Optimizing Models

It is now time to learn how to evaluate and optimize machine learning models. During the process of modeling, or even after model completion, you might want to understand how your model is performing. Each type of model has its own set of metrics that can be used to evaluate performance, and that is what we are going to study in this chapter.

Apart from model evaluation, as a data scientist, you might also need to improve your model's performance by tuning the hyperparameters of your algorithm. We will take a look at some nuances of this modeling task.

In this chapter, we will cover the following topics:

- Introducing model evaluation
- Evaluating classification models
- Evaluating regression models
- Model optimization

Alright, let's do it!

Introducing model evaluation

There are several different scenarios in which we might want to evaluate model performance, some of them are as follows.

- You are creating a model and testing different approaches and/or algorithms. Therefore, you need to compare these models to select the best one.

- You have just completed your model and you need to document your work, which includes specifying the model's performance metrics that you have reached out to during the modeling phase.

- Your model is running in a production environment and you need to track its performance. If you encounter model drift, then you might want to retrain the model.

> **Important note**
>
> The term **model drift** is used to refer to the problem of model deterioration. When you are building a machine learning model, you must use data to train the algorithm. This set of data is known as training data, and it reflects the business rules at a particular point in time. If these business rules change over time, your model will probably fail to adapt to that change. This is because it was trained on top of another dataset, which was reflecting another business scenario. To solve this problem, you must retrain the model so that it can consider the rules of the new business scenario. Reinforcement learning systems might not suffer from this issue since they can adapt to the new data by themselves.

We perform model evaluations by designing a testing approach. We have learned about holdout validation and cross-validation before. However, both testing approaches share the same requirement: they need a metric in order to evaluate performance.

This metric is specific to the problem domain, for example, there are specific metrics for regression models, classification models, clustering, natural language processing, and more. Therefore, during the design of your testing approach, you have to consider what type of model you are building in order to define the evaluation metrics.

In the following sections, we will take a look at the most important metrics and concepts that you should know to evaluate your models.

Evaluating classification models

Classification models are one of the most traditional classes of problems that you might face, either during the exam or during your journey as a data scientist. A very important artifact that you might want to generate during the classification model evaluation is known as a **confusion matrix**.

A confusion matrix compares your model predictions against the real values of each class under evaluation. *Figure 8.1* shows what a confusion matrix looks like in a binary classification problem:

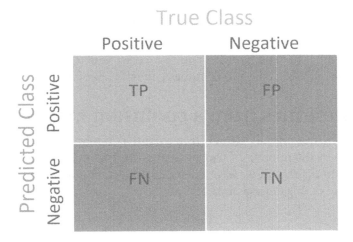

Figure 8.1 – A confusion matrix

We find the following components in a confusion matrix:

- **TP**: This is the number of **True Positive** cases. Here, we have to count the number of cases that have been predicted as true and are, indeed, true. For example, in a fraud detection system, this would be the number of fraudulent transactions that were correctly predicted as fraud.

- **TN**: This is the number of **True Negative** cases. Here, we have to count the number of cases that have been predicted as false and are, indeed, false. For example, in a fraud detection system, this would be the number of non-fraudulent transactions that were correctly predicted as not fraud.

- **FN**: This is the number of **False Negative** cases. Here, we have to count the number of cases that have been predicted as false but are, instead, true. For example, in a fraud detection system, this would be the number of fraudulent transactions that were wrongly predicted as not fraud.

- **FP**: This is the number of **False Positive** cases. Here, we have to count the number of cases that have been predicted as true but are, instead, false. For example, in a fraud detection system, this would be the number of non-fraudulent transactions that were wrongly predicted as fraud.

In a perfect scenario, your confusion matrix will have only true positive and true negative cases, which means that your model has an accuracy of 100%. In practical terms, if that type of scenario occurs, you should be skeptical instead of happy since it is expected that your model will contain errors. If your model does not contain errors, you are likely to be suffering from overfitting issues, so be careful.

Once false negatives and false positives are expected, the most that you can do is to prioritize one of them. For example, you can reduce the number of false negatives by increasing the number of false positives and vice versa. This is known as the precision versus recall trade-off. Let's take a look at these metrics next.

Extracting metrics from a confusion matrix

The simplest metric that we can extract from a confusion matrix is known as **accuracy**. Accuracy is given by the number of true positives plus true negatives over the total number of cases. In *Figure 8.2*, we have filled out all the components of the confusion matrix for the sake of this demonstration:

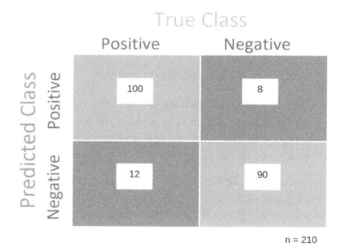

Figure 8.2 – A confusion matrix filled with some examples

According to *Figure 8.2*, the accuracy would be (100 + 90) / 210, which is equal to 0.90. There is a common issue that occurs when utilizing an accuracy metric, which is related to the balance of each class. Problems with highly imbalanced classes, such as 99% of positive cases and 1% of negative cases, will impact the accuracy score and make it useless.

For example, if your training data has 99% of positive cases (the majority class), your model is likely to correctly classify most of the positive cases but go badly in the classification of negative cases (the minority class). The accuracy will be very high (due to the correctness of the classification of the positive cases), regardless of the bad results in the minority class classification.

The point is that on highly imbalanced problems, we usually have more interest in correctly classifying the minority class, not the majority class. That's the case on most fraud detection systems, for example, where the minority class corresponds to fraudulent cases. For imbalanced problems, you should look for other types of metrics, which we will cover next.

Another important metric that we can extract from a confusion matrix is known as **recall**, which is the number of true positives over the number of true positives plus false negatives. In other words, recall is given by the number of true positive and overall positive cases. Recall is also known as **sensitivity**.

According to *Figure 8.2*, recall is given by 100 / 112, which is equal to 0.89. **Precision**, on the other hand, is given by the number of true positives over the number of true positives plus false positives. In other words, precision is given by the number of true positive and overall predicted positive cases. Precision is also known as **positive predictive power**.

According to *Figure 8.2*, precision is given by 100 / 108, which is equal to 0.93. In general, we can increase precision by the cost of decrease recall and vice versa. There is another model evaluation artifact in which we can play around with this precision versus recall trade-off. It is known as a **precision-recall curve**.

Precision-recall curves summarize the precision versus recall trade-off by using different probability thresholds. For example, the default threshold is 0.5, where any prediction above 0.5 will be considered as true; otherwise, it is false. You can change the default threshold according to your need so that you can prioritize recall or precision. *Figure 8.3* shows an example of a precision-recall curve:

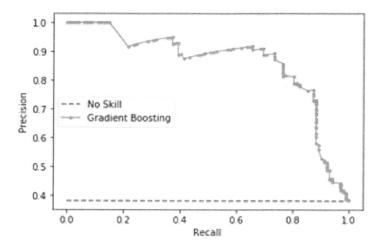

Figure 8.3 – A precision-recall curve

As you can see in *Figure 8.3*, increasing the precision will reduce the amount of recall and vice versa. *Figure 8.3* shows the precision/recall for each threshold for a gradient boosting model (as shown by the orange line) compared to a no-skill model (as shown by the blue dashed line). A perfect model will approximate the curve to the point (1,1), forming a squared corner in the top right-hand side of the chart.

Another visual analysis we can do on top of confusion matrixes is known as a **Receiver Operating Characteristic** (**ROC**) curve. ROC curves summarize the trade-off between the **true positive rate** and the **false positive rate** according to different thresholds, as in the precision-recall curve.

You already know about the true positive rate, or sensitivity, which is the same as what we have just learned in the precision-recall curve. The other dimension of an ROC curve is the **false positive rate**, which is the number of false positives over the number of false positives plus true negatives.

In literature, you might find the false positive rate referred to as inverted **specificity**, represented by *1 – specificity*. Specificity is given as the number of true negatives over the number of true negatives plus false positives. Furthermore, false-positive rates or inverted specificity are the same. *Figure 8.4* shows what an ROC curve looks like:

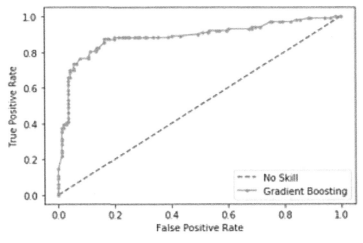

Figure 8.4 – An ROC curve

A perfect model will approximate the curve to the point (0,1), forming a squared corner in the top left-hand side of the chart. The orange line represents the trade-off between the true positive rate and the false positive rate of a gradient boosting classifier. The dashed blue line represents a no-skill model, which cannot predict the classes properly.

To summarize, you can use ROC curves for fairly balanced datasets and precision-recall curves for moderate to imbalanced datasets.

Summarizing precision and recall

Sometimes, we might want to use a metric that summarizes precision and recall, instead of prioritizing one over the other. Two very popular metrics can be used to summarize precision and recall: **F1 score** and **Area Under Curve** (**AUC**).

The F1 score, also known as **F-measure**, computes the harmonic mean of precision and recall. AUC summarizes the approximation of the area under the precision-recall curve.

That brings us to the end of this section on classification metrics. Let's now take a look at the evaluation metrics for regression models.

Evaluating regression models

Regression models are quite different from classification models since the outcome of the model is a continuous number. Therefore, the metrics around regression models aim to monitor the difference between real and predicted values.

The simplest way to check the difference between a predicted value (*yhat*) and its actual value (*y*) is by performing a simple subtraction operation, where the error will be equal to the absolute value of *yhat* − *y*. This metric is known as the **Mean Absolute Error** (**MAE**).

Since we usually have to evaluate the error of each prediction, *i*, we have to take the mean value of the errors. The following formula shows how this error can be formally defined:

$$MAE = \frac{1}{N} \sum_{i=1}^{N} |y_i - \hat{y}_i|$$

Sometimes, you might want to penalize bigger errors over smaller errors. To achieve this, you can use another metric, which is known as the **Mean Squared Error** (**MSE**). MSE will square each error and return the mean value.

By squaring errors, MSE will penalize the bigger ones. The following formula shows how MSE can be formally defined:

$$\mathrm{MSE} = \underbrace{\frac{1}{n} \sum_{i=1}}_{\text{test set}} \underbrace{(y_i}_{\text{predicted vaue}} - \underbrace{\hat{y}_i)^2}_{\text{actual value}}$$

There is a potential interpretation problem with MSE. Since it has to compute the squared error, it might be difficult to interpret the final results from a business perspective. The **Root Mean Squared Error** (**RMSE**) works around this interpretation issue, by taking the square root of MSE. Here is the RMSE equation:

$$RMSE = \sqrt{\sum_{i=1}^{n} \frac{(\hat{y}_i - y_i)^2}{n}}$$

RMSE is probably the most used metric for regression models since it can either penalize bigger errors, yet still be easily interpreted.

Exploring other regression metrics

There are many more metrics that are suitable for regression problems aside from the ones that we have just learned. We will not be able to cover most of them here, but there are a few more metrics that might be important for you to know.

One of these metrics is known as the **Mean Absolute Percentage Error (MAPE)**. As the name suggests, MAPE will compute the absolute percentage error of each prediction and then take the average value. The following formula shows how this metric is computed:

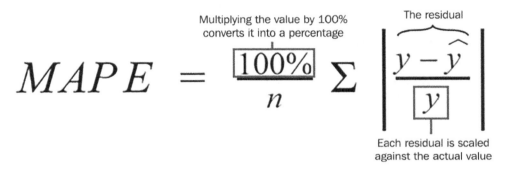

MAPE is broadly used on forecasting models since it is very simple to interpret, and it provides a very good sense of how far (or close) the predictions are from the actual values (in terms of a percentage).

We have now completed this section on regression metrics. Next, we will talk about model optimizations.

Model optimization

As you know, understanding evaluation metrics is very important in order to measure your model's performance and document your work. In the same way, when we want to optimize our current models, evaluating metrics also plays a very important role in defining the baseline performance that we want to challenge.

The process of model optimization consists of finding the best configuration (also known as hyperparameters) of the machine learning algorithm for a particular data distribution. We don't want to find hyperparameters that overfit the training data in the same way that we don't want to find hyperparameters that underfit the training data.

You learned about overfitting and underfitting in *Chapter 1*, *Machine Learning Fundamentals*. In the same chapter, you also learned how to avoid these two types of modeling issues.

In this section, we will learn about some techniques that you can use to find the best configuration for a particular algorithm and dataset. You can combine these techniques of model optimization with other methods, such as cross-validation, to find the best set of hyperparameters for your model and avoid fitting issues.

> **Important note**
>
> Always remember that you don't want to optimize your algorithm to the underlying training data but to the data distribution behind the training data. This is so that your model will work in the training data as well as in the production data (that is, the data that has never been exposed to your model during the training process). A machine learning model that works only in the training data is useless. That's why combining model-tuning techniques (such as the ones we will learn about next) with sampling techniques (such as cross-validation) makes all the difference when it comes to creating a good model.

Grid search

Grid search is probably the most popular method for model optimization. It consists of testing different combinations of the algorithm and selecting the best one. Here, we have two important points that we need to pay attention to:

- How to define the best one?

- How many combinations should we test?

The best model is defined based on an evaluation metric. In other words, you have to first define which metric you are going to use to evaluate the model's performance. Secondly, you have to define how you are going to evaluate the model. Usually, we use cross-validation to evaluate the model on multiple datasets that have never been used for training.

In terms of the number of combinations, this is the most challenging part when playing with grid search. Each hyperparameter of an algorithm may have multiple or, sometimes, infinite possibilities of values. If you consider that an algorithm will usually have multiple hyperparameters, this becomes a function with quadratic cost, where the number of unique combinations to test (also known as a model for testing) is given as *the number of values of hyperparameter a * the number of values of hyperparameter b * the number of values of hyperparameter i*. *Figure 8.5* shows how you could potentially set a grid search configuration for a decision tree model:

Criterion	Max depth	Min samples leaf
Gini, Entropy	2, 5, 10	10, 20, 30

Figure 8.5 – Grid search configuration

In *Figure 8.5*, there are three hyperparameters: **Criterion**, **Max depth**, and **Min samples leaf**. Each of these hyperparameters has a list of values for testing: 2, 3, and 3 values, respectively. That means, by the end of the grid search process, we will have tested 18 models (2 * 3 * 3), where only the best one will be selected.

As you might have noticed, all the different combinations of those three hyperparameters will be tested, for example, consider the following:

- Criterion = Gini, Max depth = 2, Min samples leaf = 10

- Criterion = Gini, Max depth = 5, Min samples leaf = 10

- Criterion = Gini, Max depth = 10, Min samples leaf = 10

Other questions that you might be wondering could include the following:

- Considering that a particular algorithm might have several hyperparameters, which ones should I tune?

- Considering that a particular hyperparameter might accept infinite values, which values should I test?

These are good questions and grid search will not give you a straight answer for them. Instead, this is closer to an empirical process, where you have to test as much as you need to achieve your target performance.

> **Important note**
> Of course, grid search cannot guarantee that you will come up with your target performance. That depends on the algorithm and the training data.

A common practice, though, is to define the values for testing by using a **linear space** or **log space**, where you can manually set the limits of the hyperparameter you want to test and the number of values for testing. Then, the intermediate values will be drawn by a linear or log function.

As you might imagine, grid search can take a long time to run. A number of alternative methods have been proposed to work around this time issue. **Random search** is one of them, where the list of values for testing is randomly selected from the search space.

Another method that has gained rapid adoption across the industry is known as **Bayesian optimization**. Algorithm optimizations, such as **gradient descent**, try to find what is called the **global minima**, by calculating derivatives of the cost function. Global minima are the points where you find the algorithm configuration with the least associated cost.

Bayesian optimization is useful when calculating derivatives is not an option. So, we can use the **Bayes theorem**, a probabilistic approach, to find the global minima using the smallest number of steps.

In practical terms, Bayesian optimization will start testing the entire search space to find the most promising set of optimal hyperparameters. Then, it will perform more tests specifically in the place where the global minima are likely to be.

Summary

In this chapter, you learned about the main metrics for model evaluation. We first started with the metrics for classification problems and then we moved on to the metrics for regression problems.

In terms of classification metrics, you have been introduced to the well-known confusion matrix, which is probably the most important artifact to perform a model evaluation on classification models.

Aside from knowing what true positive, true negative, false positive, and false negative are, we have learned how to combine these components to extract other metrics, such as accuracy, precision, recall, the F1 score, and AUC.

We went even deeper and learned about ROC curves, as well as precision-recall curves. We learned that we can use ROC curves to evaluate fairly balanced datasets and precision-recall curves for moderate to imbalanced datasets.

By the way, when you are dealing with imbalanced datasets, remember that using accuracy might not be a good idea.

In terms of regression metrics, we learned that the most popular ones, and the most likely to be present in the *AWS Machine Learning Specialty* exam, are MAE, MSE, RMSE, and MAPE. Make sure you know the basics of each of them before taking the exam.

Finally, you learned about methods for hyperparameter optimization, where grid search and Bayesian optimization are the primary ones. In the next chapter, we will take a look at SageMaker and learn how it can be used for modeling. But first, let's take a moment to practice these questions on model evaluation and model optimization.

Questions

1. You are working as a data scientist for a pharmaceutical company. You are collaborating with other teammates to create a machine learning model to classify certain types of diseases on image exams. The company wants to prioritize the assertiveness rate of positive cases, even if they have to wrongly return false negatives. Which type of metric would you use to optimize the underlying model?

   a. Recall

   b. Precision

   c. R-squared

   d. RMSE

   Answer
   In this scenario, the company prefers to have a higher probability to be right on positive outcomes at the cost of wrongly classifying some positive cases as negative. Technically, they prefer to increase precision at the cost of reducing recall.

2. You are working as a data scientist for a pharmaceutical company. You are collaborating with other teammates to create a machine learning model to classify certain types of diseases on image exams. The company wants to prioritize the capture of positive cases, even if they have to wrongly return false positives. Which type of metric would you use to optimize the underlying model?

   a. Recall

   b. Precision

   c. R-squared

   d. RMSE

   Answer
   In this scenario, the company prefers to find most of the positive cases at the cost of wrongly classifying some negative cases as positive. Technically, they prefer to increase recall at the cost of reducing precision.

3. You are working in a fraud identification system, where one of the components is a classification model. You want to check the model's performance. Which of the following metrics could be used and why?

    a. Accuracy. Since fraudulent system datasets are naturally unbalanced, this metric is good to take into consideration the assertiveness of both positive and negative classes.

    b. Precision. Since fraudulent system datasets are naturally unbalanced, this metric is good to take into consideration the assertiveness of both positive and negative classes.

    c. Recall. Since fraudulent system datasets are naturally unbalanced, this metric is good to take into consideration the assertiveness of both positive and negative classes.

    d. The F1 score. Since fraudulent system datasets are naturally unbalanced, this metric is good to take into consideration the assertiveness of both positive and negative classes.

    > **Answer**
    >
    > Option "d" is the only one that matches the explanation of the proposed metric and provides a valid measure to the problem. Accuracy cannot be used in this problem due to the unbalanced issue. Precision and recall could be potentially used together to provide a quality view of the problem, but there is no such option in the list of answers.

4. You are building a machine learning model to predict house prices. You have approached the problem as a regression model. Which of the following metrics are not applicable for regression models? (Select all correct answers.)

    a. Recall

    b. Precision

    c. MAPE

    d. RMSE

    > **Answer**
    >
    > Recall and precision are applicable for classification problems; that's why they are the correct answers. On the other hand, MAPE and RMSE are applicable for regression models.

5. Which of the following metrics help us to penalize bigger errors on regression models?

   a. Recall

   b. Precision

   c. MAPE

   d. RMSE

   > **Answer**
   >
   > RMSE computes the squared error of each prediction. Then, it takes the squared root of the MSE. By computing the squared error, RMSE will penalize bigger errors over smaller errors.

6. You are working as a data scientist for a financial services company and you have created a regression model to predict credit utilization. If you decide to include more features in the model, what will happen to R-squared and Adjusted R-squared?

   a. Adjusted R-squared will increase, whereas R-squared can either increase or decrease.

   b. R-squared will decrease, whereas Adjusted R-squared can either increase or decrease.

   c. R-squared will increase, whereas Adjusted R-squared can either increase or decrease.

   d. Adjusted R-squared will decrease, whereas R-squared can either increase or decrease.

   > **Answer**
   >
   > R-squared will increase since the extra information will help the model to capture more variance in the data. However, Adjusted R-squared can either increase or decrease, depending on the gain of adding the extra variable.

7. Which of the following metrics will compute the percentage of errors instead of absolute errors?

    a. Recall

    b. Precision

    c. MAPE

    d. RMSE

    > **Answer**
    > MAPE is applicable for regression models and it will compute the error as a percentage number.

8. You are the lead data scientist of the company. Your team wants to optimize a model that is no longer performing well in production. The team has decided to use grid search to retrain the hyperparameters; however, the process is taking a long time and does not complete. Which approach could you take to speed up the process of tuning and still maximize your chances of finding a better model?

    a) Reduce the search space to speed up the training process.

    b) Use Bayesian optimization instead of grid search.

    c) Increase the search space to speed up the training process.

    d) None of the above.

    > **Answer**
    > Reducing the search space of grid search will help to speed up the process of tuning, but you will test fewer models. This will reduce your chances of finding the best model for the problem. Increasing the search space will increase the time for tuning. Option "b" is the most resealable one since Bayesian optimization can focus on the most important search space, potentially reducing the time for processing and increasing your chances of finding the best model.

9. You are using grid search to tune a machine learning model. During the tuning process, you obtain good performance metrics. However, when you execute the model in production, the model performance is not acceptable. You have to troubleshoot the problem. Which of the following options are valid reasons for this issue? (Select all correct answers.)

   a) You are tuning and evaluating the model in the training data, which is causing overfitting.

   b) The production data does not have the same distribution as the training data.

   c) You are not using cross-validation in the training process.

   d) You are not tuning the right hyperparameters.

   > **Answer**
   > You can't tune and test the model in the same dataset at the risk of overfitting it. That's why option "a" is correct. If the production data does not follow the same distribution of the training data, the model will not work, so option "b" is also correct. Option "c" is not valid because cross-validation is not mandatory for model evaluation. Option "d" would be correct if you find bad results in the training data, not in the production data.

10. You are working for a global financial company. Your team has created a binary classification model to identify fraudulent transactions. The model has been put into production and is automatically flagging fraudulent transactions and sending them for further screening. The operation team is complaining that this model is blocking too many transactions and they would prefer to flag a smaller number of transactions. According to the preceding scenario, what is the expectation of the operation team?

   a) They want to calibrate the model threshold at 0.5.

   b) They want to prioritize precision over recall.

   b) They want to prioritize recall over precision.

   b) They want to use F-measure.

Answer

We always have to match model usage with business goals and capacity. In this scenario, the model is flagging a lot of potentially fraudulent transactions, but there isn't a big enough human workforce to evaluate all of those blocked transactions. Furthermore, what makes more sense is "calibrating" the model to the real business scenario, where it will flag fewer (but more likely) fraudulent cases for further screening.

9

Amazon SageMaker Modeling

In the previous chapter, we learned several methods of model optimization and evaluation techniques. We also learned various ways of storing data, processing data, and applying different statistical approaches to data. So, how can we now build a pipeline for this? Well, we can read data, process data, and build machine learning models on the processed data. But what if my first machine learning model does not perform well? Can I fine-tune my model? The answer is *Yes*; you can perform nearly everything using Amazon SageMaker. In this chapter, we will walk you through the following topics using Amazon SageMaker:

- Understanding different instances of Amazon SageMaker
- Cleaning and preparing data in Jupyter Notebook in Amazon SageMaker
- Model training in Amazon SageMaker
- Using SageMaker's built-in machine learning algorithms
- Writing custom training and inference code in SageMaker

Technical requirements

You can download the data used in this chapter's examples from GitHub at `https://github.com/PacktPublishing/AWS-Certified-Machine-Learning-Specialty-MLS-C01-Certification-Guide/tree/master/Chapter-9`.

Creating notebooks in Amazon SageMaker

If you're working with machine learning, then you need to perform actions such as storing data, processing data, preparing data for model training, model training, and deploying the model for inference. They are not easy, and each of these stages requires a machine to perform the task. With Amazon SageMaker, life becomes much easier when carrying out these steps.

What is Amazon SageMaker?

SageMaker provides training instances to train a model using the data and provides endpoint instances to infer by using the model. It also provides notebook instances, running Jupyter Notebooks, to clean and understand the data. If you're happy with your cleaning process, then you should store them in S3 as part of the staging for training. You can launch training instances to consume this training data and produce a machine learning model. The machine learning model can be stored in S3, and endpoint instances can consume the model to produce results for end users.

If you draw this in a block diagram, then it will look similar to *Figure 9.1*:

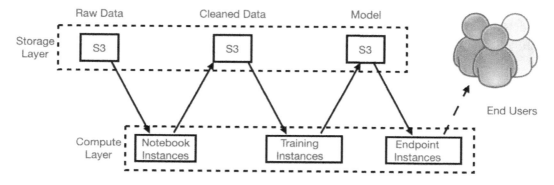

Figure 9.1 – A pictorial representation of the different layers of the Amazon SageMaker instances

Now, let's take a look at the Amazon SageMaker console and get a better feel for it. Once you log in to your AWS account and go to Amazon SageMaker, you will see something similar to *Figure 9.2*:

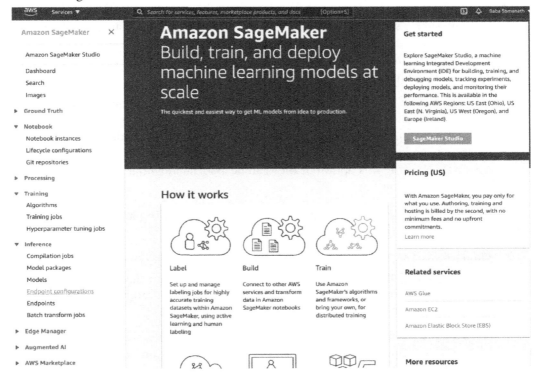

Figure 9.2 – A quick look at the SageMaker console

There are three different sections, including **Notebook**, **Training**, and **Inference**, which have been expanded in *Figure 9.2* so that we can dive in and understand them better.

Notebook has three different options that you can use:

- **Notebook instances**: This helps us to create, open, start, and stop notebook instances. These instances are responsible for running Jupyter Notebooks. They allow us to choose the instance type based on the workload of the use case. The best practice is to use a notebook instance to orchestrate the data pipeline for processing a large dataset. For example, making a call from a notebook instance to AWS Glue for ETL services or Amazon EMR to run Spark applications. If you're asked to create a secured notebook instance outside AWS, then you need to take care of endpoint security, network security, launching the machine, managing storage on it, and managing Jupyter Notebook applications running on the instance. The user does not need to manage any of these with SageMaker.

- **Lifecycle configurations**: This is useful when there is a use case that requires a different library, which is not available in the notebook instances. To install the library, the user will do either a `pip install` or a `conda install`. However, as soon as the notebook instance is terminated, the customization will be lost. To avoid such a scenario, you can customize your notebook instance through a script provided through **Lifecycle configurations**. You can choose any of the environments present in `/home/ec2-user/anaconda3/envs/` and customize the specific environment as required.

- **Git repositories**: AWS CodeCommit, GitHub, or any other Git server can be associated with the notebook instance for the persistence of your notebooks. If access is given, then the same notebook can be used by other developers to collaborate and save in a source control fashion. Git repositories can either be added separately by using this option or they can be associated with a notebook instance during the creation.

As you can see in *Figure 9.2*, **Training** offers **Algorithms**, **Training jobs**, and **Hyperparameter tuning jobs**. Let's understand their usage:

- **Algorithms**: This is the first step toward deciding on an algorithm that we are going to run on our cleaned data. You can either choose a custom algorithm or create a custom algorithm based on the use case. Otherwise, you can run SageMaker algorithms on the cleaned data.

- **Training jobs**: You can create training jobs from a notebook instance via API calls. You can set the number of instances, input the data source details, perform checkpoint configuration, and output data configuration. Amazon SageMaker manages the training instances and stores the model artifacts as output in the specified location. Both incremental training (that is, to train the model from time to time for better results) and managed spot training (that is, to reduce costs) can also be achieved.

- **Hyperparameter tuning jobs**: Usually, hyperparameters are set for an algorithm prior to the training process. During the training process, we let the algorithm figure out the best values for these parameters. With hyperparameter tuning, we obtain the best model that has the best value of hyperparameters. This can be done through a console or via API calls. The same can be orchestrated from a notebook instance too.

Inference has many offerings and is evolving every day:

- **Compilation jobs**: If your model is trained using a machine learning framework such as Keras, MXNet, ONNX, PyTorch, TFLite, TensorFlow, or XGBoost, and your model artifacts are available on a S3 bucket, then you can choose either **Target device** or **Target platform**. Target device is used to deploy your model, such as an AWS SageMaker machine learning instance or an AWS IoT Greengrass device. Target platform is used to decide the operating system, architecture, and accelerator on which you want your model to run. You can also store the compiled module in your S3 bucket for future use. This essentially helps you in cross-platform model deployment.

- **Model packages**: These are used to create deployable SageMaker models. You can create your own algorithm, package it using the model package APIs, and publish it to AWS Marketplace.

- **Models**: Models are created using model artifacts. They are similar to mathematical equations with variables; that is, you input the values for the variables and get an output. These models are stored in S3 and will be used for inference by the endpoints.

- **Endpoint configurations**: Amazon SageMaker allows you to deploy multiple weighted models to a single endpoint. This means you can route a specific number of requests to one endpoint. *What does this mean?* Well, let's say you have one model in use. You want to replace it with a newer model. However, you cannot simply remove the first model that is already in use. In this scenario, you can use the `VariantWeight` API to make the endpoints serve 80% of the request with the older model and 20% of the request with the new model. This is the most common production scenario where the data changes rapidly and the model needs to be trained and tuned periodically. Another possible use case is to test the model results with live data, then a certain percentage of the requests can be routed to the new model, and the results can be monitored to testify the accuracy of the model on real-time unseen data.

- **Endpoints**: These are used to create an URL to which the model is exposed and can be requested to give the model results as a response.

- **Batch transform jobs**: If the use case demands that you infer results on several million records, then instead of individual inference jobs, you can run batch transform jobs on the unseen data. Note that there can be some confusion when you receive thousands of results from your model after parsing thousands of pieces of unseen data as a batch. To overcome this confusion, `InputFilter`, `JoinSource`, `OutputFilter` APIs can be used to associate input records with output results.

Now, we have got an overview of Amazon SageMaker. Let's put our knowledge to work in the next section.

> **Important note**
> The Amazon SageMaker console keeps changing. There's a possibility that when you're reading this book, the console might look different.

Getting hands-on with Amazon SageMaker notebook instances

The very first step, in this section, is to create a Jupyter Notebook, and this requires a notebook instance. Let's start by creating a notebook instance, as follows:

1. Sign in to your AWS account.

2. Navigate to **Services** > **Amazon SageMaker**.

3. In the left navigation pane, click on **Notebook instances** and then click on the **Create notebook instance** button.

4. Provide a **Notebook instance name** such as notebookinstance and leave the **Notebook instance type** to its default ml.t2.medium setting. In the **Permissions and encryption** section, select Create a new role in **IAM role**. You will be asked to specify the bucket name. For the purpose of this example, it's chosen as any bucket.

5. Following the successful creation of a role, you should see something similar to *Figure 9.3*:

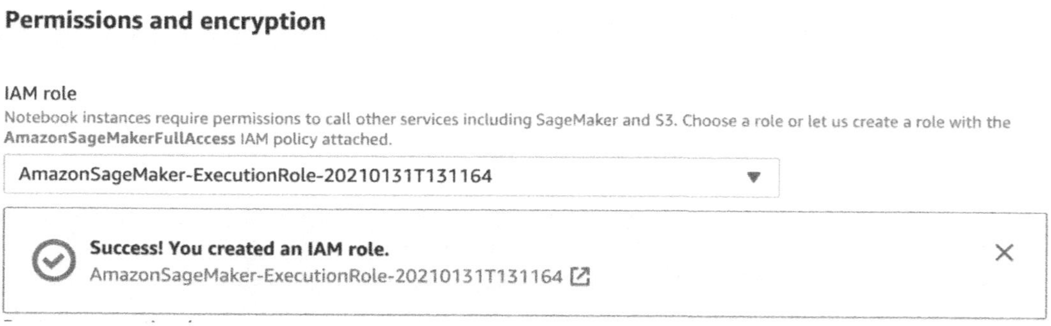

Permissions and encryption

IAM role
Notebook instances require permissions to call other services including SageMaker and S3. Choose a role or let us create a role with the **AmazonSageMakerFullAccess** IAM policy attached.

AmazonSageMaker-ExecutionRole-20210131T131164	▼

> ✓ **Success! You created an IAM role.**   ✕
> AmazonSageMaker-ExecutionRole-20210131T131164 ↗

Figure 9.3 – Amazon SageMaker role creation

6. Leave everything else in its default setting and click on the **Create notebook instance** button.

7. Once the instance is in the `InService` state, select the instance. Click on the **Actions** drop-down menu and choose **Open Jupyter**. This opens your Jupyter Notebook.

8. Now, we are all set to run our Jupyter Notebook on the newly created instance. We will perform **Exploratory Data Analysis (EDA)** and plot different types of graphs to visualize the data. Once we are familiar with the Jupyter Notebook, we will build some models to predict house prices in Boston. We will apply the algorithms that we have learned in previous chapters and compare them to find the best model that offers the best prediction according to our data. Let's dive in.

9. In the Jupyter Notebook, click on **New** and select **Terminal**. Run the following commands in Command Prompt to download the codes to the instance:

```
sh-4.2$ cd ~/SageMaker/
sh-4.2$ git clone https://github.com/PacktPublishing/
AWS-Certified-Machine-Learning-Specialty-MLS-C01-
Certification-Guide.git
```

10. Once the Git repository is cloned to the SageMaker notebook instance, type `exit` into Command Prompt to quit. Now, your code is ready to execute.

11. Navigate to `Chapter-9` in the Jupyter Notebook's **Files** section, as shown in *Figure 9.4*:

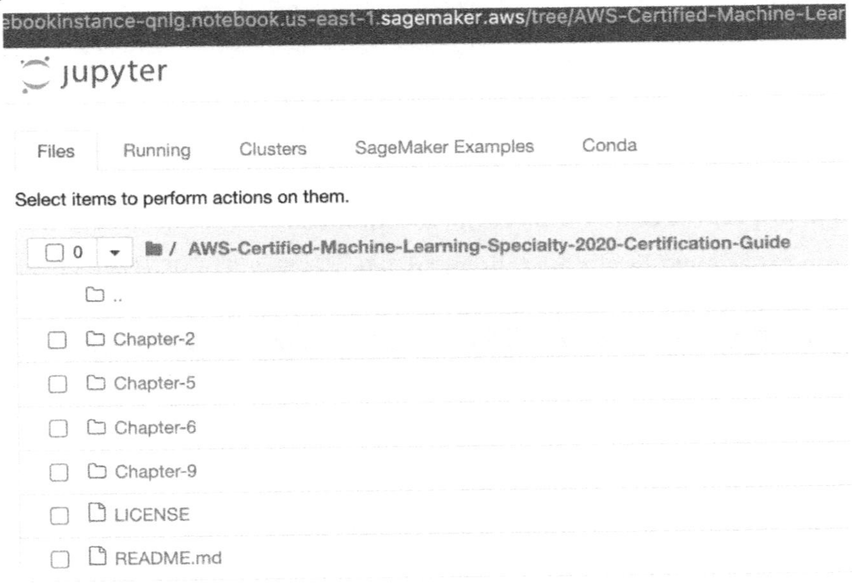

Figure 9.4 – Jupyter Notebook

12. Click on the first notebook in *1.Boston-House-Price-SageMaker-Notebook-Instance-Example.ipynb*. It will prompt you to choose the kernel for the notebook. Please select conda_python3, as shown in *Figure 9.5*:

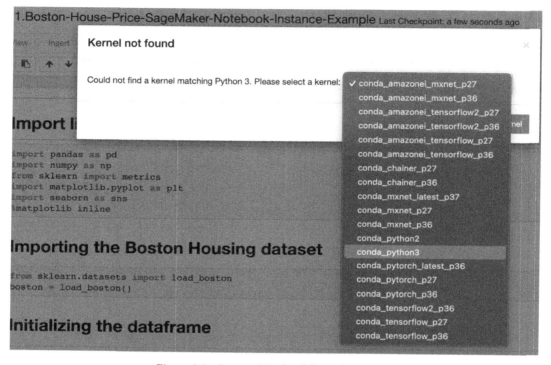

Figure 9.5 – Jupyter Notebook kernel selection

13. From the notebook, navigate to **Kernel** > **Restart & Clear Output**. Click on the play icon to run the cells one after another. Please ensure you have run each individual cell and inspect the output from each execution/run.

14. You can experiment by adding cells and deleting cells to familiarize yourself with the Jupyter Notebook operations. In one of the paragraphs, there is a bash command that allows you to install the xgboost libraries from the notebook.

15. The final cell explains how we have compared the different scores of various modeling techniques to draw a conclusion mathematically. *Figure 9.6* clearly shows that the best model to predict house prices in Boston is XGBoost:

```
models = pd.DataFrame({
    'Model': ['Linear Regression', 'Random Forest', 'XGBoost', 'Support Vector Machines'],
    'R-squared Score': [acc_linreg*100, acc_rf*100, acc_xgb*100, acc_svm*100],
    'Adjusted R-squared Score': [adj_R2_linreg*100, adj_R2_rf*100, adj_R2_xgb*100, adj_R2_svm*100],
    'MAE': [mae_linreg, mae_rf, mae_xgb, mae_svm],
    'MSE': [mse_linreg, mse_rf, mse_xgb, mse_svm],
    'RMSE': [rmse_linreg, rmse_rf, rmse_xgb, rmse_svm]})
models.sort_values(by='R-squared Score', ascending=False)
```

	Model	R-squared Score	Adjusted R-squared Score	MAE	MSE	RMSE
2	XGBoost	85.799520	84.461793	2.530958	14.828152	3.850734
1	Random Forest	82.181317	80.502745	2.500316	18.606282	4.313500
0	Linear Regression	71.218184	68.506853	3.859006	30.053993	5.482152
3	Support Vector Machines	59.001585	55.139415	3.756145	42.810575	6.542979

Figure 9.6 – Comparing the models

16. Once you've completed the execution of this notebook, please feel free to shut down the kernel and stop your notebook instance from the SageMaker console. This is the best practice to save on cost.

In the next hands-on section, we will familiarize ourselves with Amazon SageMaker's training and inference instances. We will also use the Amazon SageMaker API to make this process easier. We will use the same notebook instance as we did in the previous example.

Getting hands-on with Amazon SageMaker's training and inference instances

In this section, we will learn about training a model and hosting the model to generate predicted results. Let's dive in by using the notebook instance from the previous example:

1. Sign in to your AWS account at `https://console.aws.amazon.com/sagemaker/home?region=us-east-1#/notebook-instances`.

2. Click on **Start** next to the instance that we created in the previous example, **notebookinstance**. Once the status moves to `InService`, open it in a new tab, as shown in *Figure 9.7*:

Figure 9.7 – The InService instance

3. Navigate to the tab named SageMaker Examples in the Jupyter Notebook home page.

4. Select the `k_nearest_neighbors_covtype.ipynb` notebook. Click on **Use** and create a copy.

5. When you run the following paragraph, as shown n *Figure 9.8*, you can also check a training job in **Training** > **Training jobs** of the SageMaker home page:

```
hyperparams = {"feature_dim": 54, "k": 10, "sample_size": 200000, "predictor_type": "classifier"}
output_path = f"s3://{bucket}/{prefix}/default_example/output"
knn_estimator = trained_estimator_from_hyperparams(
    s3_train_data, hyperparams, output_path, s3_test_data=s3_test_data
)
```

```
The method get_image_uri has been renamed in sagemaker>=2.
See: https://sagemaker.readthedocs.io/en/stable/v2.html for details.
Defaulting to the only supported framework/algorithm version: 1. Ignoring framework/algorithm version: 1.

2021-02-03 22:00:05 Starting - Starting the training job...
2021-02-03 22:00:30 Starting - Launching requested ML instancesProfilerReport-1612389605: InProgress
.........
2021-02-03 22:01:51 Starting - Preparing the instances for training...
2021-02-03 22:02:32 Downloading - Downloading input data...
2021-02-03 22:02:52 Training - Downloading the training image...
2021-02-03 22:03:33 Training - Training image download completed. Training in progress..Docker entrypoint called with
argument(s): train
Running default environment configuration script
[02/03/2021 22:03:35 INFO 140457495148352] Reading default configuration from /opt/amazon/lib/python2.7/site-package
s/algorithm/resources/default-conf.json: {u'index_metric': u'L2', u'_tuning_objective_metric': u'', u'_num_gpus': u'a
uto', u'_log_level': u'info', u'feature_dim': u'auto', u'faiss_index_ivf_nlists': u'auto', u'epochs': u'1', u'index_t
ype': u'faiss.Flat', u'_faiss_index_nprobe': u'5', u'_kvstore': u'dist_async', u'_num_kv_servers': u'1', u'mini_batch
_size': u'5000'}
[02/03/2021 22:03:35 INFO 140457495148352] Merging with provided configuration from /opt/ml/input/config/hyperparamet
```

Figure 9.8 – The SageMaker fit API call

6. The training job looks similar to *Figure 9.9*. It launches an ECS container in the backend and uses the IAM execution role created in the previous example to run the training job for this request:

Figure 9.9 – Training obs

7. If you go inside and check the logs in CloudWatch, it gives you more details about the containers and the steps they performed. As a machine learning engineer, it's worth going in and checking the CloudWatch metrics for Algorithm.

8. Now, if you run the following paragraph, as shown in *Figure 9.10*, in the notebook, then it will create an endpoint configuration and an endpoint where the model from the earlier training job is deployed.

9. I have changed the instance type to save on cost. It is the instance or the machine that will host your model. Please choose your instance wisely. We will learn about choosing instance types in the next section. I have also changed endpoint_name so that it can be recognized easily:

```
import time

instance_type = "ml.t2.medium"
model_name = "knn_%s" % instance_type
endpoint_name = "knn-baba-test-%s" % (str(time.time()).replace(".", "-"))
print("setting up the endpoint..")
predictor = predictor_from_estimator(
    knn_estimator, model_name, instance_type, endpoint_name=endpoint_name
)
```

```
setting up the endpoint..
-
```

Figure 9.10 – Creating the predictor object with endpoint details

10. Navigate to **Inference** > **Endpoints**. This will show you the endpoint that was created as a result of the previous paragraph execution. This endpoint has a configuration and can be navigated and traced through **Inference** > **Endpoint Configurations**.

11. If you view the **Inference** section in the notebook, you will notice that it uses the test data to predict results. It uses the predictor object from the SageMaker API to make predictions. The predictor object contains the endpoint details, model name, and instance type.

12. The API call to the endpoint occurs in the **Inference** section, and it is authenticated via the IAM role with which the notebook instance is created. The same API calls can be traced through CloudWatch invocation metrics.

13. Finally, running the `delete_endpoint` method in the notebook will delete the endpoint. To delete the endpoint configurations, navigate to **Inference** > **Endpoint Configurations** and select the configuration on the screen. Click on **Actions** > **Delete** > **Delete**.

14. Now, please feel free to shut down the kernel and stop your notebook instance from the SageMaker console. This is the best practice to save on cost.

In this section, we learned about using the notebook instance, training instances, inference endpoints, and endpoint configurations to clean our data, train models, and generate predicted results from them. In the next section, we will learn about model tuning.

Model tuning

In *Chapter 8, Evaluating and Optimizing Models*, you learned many important concepts about model tuning. Let's now explore this topic from a practical perspective.

In order to tune a model on SageMaker, we have to call `create_hyper_parameter_tuning_job` and pass the following main parameters:

- `HyperParameterTuningJobName`: This is the name of the tuning job. It is useful to track the training jobs that have been started on behalf of your tuning job.

- `HyperParameterTuningJobConfig`: Here, you can configure your tuning options. For example, which parameters you want to tune, the range of values for them, the type of optimization (such as random search or Bayesian search), the maximum number of training jobs you want to spin up, and more.

- `TrainingJobDefinition`: Here, you can configure your training job. For example, the data channels, the output location, the resource configurations, the evaluation metrics, and the stop conditions.

In SageMaker, the main metric that we want to use to evaluate the models to select the best one is known as an **objective metric**.

In the following example, we are configuring `HyperParameterTuningJobConfig` for a decision tree-based algorithm. We want to check the best configuration for a **max_depth** hyperparameter, which is responsible for controlling the depth of the tree.

In `IntegerParameterRanges`, we have to specify the following:

- The hyperparameter name
- The minimum value that we want to test
- The maximum value that we want to test

> **Important note**
> Each type of hyperparameter must fit in one of the parameter ranges sections, such as categorical, continuous, or integer parameters.

In `ResourceLimits`, we are specifying the number of training jobs along with the number of parallel jobs that we want to run. Remember that the goal of the tuning process is to execute many training jobs with different hyperparameter settings. This is so that the best one will be selected for the final model. That's why we have to specify these training job execution rules.

We then set up our search strategy in `Strategy` and, finally, set up the objective function in `HyperParameterTuningJobObjective`:

```
tuning_job_config = {
    "ParameterRanges": {
        "CategoricalParameterRanges": [],
        "ContinuousParameterRanges": [],
        "IntegerParameterRanges": [
            {
                "MaxValue": "10",
                "MinValue": "1",
                "Name": "max_depth"
            }
```

```
      ]
    },
    "ResourceLimits": {
      "MaxNumberOfTrainingJobs": 10,
      "MaxParallelTrainingJobs": 2
    },
    "Strategy": "Bayesian",
    "HyperParameterTuningJobObjective": {
      "MetricName": "validation:auc",
      "Type": "Maximize"
    }
  }
```

The second important configuration we need to set is `TrainingJobDefinition`. Here, we have to specify all the details regarding the training jobs that will be executed. One of the most important settings is the `TrainingImage` setting, which refers to the container that will be started to execute the training processes. This container, as expected, must have your training algorithm implemented.

Here, we present an example of a built-in algorithm, **eXtreme Gradient Boosting**, so that you can set the training image as follows:

```
training_image = sagemaker.image_uris.retrieve('xgboost',
region, '1.0-1')
```

Then, you can go ahead and set your training definitions:

```
training_job_definition = {
  "AlgorithmSpecification": {
    "TrainingImage": training_image,
    "TrainingInputMode": "File"
  },
```

Next, we have to specify the data input configuration, which is also known as the data channels. In the following section of code, we are setting up two data channels – train and validation:

```
  "InputDataConfig": [
    {
      "ChannelName": "train",
```

```
         "CompressionType": "None",
         "ContentType": "csv",
         "DataSource": {
           "S3DataSource": {
             "S3DataDistributionType": "FullyReplicated",
             "S3DataType": "S3Prefix",
             "S3Uri": s3_input_train
           }
         }
       },
       {
         "ChannelName": "validation",
         "CompressionType": "None",
         "ContentType": "csv",
         "DataSource": {
           "S3DataSource": {
             "S3DataDistributionType": "FullyReplicated",
             "S3DataType": "S3Prefix",
             "S3Uri": s3_input_validation
           }
         }
       }
     ],
```

We also need to specify where the results will be stored:

```
    "OutputDataConfig": {
      "S3OutputPath": "s3://{}/{}/output".format(bucket,prefix)
    },
```

Finally, we set the resource configurations, roles, static parameters, and stopping conditions. In the following section of code, we want to use two instances of type `ml.c4.2xlarge` with 10 GB of storage:

```
    "ResourceConfig": {
      "InstanceCount": 2,
```

```
        "InstanceType": "ml.c4.2xlarge",
        "VolumeSizeInGB": 10
    },
    "RoleArn": <<your_role_name>>,
    "StaticHyperParameters": {
        "eval_metric": "auc",
        "num_round": "100",
        "objective": "binary:logistic",
        "rate_drop": "0.3",
        "tweedie_variance_power": "1.4"
    },
    "StoppingCondition": {
        "MaxRuntimeInSeconds": 43200
    }
}
```

> **Important note**
>
> Please note that we are using other variables in this configuration file, `bucket` and `prefix`, which should be replaced by your bucket name and prefix key (if needed), respectively. We are also referring to `s3_input_train` and `s3_input_validation`, which are two variables that point to the train and validation datasets in S3.

Once you have set your configurations, you can spin up the tuning process:

```
smclient.create_hyper_parameter_tuning_job(
    HyperParameterTuningJobName = "my-tuning-example",
    HyperParameterTuningJobConfig = tuning_job_config,
    TrainingJobDefinition = training_job_definition
)
```

Next, let's find out how to track the execution of this process.

Tracking your training jobs and selecting the best model

Once you have started the tuning process, there are two additional steps that you might want to check: tracking the process of tuning and selecting the winner model (that is, the one with the best set of hyperparameters).

In order to find your training jobs, you should go to the SageMaker console and navigate to **Hyperparameter training jobs**. You will then find a list of executed tuning jobs, including yours:

Figure 9.11 – Finding your tuning job

If you access your tuning job, by clicking under its name, you will find a summary page, which includes the most relevant information regarding the tuning process. Under the **Training jobs** tab, you will see all of the training jobs that have been executed:

Figure 9.12 – Summary of the training jobs in the tuning process

Finally, if you click on the **Best training job** tab, you will find the best set of hyperparameters for your model, including a handy button to create a new model based on those best hyperparameters that have just been found:

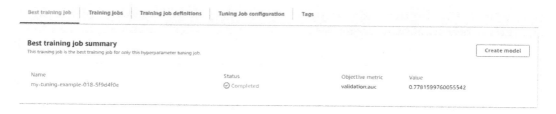

Figure 9.13 – Finding the best set of hyperparameters

As you can see, SageMaker is very intuitive, and once you know the main concepts behind model optimization, playing with SageMaker should be easier. By now, we have understood how to use SageMaker for our specific needs. In the next section, we will explore how to select the instance type for various use cases and the security of our notebooks.

Choosing instance types in Amazon SageMaker

SageMaker is a pay-for-usage model. There is no minimum fee for it.

When we think about instances on SageMaker, it all starts with an EC2 instance. This instance is responsible for all your processing. It's a managed EC2 instance. These instances won't show up in the EC2 console and cannot be SSHed either. The instance type starts with ml.

SageMaker offers instances of the following families:

- The **t** family: This is a burstable CPU family. With this family, you get a normal ratio of CPU and memory. This means that if you have a long-running training job, then you lose performance over time as you spend the CPU credits. If you have very small jobs, then they are cost-effective. For example, if you want a notebook instance to launch training jobs, then this family is the most relevant and cost-effective.

- The **m** family: In the previous family, we saw that CPU credits are consumed faster due to their burstable nature. If you have a long-running machine learning job that requires constant throughput, then this is the right family. It comes with a similar CPU and memory ratio as the **t** family.

- The **r** family: This is a memory-optimized family. *When do we need this?* Well, imagine a use case where you have to load the data in memory and do some data engineering on the data. In this scenario, you will require more memory and your job will be memory-optimized.

- The **c** family: **c** family instances are compute-optimized. This is a requirement for jobs that need higher compute power and less memory to store the data. If you refer to the following table, C5.2x large has 8 vCPU and 16 GiB memory, which makes it compute-optimized with less memory. For example, a use case needs to be tested on a fewer number of records and it is compute savvy, then this instance family is the to-go option to get some sample records from a huge dataframe and test your algorithm.

- The **p** family: This is a GPU family that supports accelerated computing jobs such as training and inference. Notably, **p** family instances are ideal for handling large, distributed training jobs, and this leads to less time required to train. As a result, this becomes cost-effective. The P3/P3dn GPU compute instance can go up to 1 petaFLOP per second compute with up to 256 GB of GPU memory and 100 Gbps (gigabits) of networking with 8x NVIDIA v100 GPUs. They are highly optimized for training and are not fully utilized for inference.

- The **g** family: For cost-effective, small-scale training jobs, **g** family GPU instances are ideal. G4 has the lowest cost per inference for GPU instances. It uses T4 NVIDIA GPUs. The G4 GPU compute instance goes up to 520 TeraFLOPs of compute time with 8x NVIDIA T4 GPUs. This instance family is the best for simple networks.

In the following table, 2x large instance types have been taken from each family for a visual comparison between the CPU and memory ratio:

t3.2x large	m5.2x large	r5.2x large	c5.2x large	p3.2x large	g4dn.2x large
8 vCPU, 32 GiB	8 vCPU, 32 GiB	8 vCPU, 64 GiB	8 vCPU, 16 GiB	8 vCPU, 61 GiB	8 vCPU, 32 GiB

Table 9.1 – A table showing the CPU and memory ratio of different instance types

> **Important note**
> To remember this easily, you can think of T for Tiny, M for Medium, C for Compute, and P and G for GPU. CPU family instance types are T, M, R, and C. GPU family instance types are P and G.

Choosing the right instance type for a training job

There is no rule of thumb to decide the instance type that you require. It changes based on the size of the data, the complexity of the network, the machine learning algorithm, and several other factors such as time and cost. Asking the right question will save money and make it cost-effective.

If the deciding factor is *Instance Size*, then classifying the problem for CPU or GPU is the right step. Once that is done, then it is good to consider whether it can be multi-GPU or multi-CPU. That would solve your question about distributed training. This also solves your *Instance Count* factor. If it's compute-intensive, then it would be wise to check the memory requirements too.

The next deciding factor is *Instance Family*. The right questions here would be, *Is it optimized for time and cost?* In the previous step, we have already figured out the problem to be solved in either the CPU or GPU, and this narrows down the selection process. Now, let's learn about inference jobs.

Choosing the right instance type for an inference job

The majority of the cost and complexity of machine learning in production is inference. Usually, inference runs on a single input in real time. They are usually less compute/memory-intensive. They have to be highly available as they run all the time and serve the end user requests or are integrated as part of an application.

You can choose any of the instance types that we learned about recently based on the workload. Other than that, AWS has **Inf1** and **Elastic Inference** type instances for inference. Elastic inference allows you to attach a fraction of a GPU instance to any CPU instance.

Let's look at an example where an application is integrated with inference jobs, then the requirement of CPU and memory for the application is different from the inference jobs. For those use cases, you need to choose the right instance type and size. In such scenarios, it is good to have a separation between your application fleets and inference fleets. This might require some management. If such management is a problem for your requirement, then choose elastic inference, where both the application and inference jobs can be colocated. This means that you can host multiple models on the same fleet, and you can load all of these different models on different accelerators in memory and concurrent requests can be served.

It's always recommended that you run some examples in a lower environment before deciding on your instance types and family in the production environment. In the next section, we will dive into and understand the different ways of securing our Amazon SageMaker notebooks.

Securing SageMaker notebooks

If you are reading this section of the chapter, then you have already learned how to use notebook instances, which type of training instances should be chosen, and how to configure and use endpoints. Now, let's learn about securing those instances. The following aspects will help to secure the instances:

- **Encryption**: When we say or think about securing via encryption, then it is all about the data. But what does this mean? It means protecting data at rest using encryption, protecting data in transit with encryption, and using KMS for better role separation and internet traffic privacy through TLS 1.2 encryption. SageMaker instances can be launched with encrypted volumes by using an AWS-managed KMS key. This helps you to secure the Jupyter Notebook server by default.

- **Root access**: When a user opens a shell terminal from the Jupyter Web UI, they will be logged in as ec2-user, which is the default username in Amazon Linux. Now the user can run sudo to the root user. With root access, users can access and edit files. In many use cases, an administrator might not want data scientists to manage, control, or modify the system of the notebook server. This requires restrictions to be placed on the root access. This can be done by setting the `RootAccess` field to `Disabled` when you call `CreateNotebookInstance` or `UpdateNotebookInstance`. The data scientist will have access to their user space and can install Python packages. However, they cannot sudo into the root user and make changes to the operating system.

- **IAM role**: During the launch of a notebook instance, it is necessary to create an IAM role for execution or to use an existing role for execution. This is used to launch the service-managed EC2 instance with an instance profile associated with the role. This role will restrict the API calls based on the policies attached to this role.

- **VPC connection**: When you launch a SageMaker notebook instance, by default, it gets created within the SageMaker Service Account, which has a service-managed VPC, and it will, by default, have access to the internet via an internet gateway, and that gateway is managed by the service. If you are only dealing with AWS-related services, then it is recommended that you launch a SageMaker notebook instance in your VPC within a private subnet and with a well-customized security group. The AWS services can be invoked or used from this notebook instance via VPC endpoints attached to that VPC. The best practice is to control them via endpoint policies for better API controls. This ensures the restriction on data egress outside your VPC and secured environment. In order to capture all the network traffic, you can turn on the VPC flow logs, which can be monitored and tracked via CloudWatch.

- **Internet access**: You can launch a Jupyter Notebook server without direct internet access. It can be launched in a private subnet with a NAT or to access the internet through a virtual private gateway. For training and deploying inference containers, you can set the `EnableNetworkIsolation` parameter to `True` when you are calling `CreateTrainingJob`, `CreateHyperParameterTuningJob`, or `CreateModel`. Network isolation can be used along with the VPC, which ensures that containers cannot make any outbound network calls.

- **Connecting a private network to your VPC**: You can launch your SageMaker notebook instance inside the private subnet of your VPC. This can access data from your private network by communicating to the private network, which can be done by connecting your private network to your VPC by using Amazon VPN or AWS Direct Connect.

In this section, we learned about several ways in which we can secure our SageMaker notebooks. In the next section, we will learn about creating SageMaker pipelines with Lambda Functions.

Creating alternative pipelines with Lambda Functions

Indeed, SageMaker is an awesome platform that you can use to create training and inference pipelines. However, we can always work with different services to come up with similar solutions. One of these services that we will learn about next is known as **Lambda Functions**.

AWS Lambda is a serverless compute service where you can literally run a function as a service. In other words, you can concentrate your efforts on just writing your function. Then, you just need to tell AWS how to run it (that is, the environment and resource configurations), so all the necessary resources will be provisioned to run your code and then discontinued once it is completed.

Throughout *Chapter 6, AWS Services for Data Processing*, you explored how Lambda Functions integrate with many different services, such as Kinesis and AWS Batch. Indeed, AWS did a very good job of integrating Lambda with 140 services (and the list is constantly increasing). That means that when you are working with a specific AWS service, you will remember that it is likely to integrate with Lambda.

It is important to bear this in mind because Lambda Functions can really expand your possibilities to create scalable and integrated architectures. For example, you can trigger a Lambda Function when a file is uploaded to S3 in order to preprocess your data before loading it to Redshift. Alternatively, you can create an API that triggers a Lambda Function at each endpoint execution. Again, the possibilities are endless with this powerful service.

It is also useful to know that you can write your function in different programming languages, such as Node.js, Python, Go, Java, and more. Your function does not necessarily have to be triggered by another AWS service, that is, you can trigger it manually for your web or mobile application, for example.

When it comes to deployment, you can upload your function as a ZIP file or as a container image. Although this is not ideal for an automated deployment process, coding directly into the AWS Lambda console is also possible.

As with any other service, this one also has some downsides that you should be aware of:

- Memory allocation for your function: This is from 128 MB to 10,240 MB (AWS has recently increased this limit from 3 GB to 10 GB, as stated previously).

- Function timeout: This is a maximum of 900 seconds (15 minutes).

- Function layer: This is a maximum of 5 layers.

- Burst concurrency: This is from 500 to 3,000, depending on the region.

- Deployment package size: This is 250 MB unzipped, including layers.

- Container image code package size: This is 10 GB.

- Available space in the /tmp directory: This is 512 MB.

Before going for Lambda Functions, make sure these restrictions fit your use case. Bringing Lambda Functions closer to your scope of alternative pipelines for SageMaker, one potential use of Lambda is to create inference pipelines for our models.

As you know, SageMaker has a very handy .deploy() method that will create endpoints for model inference. This is so that you can call to pass the input data in order to receive predictions back. Here, we can create this inference endpoint by using the API gateway and Lambda Functions.

In case you don't need an inference endpoint and you just want to make predictions and store results somewhere (in a batch fashion), then all we need is a Lambda Function, which is able to fetch the input data, instantiate the model object, make predictions, and store the results in the appropriated location. Of course, it does this by considering all the limitations that we have discussed earlier.

Alright, now that we have a good background about Lambda and some use cases, let's take a look at the most important configurations that we should be aware of for the exam.

Creating and configuring a Lambda Function

First of all, you should know that you can create a Lambda Function in different ways, such as via the AWS CLI (Lambda API reference), the AWS Lambda console, or even deployment frameworks (for example, *the serverless framework*).

Serverless frameworks are usually provider and programming language-independent. In other words, they usually allow you to choose where you want to deploy a serverless infrastructure from a variate list of cloud providers and programming languages.

> **Important note**
> The concept of serverless architecture is not specific to AWS. In fact, many cloud providers offer other services that are similar to AWS Lambda Functions. That's why these serverless frameworks have been built: to help developers and engineers to deploy their services, wherever they want, including AWS. This is unlikely to come up in your exam, but it is definitely something that you should know so that you are aware of different ways in which to solve your challenges as a data scientist or data engineer.

Since we want to pass the AWS Machine Learning Specialty exam, here, we have taken the approach to walk through the AWS Lambda console. This is so that you will become more familiar with their interface and the most important configuration options.

When you navigate to the Lambda console and request a new Lambda Function, AWS will provide you with some starting options:

- Author from scratch: This is if you want to create your function from scratch.

- Use a blueprint: This is if you want to create your function from a sample code and configuration preset for common use cases.

- Container image: This is if you want to select a container image to deploy your function.

- Browse serverless app repository: This is if you want to deploy a sample Lambda application from the AWS Serverless Application Repository.

Starting from scratch, the next step is to set up your Lambda configurations. AWS splits these configurations between basic and advanced settings. In the basic configuration, you will set your function name, runtime environment, and permissions. *Figure 9.14* shows these configurations:

Create function Info

Choose one of the following options to create your function.

Author from scratch ⦿	Use a blueprint ○	Container
Start with a simple Hello World example.	Build a Lambda application from sample code and configuration presets for common use cases.	Select a

Basic information

Function name
Enter a name that describes the purpose of your function.

    myFunctionName

Use only letters, numbers, hyphens, or underscores with no spaces.

Runtime Info
Choose the language to use to write your function.

    Python 3.8

Permissions Info
By default, Lambda will create an execution role with permissions to upload logs to Amazon CloudWatch Logs. You can customize this default role later when adding triggers.

▼ Change default execution role

Execution role
Choose a role that defines the permissions of your function. To create a custom role, go to the IAM console.

⦿ Create a new role with basic Lambda permissions
○ Use an existing role
○ Create a new role from AWS policy templates

> ⓘ Role creation might take a few minutes. Please do not delete the role or edit the trust or permissions policies in this role.

Lambda will create an execution role named <myFunctionName>-role-vio400dj, with permission to upload logs to Amazon CloudWatch Logs.

▼ **Advanced settings**

Code signing

Code signing configuration - *optional* Info
To enable code signing, choose a configuration that defines the signature validation policy and the signing profiles that are permitted to sign code.

    Choose a code signing configuration ARN

Network

To provide network access for your Lambda function, specify a virtual private cloud (VPC), VPC subnets, and VPC security groups. VPC configuration is optional unless your user permissions require you to configure a VPC.

VPC - *optional* Info
Choose a VPC for your function to access.

    Choose a VPC

Figure 9.14 – Creating a new Lambda Function from the AWS Lambda console

Here, we have a very important configuration that you should remember during your exam: the **execution role**. Your Lambda Function might need permissions to access other AWS resources, such as S3, Redshift, and more. The execution role grants permissions to your Lambda Function so that it can access resources as needed.

You have to remember that your VPC and security group configurations will also interfere with how your Lambda Function runs. For example, if you want to create a function that needs internet access to download something, then you have to deploy this function in a VPC with internet access. The same logic applies to other resources, such as access to relational databases, Kinesis, Redshift, and more.

Furthermore, in order to properly configure a Lambda Function, we have to, at least, write its code, set the execution role, and make sure the VPC and security group configurations match our needs. Next, let's take a look at other configurations.

Completing your configurations and deploying a Lambda Function

Once your Lambda is created in the AWS console, you can set additional configurations before deploying the function. One of these configurations is the event trigger. As we mentioned earlier, your Lambda Function can be triggered from a variety of services or even manually.

> **Important note**
>
> A very common example of a trigger is **Event Bridge**. This is an AWS service where you can schedule the execution of your function.

Depending on the event trigger you choose, your function will have access to different event metadata. For example, if your function is triggered by a **PUT** event on S3 (for example, someone uploads a file to a particular S3 bucket), then your function will receive the metadata associated with this event, for example, bucket name and object key. Other types of triggers will give you different types of event metadata!

You have access to those metadata through the event parameter that belongs to the signature of the entry point of your function. Not clear enough? OK, let's see how your function code should be declared, as follows:

```
def lambda_handler(event, context):
    TODO
```

Here, `lambda_handler` is the method that represents the entry point of your function. When it is triggered, this method will be called, and it will receive the event metadata associated with the event trigger (through the `event` parameter). That's how you have access to the information associated with the underlying event that has triggered your function! The `event` parameter is a JSON-like object.

If you want to test your function, but you don't want to trigger it directly from the underlying event, that is no problem; you can use **test events**. They simulate the underlying event by preparing a JSON object that will be passed to your function.

Figure 9.15 shows a very intuitive example. Let's suppose you have created a function that is triggered when a user uploads a file to S3 and now you want to test your function. You can either upload a file to S3 (which forces the trigger) or create a test event.

By creating a test event, you can prepare a JSON object that simulates the S3-put event and then pass this object to your function:

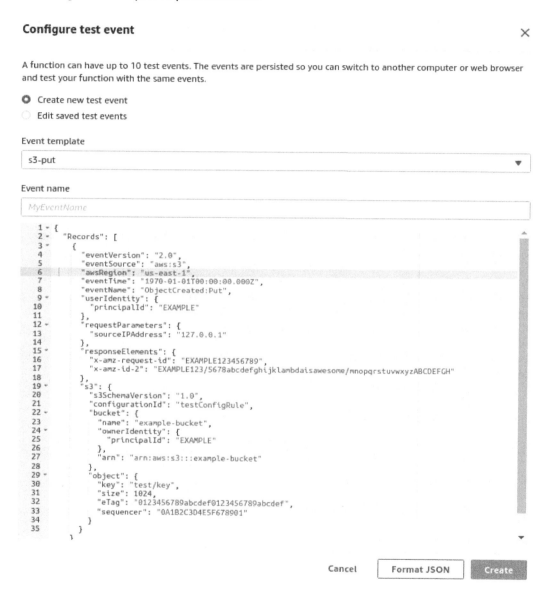

Figure 9.15 – Creating a test event from the Lambda console

Another type of configuration you can set is an **environment variable**, which will be available on your function. *Figure 9.16* shows how to add environment variables in a Lambda Function:

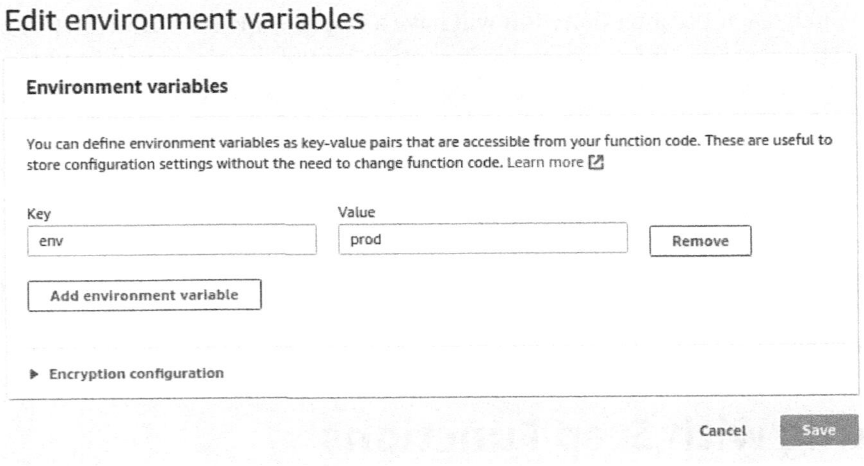

Edit environment variables

Environment variables

You can define environment variables as key-value pairs that are accessible from your function code. These are useful to store configuration settings without the need to change function code. Learn more [

Key	Value	
env	prod	Remove

Add environment variable

▶ Encryption configuration

Cancel   Save

Figure 9.16 – Adding environment variables to a Lambda Function

You can always come back to these basic configurations to make adjustments as necessary. *Figure 9.17* shows what you will find in the basic configurations section:

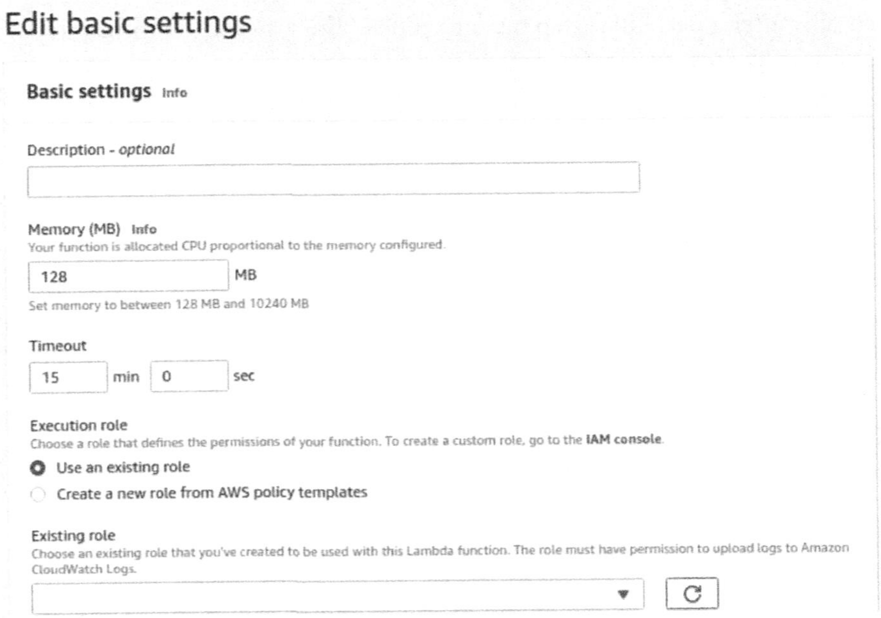

Edit basic settings

Basic settings Info

Description - *optional*

Memory (MB) Info
Your function is allocated CPU proportional to the memory configured.

128   MB

Set memory to between 128 MB and 10240 MB

Timeout

15   min   0   sec

Execution role
Choose a role that defines the permissions of your function. To create a custom role, go to the **IAM console**.

◉ Use an existing role
◯ Create a new role from AWS policy templates

Existing role
Choose an existing role that you've created to be used with this Lambda function. The role must have permission to upload logs to Amazon CloudWatch Logs.

▼   C

Figure 9.17 – Changing the basic configurations of a Lambda Function

In terms of monitoring, by default, Lambda Functions produce a **CloudWatch** Logs stream and standard metrics. You can access log information by navigating through your Lambda Function monitoring section and clicking on *View logs in CloudWatch*.

In CloudWatch, each Lambda Function will have a **Log group** and, inside that Log group, many **Log streams**. Log streams store the execution logs of the associated function. In other words, a log stream is a sequence of logs that share the same source, which, in this case, is your Lambda Function. A log group is a group of log streams that share the same retention, monitoring, and access control settings.

We are reaching the end of this section, but not the end of this topic on Lambda Functions. As we mentioned earlier, this AWS service has a lot of use cases and integrates with many other services. In the next section, we will take a look at another AWS service that will help us to orchestrate executions of Lambda Functions. These are known as **AWS Step Functions**.

Working with Step Functions

Step Functions is an AWS service that allows you to create workflows in order to orchestrate the execution of Lambda Functions. This is so that you can connect them in a sort of event sequence, known as **steps**. These steps are grouped in a **state machine**.

Step Functions incorporates retry functionality so that you can configure your pipeline to proceed only after a particular step has succeeded. The way you set these retry configurations is by creating a **retry policy**.

> **Important note**
> Just like the majority of AWS services, AWS Step Functions also integrates with other services, not only AWS Lambda.

Creating a state machine is relatively simple. All you have to do is navigate to the AWS Step Functions console, then create a new state machine. On the *Create state machine* page, you can specify whether you want to create your state machine from scratch, from a template, or whether you just want to run a sample project.

AWS will help you with this state machine creation, so even if you choose to create it from scratch, you will find code snippets for a variate list of tasks, such as AWS Lambda invocation, SNS topic publication, running Athena queries, and more.

For the sake of demonstration, we will create a very simple, but still helpful, example of how to use Step Functions to execute a Lambda Function with the retry option activated:

```json
{
  "Comment": "A very handy example of how to call a lamnbda function with retry option",
  "StartAt": "Invoke Lambda function",
  "States": {
    "Invoke Lambda function": {
      "Type": "Task",
      "Resource": "arn:aws:states:::lambda:invoke",
      "Parameters": {
        "FunctionName": "arn:aws:lambda:your-function-identification",
        "Payload": {
          "Input": {
            "env": "STAGE"
          }
        }
      },
      "Retry": [
        {
          "ErrorEquals": ["States.ALL"],
          "IntervalSeconds": 60,
          "MaxAttempts": 5,
          "BackoffRate": 2.0
        }
      ],
      "Next": "Example"
    },
    "Example": {
      "Type": "Pass",
      "Result": "Just to show you how to configure other steps",
      "End": true
    }
  }
}
```

In the preceding example, we created a state machine with two steps:

- Invoke Lambda function: This will start the execution of your underlying Lambda.

- Example: This is a simple pass task just to show you how to connect a second step in the pipeline.

In the first step, we have also set up a retry policy, which will try to re-execute this task if there are any failures. We are setting up the interval (in seconds) to try again and to show here the number of attempts. *Figure 9.18* shows the state machine:

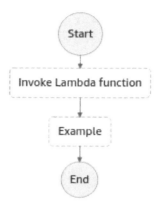

Figure 9.18 – The state machine

We have now reached the end of this section and the end of this chapter. Next, let's summarize what we have learned.

Summary

In this chapter, we learned about the usage of SageMaker for creating notebook instances and training instances. As we went through we learned how to use SageMaker for hyperparameter tuning jobs. As the security of our assets in AWS is an essential part, we learned about the various ways to secure SageMaker instances. With hands-on practices, we created Step Functions and orchestrated our pipeline using AWS Lambda.

AWS products are evolving every day to help us solve our IT problems. It's not easy to remember all the product names. The only way to learn is through practice. When you're solving a problem or building a product, then focus on the different technological areas of your product. Those areas can be an AWS service, for example, scheduling jobs, logging, tracing, monitoring metrics, autoscaling, and more.

Compute time, storage, and networking are the baselines. It is recommended that you practice some examples for each of these services. Referring to the AWS documentation for clarifying any doubts is also the best option. It is always important to design your solutions in a cost-effective way, so exploring the cost-effective way to use these services is equally important as building the solution. I wish you all the best!

Questions

1. Which of the following models are supervised algorithms? Select two options.

    A. Clustering

    B. Classification

    C. Association rule mining

    D. Regression

2. You would like to turn your Amazon SageMaker machine learning models and endpoints into customer-facing applications. You decide to put these on a single web server that can be accessed by customers via a browser. However, you realize that the web server is not inherently scalable; if it receives a lot of traffic, it could run out of CPU or memory. How can you make this approach more scalable and secure? Select three answers.

    A. Create an IAM role, so the webserver can access the SageMaker endpoints.

    B. Deploy a load balancer and set up autoscaling.

    C. Make all customers IAM users so that they can access SageMaker.

    D. Keep the operating system and language runtimes for the web server patch secured.

3. For the preceding situation, what would be a better AWS service to automate server and operating system maintenance, capacity provisioning, and automatic scaling?

    A. AWS Lambda

    B. AWS Fargate

    C. AWS ELB

4. Amazon SageMaker is a fully managed service that enables you to quickly and easily integrate machine learning-based models into your applications. It also provides services such as notebook, training, and endpoint instances to help you get the job done.

    A. TRUE

    B. FALSE

5. Chose three correct statements from the following:

    A. Notebook instances clean and understand data.

    B. Training instances use data to train the model.

    C. Endpoint instances use models to produce inferences.

    D. Notebook instances clean, understand, and build models.

    E. Training instances are used to predict results.

6. What is the first step of creating a notebook?

    A. Give it a name.

    B. Choose a kernel.

    C. Starting developing code in paragraph format.

7. Linear learner and XGBoost algorithms can be used in supervised learning models such as regression and classification.

    A. TRUE

    B. FALSE

8. Which of these statements about hyperparameter tuning is true?

    A. Hyperparameter tuning is a guaranteed way to improve your model.

    B. Hyperparameter tuning does not require any input values.

    C. Hyperparameter tuning uses regression to choose the best value to test.

    D. Hyperparameter tuning is an unsupervised machine learning regression problem.

Answers

1. B and D

2. A, B, and D

3. A

4. A

5. A, B, and C

6. B

7. A

8. C

Packt.com

Subscribe to our online digital library for full access to over 7,000 books and videos, as well as industry leading tools to help you plan your personal development and advance your career. For more information, please visit our website.

Why subscribe?

- Spend less time learning and more time coding with practical eBooks and Videos from over 4,000 industry professionals

- Improve your learning with Skill Plans built especially for you

- Get a free eBook or video every month

- Fully searchable for easy access to vital information

- Copy and paste, print, and bookmark content

Did you know that Packt offers eBook versions of every book published, with PDF and ePub files available? You can upgrade to the eBook version at packt.com and as a print book customer, you are entitled to a discount on the eBook copy. Get in touch with us at customercare@packtpub.com for more details.

At www.packt.com, you can also read a collection of free technical articles, sign up for a range of free newsletters, and receive exclusive discounts and offers on Packt books and eBooks.

Other Books You May Enjoy

If you enjoyed this book, you may be interested in these other books by Packt:

Learn Amazon SageMaker

Julien Simon

ISBN: 978-1-80020-891-9

- Create and automate end-to-end machine learning workflows on Amazon Web Services (AWS)
- Become well-versed with data annotation and preparation techniques
- Train computer vision and NLP models using real-world examples
- Cover training techniques for scaling, model optimization, model debugging, and cost optimization
- Automate deployment tasks in a variety of configurations using SDK and several automation tools

Mastering Machine Learning on AWS

Saket Mengle, Maximo Gurmendez

ISBN: 978-1-78934-979-5

- Manage AI workflows by using AWS cloud to deploy services that feed smart data products
- Use SageMaker services to create recommendation models
- Scale model training and deployment using Apache Spark on EMR
- Understand how to cluster big data through EMR and seamlessly integrate it with SageMaker
- Build deep learning models on AWS using TensorFlow and deploy them as services
- Enhance your apps by combining Apache Spark and Amazon SageMaker

Packt is searching for authors like you

If you're interested in becoming an author for Packt, please visit authors. packtpub.com and apply today. We have worked with thousands of developers and tech professionals, just like you, to help them share their insight with the global tech community. You can make a general application, apply for a specific hot topic that we are recruiting an author for, or submit your own idea.

Leave a review - let other readers know what you think

Please share your thoughts on this book with others by leaving a review on the site that you bought it from. If you purchased the book from Amazon, please leave us an honest review on this book's Amazon page. This is vital so that other potential readers can see and use your unbiased opinion to make purchasing decisions, we can understand what our customers think about our products, and our authors can see your feedback on the title that they have worked with Packt to create. It will only take a few minutes of your time, but is valuable to other potential customers, our authors, and Packt. Thank you!

Index

Made in the USA
Middletown, DE
08 August 2022

70797416R00190